BEHIND THE
SHADES

The Autobiography

Duncan Fletcher

with Steve James

POCKET
BOOKS

LONDON • SYDNEY • NEW YORK • TORONTO

First published in Great Britain in 2007
by Simon & Schuster UK Ltd
This edition first published by Pocket Books, 2008
An imprint of Simon & Schuster UK Ltd
A CBS COMPANY

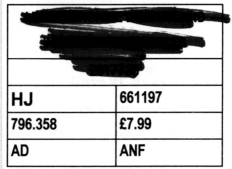

PICTURE CREDITS
1, 2, 3, 4, 5, 6, 7, 8, 10, 13, 14, 23, 24, 32, 33, 34, 35,
36, 37, 40, Courtesy of author's private collection
9, 12, 21, 28, © Mirrorpix
11, 18, 26, 30, © Philip Brown Photos
15, 16, 17, 19, 29, 38, 41, © Getty Images
20, 22, 25, 27, 31, 39, © Corbis

A CIP catalogue for this book is available
from the British Library.

ISBN: 978-1-4165-1102-1

Typeset in Garamond by M Rules
Printed and bound in Great Britain by
Cox & Wyman Ltd, Reading, Berks

To my ever-understanding and loving wife, Marina.

And to our children Michael and Nicola for
their constant love, help and support.

Contents

Acknowledgements

Thanks to:

My wife Marina and children Michael and Nicola, for their passionate and continual support, particularly their patience in many lonely times;

My parents Desmond and Mary, and brothers John, Colin, Gordon, Allan and sister Ann, for a great family upbringing on Carswell Farm. Special thanks to John for his sound advice;

Marina's parents, Alex and Elisa, for their help and support, especially when we emigrated to Cape Town;

Nick Erskine, for giving me the break at Prince Edward High School;

Zimbabwe Cricket and in particular Alwyn Pichanick, for being such a very important mentor;

Western Province Cricket, for starting the journey;

Glamorgan County Cricket Club, for giving me the opportunity to make people notice;

Simon & Schuster, for letting me put my story down on paper;

Steve James, for his patience and enthusiasm;

England Cricket and especially the England players, who allowed me to try to be successful at the job that I am so passionate about.

Preface

It all ended in tears. They say that the tenures of most sporting coaches end that way, but I would like to think this was a little different. Those tears offered me the most humbling of stories. They told me that I had been successful in my seven-and-a-half-year reign as coach of the England cricket team; that I had earnt the respect of the England players.

Those are the things that matter most to a coach. I had never demanded respect, always expecting to earn it. Now I had final confirmation that I had done that. In the space of a minute or two, I discovered everything I needed to know about my coaching stint with England. Things had gone horribly wrong in that winter of 2006/7, and yet I was being afforded such a heart-warming send-off. Anyone who offered the opinion that I had 'lost' the England dressing room at the end of my tenure should have been there. It truly was special.

The tears came at the Police ground in Bridgetown, Barbados, on 19 April 2007. It was there that I announced to the England team that I had resigned as England coach and that their final World Cup Super Eight match against the West Indies in two days' time would be my last. And, yes, I did resign of my own volition. It was wholly my decision. I was not pushed in any way, as some have suggested.

I knew it was going to be an emotional moment, but not this

emotional. That is because, contrary to popular belief, the tears were not just mine. I actually thought that I had been holding myself together pretty well. I had called all the players together mid-practice because I knew that England and Wales Cricket Board (ECB) chairman David Morgan was about to give a press conference elsewhere on the island to announce my resignation. I wanted the players to know before that happened.

But I did not really know what to say. So I just told them the bare facts and thanked them very much for their efforts. 'Right, that's it,' I said and prepared to walk away, hoping the net practice could continue. It was then that skipper Michael Vaughan stopped me.

'Hold on, Fletch, I want to say something,' he said. But as he was saying this, tears were appearing in his eyes. I lost it then. But remarkably, despite his overly emotional state, Vaughan continued speaking, even if he was struggling to control his breathing. I am not sure I could have done that. Vaughan thanked me sincerely for what I had done. I looked around and there were other players with tears in their eyes. I lost it a bit more. Even my old mate, physiotherapist Dean Conway, certainly not one for excessive emotion, said to me afterwards, 'I was lucky I had my sunglasses on.' I had mine on – as usual – but they were misting up. And it was Conway who later mentioned to me that Vaughan had sent him a text message. 'I cannot believe I have just cried in front of grown-ups,' was the gist of it. Apparently Vaughan had never done that before.

I walked away wiping those tears from under my shades as players came up to shake my hand. But there was a strange silence which added to the unforgettable feeling. Players just drifted away to the tent area provided for shade and changing. No one was saying a word.

So I said, 'Come on, guys, we've got a game on Saturday.' And then something even stranger happened. As the two batsmen returned to the nets they had been in before I called them out, everybody else went to have a bowl. I could never remember that happening before. Even the non-bowlers were turning their arms over to occupy their minds. The net became chaos. I just think the players were shocked. Questions had been asked because of the scheduling of Morgan's press conference but only Vaughan, Conway and the relevant people at the ECB knew. As bowling coach Kevin Shine later said: 'That was really classy the way you handled that, not letting on you were going to resign.'

As you may have gathered, I always was pretty good at keeping my cards close to my chest. But the resignation had been brewing for some time. It had hardly been a glorious winter, with the 5–0 Ashes thrashing. There were, however, reasons for that which we will come to. But nothing had prepared me for the thunderbolt with which Mike Atherton struck me after we had lost the final Test in Sydney. Doing an interview for Sky Sports he asked me about an independent review which he had learnt was to be conducted into our defeat.

I knew nothing about it. This was a terrible way to find out. Nobody had had the decency to tell me. I can say honestly that was the lowest point of my cricketing career. The ECB media people Colin Gibson and Andrew Walpole apologized afterwards, but the damage had been done. I felt completely isolated. Not even my employers were backing me up during such a difficult time.

Why was a review needed? Without wishing to brag, England's Test record under me had been very, very good. In the previous twelve Test series we had lost only two. In twenty-two Tests at home before 2007 we had only lost two. We were ranked number two in the world. One very poor series against one of the best teams in the history of the game and this review had been called for. It just did not seem right.

It later transpired that the review was to be headed by Ken

Schofield, a golf man. But still nobody spoke to me about it. Nobody spoke to me about its setting-up, and of its committee only Nasser Hussain, Nick Knight and Micky Stewart later spoke to me about its purpose.

In Australia a couple of days after the review's announcement I even had to phone Morgan and ECB chief executive David Collier for a meeting about it. When I questioned them they allowed me to look through their terms of reference. Some of them did not exactly give me a confidence boost. My mood sank a little lower.

I can only assume Morgan was supporting me but was being outnumbered by his board in the desire for the review. Morgan understood what was going on amongst the squad but, in fairness to him, he was displaying the confidentiality which brought such great mutual respect between us. He was probably not relaying the private one-on-one chats we had had about this. And vice versa he was not relaying to me his conversations with the board. If only others had had such standards of confidentiality. There is no way news of the Schofield Report should have leaked out, but sadly this was typical of my dealings with the ECB. There are people there who think it is their right to inform the media because it makes them look important, certainly a lot more important than they actually are.

I walked away from that meeting in Sydney with Morgan and Collier a depressed man. I wandered the ten-minute walk back to my hotel and for the first time resignation thoughts entered my mind. 'Hold on, what's going on here?' I thought. 'Is it really worth carrying on?'

For then, though, I snapped out of it quickly enough. But the Schofield Report hung like the sword of Damocles over the team's every movement from then on. It definitely affected morale and would have done so even more if the initial, ridiculous, intended date of release – two days before our first World Cup match against New Zealand – had been adhered to. It certainly affected me when Micky Stewart asked to see me at Gatwick airport prior to our departure for the World Cup.

I have a lot of admiration for Stewart. He was always very supportive of me as England coach, always there with a cheering phone call when things were going badly. We chatted about the matters in hand, but then at the end of our conversation he said: 'One criticism of you, Duncan, is your lack of communication.'

'I would communicate a lot more,' I said, 'if there was more confidentiality. I know there is none so I keep things to myself. Why talk if people are going to blab?' He said he appreciated that and then he was on his way. It was not talking to Stewart that frustrated me, just the general situation. 'Why am I having to explain all these things just before such a big tournament?' I asked myself. It was all so very wrong.

That was it. Everyone has a tipping point, and this moment now provided mine. I decided to resign once the World Cup was over. As soon as we landed in St Vincent to begin our World Cup preparations I phoned my wife, Marina. I asked that, when she came out to Antigua later in the tournament, she bring my contract so that I could check the exact wording.

I told no one else then, though, and, as I suppose is the case with many people faced with my sort of situation, vacillated constantly between resignation and carrying on over the next couple of weeks.

The final straw then came with the manner in which the ECB handled an incident concerning Darren Gough. Gough had criticized me at a function in London and it had found its way into the papers. Gough denied doing so and said his words had been taken out of context, but, from the information I received, they had not.

I was heartened when John Carr, the ECB's director of England cricket, told me that action was being taken. So it should have been. But to my dismay the next I heard of it was when we were in Antigua.

While there I received an ECB internal circular e-mail, detailing an imminent press release with the final words being something like 'Let's support Darren Gough in his support of the England cricket team.' That is OK then. Let us all feel sorry for Darren Gough, and let us forget about the feelings of the England coach.

I asked Carr, who was in Antigua, for a meeting and queried the e-mail. 'Is this the way the ECB are handling this?' I said to him in reference to its ending. He had some sympathy for me, but that was not enough. I left him and went to my room. I sat down at my laptop and wrote my letter of resignation. It was 7 April 2007, and I indicated that I intended my twelve-month period of notice to begin on 1 May.

Before printing it, though, I thought it might be best if I spoke to Carr again to clarify a few things, notably to ensure the wording of the letter was correct. But we were playing Australia the following day so it was two days after that, the day before we played Bangladesh, that I eventually spoke to Carr and told him of my intention. He told me to wait, saying he wanted to speak to Morgan and Collier.

In return I told him I was happy to do whatever the board wanted in terms of the notice period. For I had always been fair with them in contractual negotiations. For instance when they first offered me the job in 1999, I asked for a two-year deal rather than the three years on the table.

I said that I would not mind carrying on until the end of the summer of 2007. For, at the back of my mind, I had one last ambition: to beat India in a Test series. They were the only country I did not do that against as coach. I doubt if too many people realize that.

Morgan arrived in Barbados for the Super Eights and we sat down to lay out the terms of my departure. Having accepted my resignation, he told me the West Indies game was to be my last. I was happy with the terms and he said he would make an

announcement after the game against South Africa, the penultimate match of the Super Eights.

Much was made of the fact that I did not speak to the media
the day after the subsequently heavy loss to South Africa – the
only time in my tenure they were denied, when we had done
badly, what they always called a 'Duncan Day' – but that was my
instruction from the ECB. They told me to relax and go off and
play golf. Given my relationship with the media I was hardly
going to argue.

After golf I spoke to Vaughan and told him I was resigning. In
fact, we went to the pub and had a few drinks – a few too many –
reminiscing about the good times.

For there had been many good times. I thoroughly enjoyed
being England coach. I became and felt very English during that
time – still do, if I am honest. Or is that Welsh? After my two seasons at Glamorgan I became rather attached to the other side of
the Severn Bridge. I never bought a house in Cardiff as some
thought, but did rent a place there every summer. And every time
Marina and I came near that bridge on the M4 we would joke
'nearly home now'. Sometimes I wish I had bought a house there,
but it would not be much use now, would it?

But the England job was also damn hard work, extremely stress-
ful stuff at times. I know that I may have often come across to the
media as dour, inscrutable, miserable and all those other adjectives
they so liked to attach to me, but those were more often than not
characteristics brought on by the people I was dealing with.

The key for me was that my dressing rooms were always happy
places, whether playing, captaining or coaching. And that's not
just me saying that, that comment has always been passed by
those involved in teams from Old Hararians back in Zimbabwe
right the way through to the England team.

I first began thinking about this book in 2004. I always recognized the volatility of coaching England and was worried then that

a poor tour of South Africa that winter and then something similar at home to Australia in 2005 might prove terminal. Thankfully that did not prove to be the case then, but it has now. But at least all the notes and updating since then have at last proved useful.

In the pages that follow I would like you to find out what it is really like to coach England. I also want you to know what I am really like; about my background, my family, my philosophies, my friends, my gripes, my mistakes, my capers and much, much more. People who know me recognize that I am a very different person from the public perception. I would like you to find out more about that very different person. In a nutshell, as the title says, I would like you to discover what really lies behind those shades.

Duncan Fletcher
Cape Town, July 2007

1

Born in Rhodesia

You may have noticed that whenever I was interviewed as England coach there were a number of phrases which I used rather frequently. 'Coming to the party' was probably the first one picked up on – my way of describing how a player should contribute sufficiently to the team effort – and there were to be many more.

One phrase I use quite frequently is 'one hell of a . . .'. That is generally for more private conversations but if I attach that to a noun, it is my way of saying that it is so special that I struggle to describe it. So if I say that I had 'one hell of an' upbringing, then you might begin to understand what I mean.

I grew up on Carswell Farm, which is near the town of Nyabira, some thirty kilometres north out of Harare on the road to Lake Kariba. So, unsurprisingly, it was a typically African upbringing: outdoors and active, at times tough – sometimes even extremely hard work – but certainly not closeted or restricted, and importantly it issued me with responsibility and authority at a young age, as well as immediately settling me into a team environment. That was inevitable because I was one of six children, five boys and a girl; all coincidentally with Christian names ending in n – John, Colin, Duncan, Gordon, Allan and Ann, born in that order – and

all mad keen on sport. Ann had little choice but to be brought up
as a tomboy, joining in all the sports we played, even the
impromptu rugby matches on the lawn with the African labourers' sons, where she would act as scrum half. But, to the great
pleasure of the rest of us, she became a brilliant sportswoman in
her own right, playing hockey for South Africa and then captaining the Zimbabwe women's team to gold in the 1980 Moscow
Olympics.

There was little doubt, though, that it was Colin, the second
eldest, who possessed the most sporting talent. I genuinely believe
that he is one of the most talented sportsmen I have ever known.
A big statement when you consider some of the top sportsmen I
have had the pleasure to encounter since, but I stand by it. He was
almost *too* talented, the ease with which he performed at every
sport meaning that he found it mentally difficult to fulfil his
potential in any one of them.

But he is one of only two pupils ever to have achieved full
colours in four sports at Prince Edward School, Salisbury (or
Harare as it is now), which all the Fletcher brothers attended;
Ann going to Prince Edward's sister school, the Girls' High
School, where our mother, Mary, had once been head girl. Colin's
colours came in cricket, hockey, rugby and squash, and he played
for Rhodesia Schools at cricket and hockey, and later went on to
play cricket for Transvaal B, as well as being Rhodesian Schools
squash champion and captain of the Knights squash team to tour
the UK – in essence the South African team, but it could not be
termed so because of the political situation at the time. He now
lives in Switzerland, whose national team he has represented at
squash.

When you consider that eldest brother John attained colours in
rugby and cricket, as did Gordon (who was also a South African
Universities baseball pitcher, as well as playing in the front row for
the Border U20s rugby side), and that Allan earnt his in hockey

(as captain) and cricket (representing Rhodesia Schools and subsequently Rhodesia at both, becoming the only other brother apart from myself to play first class cricket), then you can understand that we were a fairly sport-oriented family.

And the reason why I have listed these achievements of my siblings, as well as, of course, being extremely proud of them all, is to underline the rather obvious fact that I was the weakest in terms of overall sporting ability. All the others were more proficient in a greater number of sports than me. But in a way that might have been to my advantage, because it meant I could have the greater focus to make myself mentally stronger in my one sport.

To use that phrase again, my father, Desmond, naturally played one hell of a role in my early life. He was a pillar of authority, decency and common sense. But the character trait I admired in him most was that which allowed him, despite the remarkable sporting success of all of his children at school, never to be seen as pushy; never the type of father to be accepting the plaudits from other parents at the many sporting events in which his children were always involved. He was quiet, and would sit in his car away from everyone else, observing proceedings with a calm and analytical detachment. Sound familiar to anyone who has seen me watching a cricket match?

I remember one school cricket match when I was captain against our rivals St George's College, Salisbury. Now they had a Reverend Nixon in charge of cricket, a man of the cloth maybe, but when it came to cricket umpiring a man prone to the odd dubious decision. So at teatime he made a complaint to our master-in-charge. Ridiculously he accused my father of sending messages to me from his car.

In reality the lights of the car were indeed flashing, but in no way was it intentional. We had an old Peugeot 404, where the light switch was low down near your leg, and as my father occasionally moved around in the car, he was inadvertently flashing the lights. The Reverend Nixon was interpreting this as some sort of signal to his son, who was busy captaining on the field.

That accusation was made all the more laughable by the fact that my father was never overflowing with sporting advice. He believed in letting us all develop independently. That made us think about our games and so become more streetwise as a result. In contrast to my father's measured objectivity, though, was the frenzied involvement of my mother, who was constantly at the hub of every occasion, making teas and helping out at every opportunity; a truly remarkable woman with unceasing energy, for whom life can never have been totally easy at the time when all her children were away at boarding school.

To my delight my father managed the Nyabira Country Club, which was about two miles from our farmhouse, and he would captain the side that played winter districts cricket there, as well as involving himself and the rest of the family in all the attendant social activities. Some years later the club moved to new premises – only a few kilometres – and I, aged twelve, proudly opened the batting in the inaugural match there.

Interestingly my opening partner was a man named 'Boss' Lilford, a well-known local farmer, who in 1962 helped Ian Smith form the Rhodesian Front movement, which oversaw white rule in Rhodesia until 1979. My father was invited to the preparatory meetings of that party, but preferred to stay loyal to the United Federal Party, which believed that Britain should continue its involvement in the governance of Rhodesia. Our family was much more liberal than many other white families in the area, eventually leading to our ostracism, forcing my father to sell up and move into town (as the city of Salisbury/Harare is always referred to by the locals).

My father passed away in 1979, which sadly meant that he missed my best cricket-playing days (which came after Independence in 1980) and obviously all of my coaching career. But probably most tragic of all was that he missed Ann's Olympic gold, which came only months after his death. How proud he would have been of that.

My brother John, who as the eldest son took over the paternal role, recently said to me that our father would also have taken great pleasure from my coaching England, maybe more so than if I had coached South Africa; this despite us all considering ourselves South African. My father was born in Salisbury but always had an affinity with Britain, not to mention a good deal of ancestry, his father coming from Devizes in Wiltshire and his mother from Tewkesbury in Gloucestershire. Although my mother, a fine tennis player incidentally, was born in Kimberley in South Africa, she hails from the Auld family of Glasgow, Scotland.

Ours was primarily a tobacco farm of modest return, but with plenty of cattle too; not particularly unsuccessful, not particularly successful either. So when we were not at school all the children were expected not just merely to help our parents, but to assume some degree of responsibility too. Often when the time came for reaping tobacco, we might either be in charge of five labourers working on a particular piece of land or in charge of the tractor driving the reaped tobacco back to the farm; not bad for teenagers, who had to grow up pretty quickly.

Saturday mornings would also often mean being placed in charge of our own herd of cattle for dipping. On a Friday evening one of us would be allocated a paddock from which to fetch the cattle. We would round them up, counting them carefully, and then on horseback guide them down to the dip. You had to ensure the cattle did not run because, if they did so in the heat, they would be thirsty and might want to lick the dip. That could poison them. In truth on your own it was difficult to stop one or two running, so usually you would have to take them to the dam nearby for a drink before putting them in a resting pen.

Once dipped you had to guide them all back to the paddock. In all it was probably six or seven hours' hard graft.

And during the wet season when there was a rare dry spell it could often mean a twenty-four-hour session of harrowing the maize. The tractor would have to be driven through the night and my father would set up a roster of two-hour stints, always ensuring that he did the worst one from midnight to 2 a.m.

There might have been responsibility, but there was much freedom too, and naturally that led to us all getting into some scrapes. Yes, even me; a once mischievous, fun-loving child who grew up into what most of the world's cricketing media perceived as the most stern, deadpan coach it had ever encountered.

It might surprise you, but it is wholly true that I was once responsible for burning down almost a third of the farmlands when a prank of mine went badly wrong. It happened when I was trying to play a practical joke on Michael, one of the sons of one of the African labourers, and my brother Allan, who were riding their horses in front of me.

I spent a lot of time horse-riding and became especially friendly with Michael, who was given responsibility for looking after all the horses on the farm. But on this occasion I tried to be too smart in seeing if I could give them a fright by setting off a flash bomb behind them and waiting for their reaction. Unfortunately it just succeeded in creating a blaze which very quickly got out of control. For three or four hours we battled to put it out, and to say that my father, whom we had quickly summoned along with all the farm-labourers, was a little unhappy is an understatement.

My inquisitive nature could court danger in other ways too, as I discovered once when I was attacked by a cobra. It began because, while out riding, I had noticed that a huge number of weavers' nests had been destroyed by a very large monitor lizard. I did not like this, as I did not want it ruining all the birdlife. So I thought the best thing would be to go back to the farm house, collect the shotgun and try to kill it. My brother Colin asked me what I was doing, and, when I told him, he suggested we jump into the Land Rover (we all learnt to drive from about the age of eight) and take the dog. Shooting was also something we learnt early, often walking around with a .22 rifle. Arriving at the area where the nests had been destroyed, we abandoned the Land Rover and decided to walk along the bank of the small river, hoping to disturb the lizard.

I was in front with the shotgun, Colin behind with the dog, when suddenly I heard something rustling to the left. I thought that it was the lizard. I looked and was aghast to see a cobra. It was about two metres long. Luckily it had got a fright – like many animals, most snakes are only dangerous when cornered – so it quickly slithered away up an ant hill made of sand. Immediately I shouted to Colin to get the dog because I was scared it would attack the snake. He managed to grab the dog and scamper across the river to get away.

But in the short time that took to happen, the snake came sliding back down the sand towards me and set off again. As it set off I tried to shoot it. My first shot missed and my second just clipped it. This was when it realized it was in danger and turned and stood up on itself. It started coming at me from about three metres away.

My only thought then was: 'Hold on, I've got to get the hell out of here!' I realized I did not have any ammunition left and because of the U shape of the river, with the angry snake in the middle, the only way out was to jump across it without damaging the gun. Thank goodness it was only a small river so that I could get to the other side to Colin, who had all the spare ammunition.

We immediately killed the cobra. Talk about relief. Those wondering why so many Rhodesians/Zimbabweans, especially the farmers, appeared to make such good cricket fielders over the years need look no further for one possible explanation. You will do well to acquire such natural agility, alertness and awareness through an urban upbringing.

I had another, much weirder, experience with a cobra. It occurred one day when an African approached me in a state of some panic, complaining that there was a snake in his hut. The Africans are very superstitious about snakes and he wanted me to kill it in order to exorcize all the bad spirits from his house.

But for that to happen, it had to be killed inside. And that was where the problem lay, because the hut was merely a mud rondavel, which the Africans build for themselves. One shot and a lot of damage could be done. Indeed, one shot and you could be looking at an African family not having any shelter from the elements.

So with shotgun in hand I decided to look through the doorway of the hut. Because these huts do not have any windows there is no light inside except the tiny bit afforded by the doorway. Even that was being blocked now, so I had to get down on my knees to have a look. I had no idea how big this snake was. The Africans would try to describe them in comparison with the size of their arms and legs. Up to their wrist was maybe a cobra or mamba; when they started comparing it to their calf then you knew it was a python. The African was indicating his wrist in this instance, which meant this snake was pretty dangerous.

On the far side of the hut I could see under a table the silvery shadow of a snake. It seemed motionless, though. Having spotted it I turned to the African. 'I've seen it but there are some pots and things around the table that I could damage. I might blow out the back of your hut,' I said. He was more than happy. 'You just shoot that thing,' he said. 'Are you positive?' I asked. 'Yes,' he said.

But unbeknown to me the snake had been moving around the edge of the hut. I now turned back and looked to see where it was. It had disappeared. I was moving myself so that I could have a look when suddenly over the step, no more than half a metre away, the cobra's head appeared. It was looking at me eye to eye.

Thank goodness it got a fright, just like me, and, as I jumped back, it slithered back into the hut. Now as it made its way under the table again I could see it clearly. So it was then that I let go with the shotgun. Part of the hut and all the cooking utensils were destroyed. That saddened me. But not my African friend; he was smiling from ear to ear. Forget about the lack of accommodation, there were to be no evil spirits for him.

There were many other brushes in the wild, and when I look back, some of our escapades – like riding the horses at full gallop and then leaping off into a haystack – were downright reckless and foolhardy, certainly not of the sort in which I would ever knowingly let my children indulge. There were so many adventures, involving snakes, serval cats and other wild animals, that I could probably write another book on its own about them. Often many years later some of the England players would be seated in a bar somewhere and say: 'Come on, Fletch, tell us about your Zim days.' And then these sorts of tales would come out. To me they were nothing extraordinary, but I soon came to realize that others found them fascinating, so different from anything they had experienced.

However, there was a downside to this life. I had to attend boarding school. The drive into Salisbury, mainly along a tarred strip of road, was too demanding and time-consuming to be made every day, so at the age of seven I was packed off to Blakiston Junior School. Because there were no boarding facilities there, all the Fletcher children stayed in the Braemar Hostel, which was a privately operated concern in town, run by a matron, specifically for children aged between six and fifteen from the farming community. Every morning we would cycle the mile and a half to the school, back to the hostel at lunchtime and then back to school for sport in the afternoon. Relief came in the form of a return to the farm at weekends.

Of course, the sport was thoroughly enjoyable and an early memory is of being made captain of the junior school cricket team, mainly because it began a succession of appointments throughout my life which took me utterly by surprise. I never expected to be captain then, nor later of Rhodesian Schools, because there were players like Rob Berry and Jack Heron whom I thought way ahead of me in the pecking order.

Even when I eventually became captain of Rhodesia, that was also a shock. I remember being called to a selection meeting at Salisbury Sports Club and thinking: 'Jeez, my place could be in doubt here.' When the selectors asked me to become captain, I can clearly recall my response: 'You've got to be joking!' I was so stunned that I told them that I needed some time to consider it before accepting.

It would be easy to dismiss this as false modesty, but I genuinely believe that it is just an indication that captaincy was never something I coveted. Others seemed preoccupied with becoming leaders while I just went quietly about my business. In a way I suppose it was another confirmation of that old, clichéd saying: 'If you look after the pennies, the pounds will look after themselves.' That was all I was doing. Later I used that cliché often with the England team, telling them that if they looked after the controllables the result would look after itself.

However, it is not as if that early elevation at junior school suddenly alerted me to the prospect of a career in cricket. As we did not have access to television I did not even know that a Rhodesian senior cricket team existed. Nowadays all the youngsters in England at that age can switch on their televisions and see the likes of 'Freddie' Flintoff smashing the ball to all parts and think: 'I want to be like him one day.' My mates and I had none of that; we were just having fun.

From Blakiston I was lucky enough to progress to Prince Edward School, as fine a senior educational establishment as I could have entered. It is a special school, which has produced some special people – golfers Mark McNulty and Nick Price, cricketers Graeme Hick, David Houghton and Trevor Penney to name but a few sportsmen. When people refer to its alumni as possessing 'blue blood' that is no jocular bowing to perceived nobility. The bond between its old boys is solid, lasting and respected. Just to illustrate, in 2004 I visited a heart specialist in Cape Town for a check-up. His name was Tommy Maybairn, one of the best in his field in South Africa and formerly of Prince Edward. When I got on the treadmill to be tested, I enjoyed what he said to the nurse: 'Don't worry about him. He's blue blood – strong as concrete – you can top up the speed as much as you want.'

From the outside such talk might seem piffling but loyalty is at the crux of the Prince Edward ethos, and thus ingrained it has stayed with me for the rest of my life. It was one standard I demanded from every cricketer I either captained or coached. First it was to your house (boarding hostel) and then to the school. I have experienced few greater thrills than being able to pull on the emerald green socks of Selous House to play house sport. That always meant so much, as did all the house sporting competitions which were always fanatically contested.

It is all the way back to here that you can trace the roots of my uneasy relationship with the media. It was all about loyalty. Once someone had been disloyal to me I could never show them respect or warmth. Rightly or wrongly that was my biggest problem with the media. I saw it as disloyalty; they just saw it as doing their job.

I will not pretend that it was all smooth running for me at Prince Edward either. For when I arrived at the school my life was made anything but easy. My brother Colin was so talented that there were a lot of people who were jealous and subsequently took it out on me, even though I was the third brother and they did not know my personality or character.

But in a way that was a good experience for me and for my future career in cricket, because it taught me how to handle people in difficult circumstances. That has definitely stood me in good stead ever since, especially as I was at boarding school and obviously could not rush home to my parents with any problems. Also there was no way that you could be seen to be running to your brother for help. I had to fight my own battles.

The other pupils thought Colin arrogant. He was definitely not so, but he was so gifted he would have had every right to have been. It is interesting that, very often in talented individuals, shyness can be mistaken for arrogance, and that was the case here. Likewise I think that much of my so-called grumpiness can be attributed to shyness. Also there is a genetic trait to be considered. All of my family are alike in that our jowls are so low it makes us look as if we are scowling when, in fact, a slight elevation of them will bring about a smile. And we do smile. Even me.

Things were going well for me at school as I was made captain of the U13 and then U14 cricket teams, again unexpectedly on both occasions especially as I was then so small for my age, until I was curiously overlooked for the leadership of the U15 team. Ian Tinker, the master in charge, had this new idea of allowing the players to choose their own leader. They had clearly had enough of listening to me. A chap called Peter Whaley was picked instead. It was the only time during my whole cricketing career that I was dropped from a position or team.

There might have been a perception that I was not suited to it. I was a little bit mischievous and wayward at times, but certainly no delinquent and certainly nothing like my brother Gordon, who was definitely the naughtiest of the Fletchers. He later went on to Rhodes University in South Africa and apparently tales of his revelry still live on there.

He was also very accident-prone. There was one occasion when we were playing touch rugby on the farm and I bumped into him rather forcibly. He stuck his hand out to stop himself against a wall of the house. Unfortunately that wall turned out to be a window and he cut his wrist severely as his hand went through the windowpane. Luckily my mother, a qualified sister trained at Edinburgh Royal Infirmary before the war, was quickly on the scene, tying a towel around his wrist as a tourniquet before rushing him to hospital thirty kilometres away in Salisbury. Having been stitched up everything seemed fine, until a month later when it was discovered that he had no feeling in his thumb and his first two fingers. An operation to repair a nerve followed, which was not entirely successful because to this day he does not have full movement in his right index finger. That meant more time off sporting activity, not something he could endure easily.

So one day back at boarding school a group of us were playing touch rugby with Gordon watching from the sidelines. Of course, he could not resist the temptation for long and soon became a one-handed winger as we played across the width of the rugby field with the 25-yard line and the try line as our touchlines. What happened next almost defies belief. He took a pass in his (good) left hand and, in his enthusiasm to do so, he had forgotten about the goalposts on his right, which in those days were made of wood, with an iron framework holding the crossbar. Smashing into the posts he went, cutting his forehead and suffering a black eye.

But there was more. He did so with such force that he dislodged the crossbar, which came crashing into the back of his head, splitting that too! Can you imagine us explaining that to our mother when she visited us a few days later? It was pretty difficult to hide the bandages – they were covering stitches to the back and front of his head.

Sometimes you need a tiny bit of luck to move upwards and so my first opportunity to play for the Prince Edward first team at cricket came as a result of a chap called Johnny Spence being called away to represent Rhodesia's hockey team at the 1964 Tokyo Olympics – some achievement for a schoolboy. But I took my unexpected chance and never lost my place after that. I was primarily a left-handed opening batsman in those days but was soon to stumble upon bowling by accident.

The Rhodesian Schools trials were being held in Umtali (now called Mutare) and I was part of a composite side comprising those who were not selected by their provinces (in my case Mashonaland). On the second day our opening bowler was promoted to the Mashonaland team because of an injury to their opening bowler. We had no one left to fill that position. 'I'll open the bowling,' I said with much enthusiasm, but little conviction. 'OK,' said the captain. I had not expected him to say that. I turned to a mate of mine and said: 'What run-up do I take?' I just did not have a clue. 'Ten paces,' he said. And that was it; my run-up for the rest of my bowling career. We played the Midlands province and remarkably I took 6–19 bowling away swingers. The next day I took five wickets too. I bowled so well that I almost made the Rhodesian Schools side to play in the famous Nuffield Schools week in South Africa. Not quite though, and sadly I never did play in the Nuffield week, in which Rhodesia then competed against all the South African provinces. When I was eventually selected (as captain), I contracted a nasty dose of the mumps, which developed into orchitis. If I had made it that would have meant a Fletcher being captain for two years running because Colin had had that honour the year before.

However, I did eventually become captain of cricket at Prince Edward. Another complete shock, after those years of only being classed as good enough to be an underling. I was never a school prefect, not even a house prefect or house sub-prefect, so to be chosen as captain of cricket was very rare, probably unique. Those in such a position usually became head boy or at least deputy head boy. I have always wondered why I was suddenly elevated. The previous cricket coach, Ian Lamont, had advised new coach, Nick Erskine, not to select me as captain, but thankfully Erskine went against that.

Out of the blue I saw Lamont in 2001 when I toured Zimbabwe with the England team. We were playing at Alexandra Sports Club in Harare and I was sitting in the viewing area tent when Lamont approached. I still wonder why he came to see me after all that time. Was it guilt? I do not know. I did not speak about school, just exchanged pleasantries and that was that.

Ironically a year later I bumped into Erskine, at Brisbane for the first 2002/3 Ashes Test, a far more convivial meeting with a man for whom I have always had the utmost respect. I said to him: 'Nick, there is something I have been wanting to ask you all these years: why did you make me captain?' He just burst out laughing. 'You know, Duncan, it's been something that has been on my mind all these years too,' he said. 'I don't know why I did it. I just did. You know, I went against the advice of at least five other teachers. They all said: "Don't make that Fletcher captain whatever you do." When you were selected as Rhodesia's Nuffield Schools captain, that was one of my proudest moments because I could go back to them and say: "I think I was right".' It might be overstating the importance of that decision to say that it was life-changing, but you never know what might have happened to me if Nick Erskine had not followed his gut feeling.

I should point out that I also did some academic work at Prince Edward, obtaining my matric passes in four subjects, English, History, Biology and Maths (with a distinction no less), but naturally sport took centre stage for the most part. As further evidence of this, Prince Edward was where my love of rugby union began. To me it is the ultimate game. I especially like the physical aspect of it, but where I feel that it is unique is the way one can watch the build-up to a try. In most other sports the crucial moments usually take you by surprise, for instance in cricket you suddenly say, 'Oh, he's out,' or in soccer, 'Oh, it's a goal,' but in rugby you can see the try being constructed and urge your side to the line. This may sound rather strange but I actually prefer watching rugby to cricket. But, having said that, I reckon that there is no greater thrill in sport than being in control when you are batting in cricket. If things are going well, you are basically saying to the fielders: 'Now, my slaves, go and fetch that ball for me to hit again.' That is some feeling.

Not that I was much good at rugby. In my dreams I delude myself that a glorious career was curtailed by injury. It was ended by injury, yes, but it was hardly going to be glorious. I was, in fact, advised to give up because of three nasty concussions I received. The first was playing soccer as an eleven-year-old (we played only soccer at junior school, because rugby was considered too physical at that age), the second while riding on the farm with my brothers.

The latter was the most scary because of the serious memory loss I incurred. All I can remember is going for a ride with a couple of my brothers one Sunday morning and shutting the gate after going through it last. The next thing I knew it was two o'clock in the afternoon and I was waking up in bed with my mother standing over me.

My brothers later filled me in as to what happened. Apparently, as we galloped off, my horse had slipped on the wet road in the tobacco lands and rolled over me, leaving me hanging upside down with one foot in the stirrup. Thank God the horse did not run off or otherwise I might not be here today. But the others had asked me if I was OK and I had said yes. So off we'd gone riding for a couple of hours. It was only when we got back home that my mother, having been told about the accident by my brothers, checked me out and realized something was wrong; her valuable nursing experience coming to the fore again.

The third concussion came while playing house hockey when a clumsy opponent, a rugby player, hit me on the back of the head as I tripped in front of him – equally clumsily I suppose. 'Get up you wet,' the teacher screamed at me and made me play on. This happened on a Friday afternoon, and that evening my mother, as always, was coming to the school to visit her sons. But when she arrived I was nowhere to be seen. My brothers eventually found me lying in bed and managed to coax me down the stairs (parents were not allowed in the dormitory). She took one look at me and, having been told what had happened, took me to hospital, where I stayed for two nights. X-rays revealed that I had two fractures in my skull. Even though I'd sustained the injury playing hockey, I was advised never to play rugby again.

We do not always do as we are told though, do we? I did play rugby again. In a house match, which to this day is one of the best sporting matches in which I have ever been involved. My brother Colin was captain of the Selous House rugby team, which was full of very good players, their only problem being that they did not have a scrum-half for the final against Rhodes House. Now, I had been a fly-half in my early days but had moved inside to scrum-half before my enforced 'retirement'. 'I'll play. Mum will never find out because it is a house match,' I told him. He reluctantly agreed.

Rhodes house was captained by Brian Murphy, who went on to become one of Rhodesia's finest number eights, coached Zimbabwe at the 1991 Rugby World Cup, and whose son, also called Brian, captained the Zimbabwe cricket team as a leg-spinner in 2001. It was one of those games where the sides just could not be split. We played extra time, which did not produce a winner. So it was decided to play to sudden death. Sure enough, after about three minutes we had a scrum near their line and Colin, who was at fly-half, called for the ball. I would like to think that it was a great pass, but whatever it was, it did its job, and Colin dropped the goal to win the game. I can still see it as if it were yesterday. I loved that day.

Talking of love, it is high time I mentioned a young lady called Marina Nicholas. That we met in the first place was down to a chap called Brian Bagnall, with whom I had become friendly in my final year at Prince Edward. That year I became a day scholar because of the family's politically enforced move into town and Brian, with whom I played in the hockey first team, introduced me to horse-racing.

Every Saturday afternoon after our morning hockey match we would go to the Borrowdale races in Salisbury where we would also meet up with three brothers – Robert, Bruce and Howard – whose surname was Nicholas. Their father, Alex, a very successful businessman in the stationery trade, then became a professional racehorse trainer, but more importantly they had a sister called Marina. Ironically, at first, she was being taken out by Brian, but that relationship soon broke up. I wanted to ask her out but felt uncomfortable about doing so, because of my close friendship with Brian. Eventually it took the prompting of her brother Bruce to persuade me to do so and I plucked up the courage to ask her to the movies. That was in 1967 and by 14 August 1971 we were married.

I am not very good at expressing my emotions in such matters, but I know that I am a very fortunate man to have found such a loving, considerate and understanding lady. I hope that the very fact that this book is dedicated to her illustrates my debt to her. She has never once stood in the way of my cricket, and at times that must have been very difficult for her. From the time we met until Independence in 1980 I did not spend one Christmas at home as the Rhodesian team was always in South Africa playing in the Currie Cup around the festive period. Wives were not allowed on tour in those days, because that time was used for bonding, but nowadays cricketers, especially the international ones, play so much cricket that it is imperative that wives and families are allowed on tour.

As an amateur cricketer in Rhodesia I would work until 5 p.m. and then be off to practise until darkness set in, at the latest at 7 p.m. All day Sunday would invariably be spent playing club cricket if there was no first class game on. So for much of the time Marina was left to bring up our two children on her own. Michael was born in 1975 and Nicola in 1978. And I have to say that she did a magnificent job. Both of them are now married; Michael, with our first grandson Jason, lives back in South Africa with his wife Cindy after spending time in London, working in the finance department at Surrey County Cricket Club, while Nicola, with husband Jared, is in Cape Town.

Both children excelled at sport at school. Nicola represented Western Province Schools at synchronized swimming at the national championships, where she won the solo routine as well as joining forces with others in her team to take the figures routine. Michael was a good enough cricketer to captain Jacques Kallis for a few seasons at Wynberg Boys' High School, and also skippered the hockey first team. He also captained Western Province Schools B team at hockey before going to the University of Cape Town, where he obtained a Business, Science and Finance degree. Nicola has recently set up her own business in graphic design.

Marina's family's interest in racehorses meant that I came to breed and own some for a while. This very nearly landed me in trouble in the early days of my first class cricketing career, when my youthful mischievousness was still being drummed out of me. I was playing in a first class match against Western Province at the old Police ground in Salisbury, where we were batting and I, as opener, was the only man out. I had had a bet on one of my horses and it was running at 2.15 p.m. at Borrowdale, no great distance from the ground. So, in a rascally moment, I thought it would be a good idea to sneak away on my motorbike, which I was using to get around at the time, and watch the race. My only concession to common sense was that I took a radio with me so that I could keep up to date with the cricket in case something calamitous occurred. I must have looked a sight sitting, peering through my binoculars and with my cricket whites on, atop one of the buses which was conveniently parked next to the track and had been used to transport racegoers.

I saw my race – I cannot even recall whether my horse won – but then got a little too comfortable and decided to watch a second race. Sod's Law now intervened and my radio announced that four wickets had suddenly fallen. I panicked and quickly got on my bike for a speedy return. As I screeched down the road, though, suddenly my back wheel seized. The chain had broken and locked in the wheel. I was fortunate not to have had a serious accident.

More important to me at the time though was how on earth I was going to get back to the match. By the largest stroke of sheer luck, who should pull up in the car behind but Marina? She was on her way to the cricket, and incredulous as to what she was seeing. 'What on earth are you doing here?' she said in surprise. We left the bike and managed to make it back with the team seven wickets down. Thankfully, no one had even noticed my absence.

I was unsure what to do when I left school. I had wanted to be a veterinary surgeon at one stage, but in order to do that I would have been required to learn Afrikaans and the only university which allowed you to study that was at Onderstepoort in Pretoria. Another possibility was training to become a fighter pilot but, in the end, I took a job in the government valuation department. Not for long though, as in 1968 I was called up into the Rhodesian Air Force. And there I did my nine-month training stint, alternating between Salisbury and Kariba. Mostly it was pretty boring stuff, mundane security work, so there are to be no heroic war stories from me. But I did experience a couple of nerve-jangling incidents during this time, which gave me enough of a reminder that there were rebels at work, vigorously opposing Ian Smith's Unilateral Declaration of Independence in 1965, which had led to comprehensive United Nations sanctions and Rhodesia being deemed an illegal regime by the rest of the world.

The first came one day when we were ordered to escort a convoy of army vehicles carrying supplies and ammunition from the capital out to a nearby airfield. I was in the hindmost vehicle, but as we drove at dusk the first vehicle hit a landmine and all hell broke loose. It was the first time I had ever experienced fear, real fear that is. You can feel your heart pumping so much that you almost seem bruised afterwards, and every shadow in the darkness assumes life.

I felt exactly the same on the second occasion when we were in Kariba and some flares went up. We thought that we were under attack. I jumped into a trench with just my running shorts on and readied myself. Allied to the fear element was a strange emotion of wanting to see how brave I was, almost willing for some combat. It did not come, though, and I can honestly say that I never fired a shot in anger.

In fact, some of my time at Kariba was spent on the lake learning to waterski, but the primary duty was to guard military aircraft. This guard duty entailed a rota of two hours on, four hours off for forty-eight hours, and then twelve hours off. And then back to two hours on, four hours off again. The most dreaded shift was from eight till ten at night because then you were back on duty at two in the morning. Only on the very odd occasion when a pride of lions passed close to the camp would things liven up.

The extent of our boredom through this monotonous roster is probably best illustrated by our daft attempts to create some entertainment. One way of doing this was to encourage elephants, of which there were many outside our camp, to charge. We would sneak outside the confines of our base and entice the elephants to charge us so that we could take photos – with our old box cameras – before running back inside. The skill was to take the photo just as the elephant began its charge. There were some close escapes, however, because the animals seemed further away than they actually were through the camera lens. It was all a bit silly, yes, and at the time we did not know the difference between a mock charge (trunk down) and a real one, but we were nineteen-year-olds being asked to live a mind-numbingly dull existence.

Probably most unnerving was an incident which occurred years later when I had long been out of the Air Force full time and was back living in Salisbury. One night in 1979 I was awoken by an enormous explosion, a bang which made the house rattle, followed by two rapid, and very near, bursts of machine-gun fire. In these circumstances we had always been told to move the family into the shower area, so I took Marina and the two children there and grabbed my Uzi submachine gun to go outside to see what was going on. Luckily for me I did this immediately because if I had waited then I might have been in trouble. I later ascertained why.

Basically there were two rebels in the area, but they were not particularly sophisticated or sharp operators. They were looking for the residence of Bishop Muzorewa, the leader of a political party which that year formed a coalition government with Ian Smith's Rhodesian Front, but in their ignorance asked its location from a couple of lurking street kids, who were no doubt drunk. These youngsters wrongly pointed out the Greek Archbishop's residence, a house not much more than 500 metres from our own in the Borrowdale area near the racecourse.

So that was the house they attacked, firing an RPG (a rocket-propelled grenade, which was normally used to take out large military vehicles) at the front door, but missing and hitting the roof instead. And then they fired shots at the Archbishop when he appeared to investigate. He was lucky to survive. His attackers fled to hide behind the entrance wall of another house around the corner, only four houses down from ours, hoping that they could then ambush the security forces when they arrived on the scene. Quite funnily, though, the owner of that house then came out in his pyjama shorts to have a look, just as I had done. That disturbed the rebels, who then fired some shots at him (miraculously he survived too) before running down the road past my house, thankfully after I'd gone back inside. The rebels were eventually cornered, and after a shoot-out were killed by the security forces in the stables down at the racecourse.

I was glad to get out of the Air Force and begin working again for a living. Computers had always fascinated me, even though there was a dearth of them in our country because of the international sanctions. So when a friend, Clive Kluckow, offered me the chance of a job working with them, I jumped at it. I still had to do a four-week Air Force camp stint each year, as did everyone, but this was much more enjoyable.

I have always had an inventive mind, rarely accepting the norm and always seeking means of improvement, whichever field I have been in. So quite a lot has been made of the fact that I helped develop the Rhodesian/Zimbabwean number-plate system which still exists today. But personally I am more proud of a document I designed when I later joined CIMAS, the medical aid society. I could not understand why they needed to send out two documents to claimants, one a statement containing the financial details and the other with the cheque for that amount. 'Why not have one page with the statement at the top and the cheque section at the bottom which can be torn off by having a perforated line?' I suggested. It sounds incredibly simple now, but it had not been seen before and I was told that only sanctions prevented it from winning a new form design competition in America.

At least because I was called up to the Air Force in April 1968 I did not miss too much of the cricket season, coming out in December to resume playing club cricket for Old Hararians, my club side, known simply as Old Boys, of Prince Edward that is, of course. The club cricket in those days was competitive and of a good standard, with all the Rhodesian players available to play in most of the fixtures; there were only eight first class fixtures a season, four home and four away.

And we were the stand-out side, being league and knockout champions on numerous occasions. It was a hugely enjoyable time, playing for Rhodesia with some very good cricketers and one great one in all-rounder Mike Procter, who spent most of the 1970s with us. His influence upon me was profound, as I especially marvelled at the way he always led courageously from the front.

I was named one of the five *South African Cricket Annual* cricketers of the year in 1975 when I took 33 wickets for just 18, including one spell I particularly remember against Eastern Province in Bulawayo. I had opened the bowling and gone wicketless for 18 runs in 6 overs, but returned for a second spell and took 6–13 in 7 overs, including four South African Test batsmen (one of whom was the great Graeme Pollock). I also took 5–61 in the second innings for my career-best match analysis.

But I did not really play my best cricket until after Independence in 1980. Playing Currie Cup cricket against the South African provinces was good, but by its very nature it was insular and there was no goal for which to aim, especially after South Africa were banned from international cricket.

On one occasion I was close to selection for South Africa, for the 1971/2 tour to Australia. In fact, Charles Fortune, the great South African cricket commentator, and a couple of other senior journalists picked me in their squads as the all-rounder. Instead, the selectors went for Transvaal's Clive Rice, with his provincial skipper Ali Bacher as captain. I was reminded of this sort of selectorial favouritism when I went to coach in county cricket with Glamorgan in 1997 and heard tales of it being an unfashionable county, whose players were often spurned by the national selectors in favour of those from, say, Surrey. I could identify with that, because I came from a similar environment. We all knew we had to be a lot better than someone from Transvaal. I would like to think that when I took over with England we got away from such thinking.

Anyway that South Africa tour was cancelled, but it would have been interesting to have known whether I was good enough to play for South Africa. It would, though, have been a difficult side to break into because I think that, but for the years of isolation, they would have dominated world cricket for a decade at least.

I always thought that Old Boys would be my only club, but one day I was at the races with Richie Kaschula, a good friend who was a legendary figure in Rhodesian cricket. He was a left-arm spinner who, weighing in at somewhere near twenty stone, was a larger than life character in more ways than one. He said to me: 'Why don't you come and play for Alex [Alexandra Sports Club]?' expecting me to say no because of my 'blue blood' connection. But I was at a stage in my career where I needed a fresh challenge, and maybe a bit of extra cash too (as I was still a relatively low-paid civil servant), so I said I would, as long as they paid me. I asked for what I thought was a ridiculously high figure at that time. He went away and returned to say: 'You're on.' I think I became the country's first professional club cricketer, setting a new trend in that respect.

I was also beginning a personal trend. Alex were a very average second division side when I joined them, but in my first year I delighted in first helping them win the knockout cup, which involved all the first and second division teams, and then taking them up into the first division by winning the second division. We won the first division immediately and Alex became a top side for many years. I hope that I am not being arrogant when I say there should be sufficient evidence throughout this book of how I have joined teams, both as player and coach, and then made a difference. That has given me great satisfaction. I must add, though, that I did ensure that my last season of Rhodesian/Zimbabwean club cricket was back at Old Boys. The 'blue blood' ensured as much.

In 1977 I experienced club cricket of another kind; a year with Rishton in the Lancashire League, following in some famous footsteps as their overseas professional. But what a palaver to get there. For a start I only had a Rhodesian passport, which, at the time of sanctions, would only allow me to visit South Africa. I could go nowhere else in the world on it, unlike both my parents, my two younger brothers and sister, who all had British passports. This British passport saga was one which ran and ran, naturally becoming more of an issue when I became coach of England. And it took until after England won the Ashes in 2005 for me to be granted one.

Most people I spoke to before then thought it ridiculous that some members of a family could have British passports, while others could not. Indeed, I remember being on tour in Pakistan with England and speaking to a member of the British High Commission about it and he was adamant that I could get one. I told him I could not, because, bizarrely, I was born before 1 January 1949, when the British Nationality Act of 1948, which conferred British citizenship on all Commonwealth citizens, finally came into force.

He checked it out and came back to me. 'You're right,' he said. It has always been a sensitive issue and one in which it was unwise to seek influential help.

I first applied for a British passport in 1991, but I really started to panic in 2002 when I knew that my Zimbabwean passport was soon to expire. With the problems in that country I knew that it was highly unlikely that it would be renewed. Fortunately at that time I was able to obtain a South African passport.

What always confused me was that I could spend no more than

450 days out of the UK over a five-year period to qualify for a British passport. But that was obviously very difficult when I was away with the England cricket team for such long periods. People were arguing that I spent a lot of time at my home in Cape Town, but I did not. I spent my northern hemisphere summers living in Cardiff and most of the winters abroad, somewhere on the long tours England always embark upon. Anyway, I got there in the end. On the day after we had won the Ashes, during the chaotic celebrations, I received the good news, via a text message, that I was to receive a British passport. A British citizen at last.

If only that had been the case back in 1977. I had agreed a contract with Rishton, but with barely a month to go before my intended departure I still had no passport. It was then that I had a stroke of luck. Rhodesia were playing a match against Western Province in Salisbury where we were introduced to a dignitary on the first morning of the game, by chance the South African ambassador. I could not let this opportunity slip, so I got hold of his phone number and called him immediately after the three-day game had finished. 'Remember I met you on Saturday?' I said, and proceeded to ask him about a travel document. He probably did not remember me, but he did at least say: 'Come and see me tomorrow.'

Up until then I had been doing some extensive research, and as a result I knew all about passports, having looked at ways of obtaining Spanish, Italian, even Greek ones. I knew where I could buy any of those. But this was a slightly more legitimate method. The ambassador asked where my mother was born. 'Kimberley,' I replied. 'Can I trust you not to get into any trouble?' he asked, with a tentativeness pre-empting the lack of conviction in my reply. 'Yes,' I mumbled.

Thank goodness he was unaware of my proposed method of travel, but he was sufficiently persuaded to instruct one of his employees to issue South African passports for myself, Marina and Michael. He took our Rhodesian passports and before he put them in a safe he was adamant that we must return the issued passports as soon as we came back. We collected our Rhodesian passports on our return and I travelled on a Rhodesian/Zimbabwean passport until September 2004 when I gained that South African passport.

However, the problem in 1977 was that flights to England were not easy to book, and expensive too. So I had a plan. My brother John was general manager of an air transport company called Air TransAfrica, which was helping Rhodesia break sanctions in importing and exporting goods, especially tobacco. And his company were organizing a lot of cargo flights to Europe, leaving at night via, say, Mauritius and going through Iran.

So he managed to get us on one of these flights, albeit one which was full of day-old chicks (what a noise!) which were to be taken to Iran. Also on board was some meat being delivered to Mauritius, and then it was on to Holland where the flight would pick up some imports which were to be returned into Rhodesia. It was one way of not using up too much of the lump sum being offered by Rishton.

First, we had to fly over Mozambique in the dark, which was a bit jittery. We had to do this because the terrorists (freedom fighters) were using SAM-7 heat-seeking missiles and there had been incidences of planes being shot down. In fact, when I was on Air Force duty this had happened to an Air Rhodesia commercial flight taking off from Kariba. There were many women and children on board and, sadly, on that flight was a lady whom I knew well because she had been my father's secretary. The pilot did incredibly well to crash land the plane but after this, while some of the men went looking for help as dusk had descended, rebels found the plane, raped the women and then shot all the survivors.

From our base at Kariba some troops were sent out to find the perpetrators of this ugly crime and three days later, after a fierce firefight, some rebels were duly brought back to the camp, two or three of them dead and a couple alive. I was ordered to take the dead bodies from a Land Rover. That is not something you can forget easily.

Neither could I forget the possible consequences of later events after landing at Tehran. We dropped off all the cargo and a new crew took over, because the first one had exceeded its permitted flying time. I was standing near the window over the wing, as the plane was now empty, and as the engines were being started I noticed a short burst of flame in one of them. I thought little of it because I reckoned it must be how they started, a bit like the piston engines backfiring on the Dakotas I had seen during my Air Force days. So there we were flying over Turkey and suddenly the plane dropped significantly out of the sky. The first batch of pilots, who had been sleeping at the back on mattresses, quickly jumped up and rushed to the cockpit. They then came back to the window out of which I had been peering when we took off. 'What's the matter?' I asked nervously. 'We've lost an engine,' was the reply. I then told them what I had seen. So we were forced to fly over Germany and France, even though those countries would not give us permission to do so because this was not a properly registered flight, before landing at Amsterdam.

It was only later when I phoned John from the UK that he told me the startling truth: 'You don't know how lucky you were. If someone else had seen that flame, you would not have been allowed to take off. And then the trouble would have started, because a new engine would have had to have been sourced in the USA. But because of sanctions it would not have been able to go straight to Tehran. It would have had to go via South America, to South Africa and then up to Tehran. That might have taken a minimum of a month and a half or up to four months, and you would not have been allowed to move.' Stuck on the tarmac at

Tehran for a month or more, now there is a thought, especially as Michael was only two at the time.

We had such a wonderful time at Rishton, though, that I promised to go back some time, if only for a brief visit. And I stuck to that pledge, making the trip just before Independence, during the interim government led by Bishop Muzorewa, by which time we were allowed to use our Rhodesian passports abroad. John said I could take one last free flight so that I could go on my own to see my pals in Rishton, especially David Lomas, Ronnie Smith and Wilf Woodhouse, so that we could reminisce about that successful season when we had finished third in the table.

Later Lomas and Smith, with two friends Brian Bowling and Maurice Davies (and sometimes Woodhouse), were regular visitors when I was England coach at a day of a Test at either Headingley or Old Trafford. The only problem was getting rid of them in the evening (only joking, guys!), trying to get them out of the hotel so that I could get to bed in readiness for the next day's play. People more passionate about cricket you will struggle to find anywhere in the world.

But that second trip to Rishton was another hair-raising experience which might easily have led to trouble. On the way back we had to stop off in Valencia to pick up some tomatoes. As we were preparing to take off, I remember being at the back of the plane with the loadmaster, who I noticed was most agitated and was sweating profusely. 'What's the matter?' I asked.

'We should not be taking off with a full load of tomatoes and a full load of fuel,' he replied. And sure enough I have never seen a plane take so long to get into the air, inch by inch it seemed as we climbed over the Mediterranean, with the loadmaster clinging furiously to his seat. It later transpired that the pilot should only have initially half-filled the plane with fuel and then refuelled in Kano, Nigeria, before dropping off the tomatoes in Brazzaville in the Congo. But straight to Brazzaville we went, despite all the dangers; the only consolation was that that pilot was subsequently suspended from flying for some time. The things I went through on my trips to Rishton!

When the country of Rhodesia became Zimbabwe in 1980, our cricket underwent significant change too. We were now on our own, divorced from South Africa and exposed to the big wide world of international cricket. We needed a plan. As I had been appointed captain in 1979, it was natural that I should be heavily involved in those important thought processes. But I was very fortunate that Alwyn Pichanick was president of the Rhodesia Cricket Union at the time (he had been so since 1965). Not only was he a good friend, a mentor I suppose, but an ever-willing ally and kindred spirit too – not always the case when talking of the player and administrator relationship. Indeed, Pichanick often remarked how refreshing it was for this to be the case between us. But I have always strived for that to be the case, whether as captain or coach, even though the ECB at times made that scenario very difficult.

Having applied for associate membership of the International Cricket Coucil (ICC) (granted in 1981) we made it our goal for Zimbabwe to reach the 1983 World Cup. But in order to do that we had first to win the ICC Trophy staged in the UK in 1982. And for that to have a chance of happening we needed to play some high quality opposition beforehand. So we invited a number of teams to tour Zimbabwe. The first of these was Middlesex, who came as county champions at the end of the 1980 season. They were clearly a strong side, captained by Mike Brearley and with internationals – past, present and future – like Mike Gatting, John Emburey, Paul Downton, Roland Butcher, Mike Selvey and Norman Cowans in their squad.

I shall never forget the first game of that trip because it was probably one of the most bizarre games I've ever been involved in.

It was a one-day match reduced to 38 overs per side, and I was pretty pleased to have scored a hundred, which I thought would be sufficient for us to overhaul Middlesex's 237. But what happened afterwards illustrates the old adage that a batsman's work is never fully done until the last ball of the innings is bowled. 'Never leave to someone else what you can do yourself' is an appropriate motto. But I did. It came to the last over with us needing one to win with six wickets in hand, but somehow we managed to contrive a tie. If match-fixing had been an issue at the time eyebrows would surely have been raised, so much did it seem that we wanted the result to be a tie.

Leicestershire, with Yorkshire's John Hampshire and David Steele, then at Derbyshire, as guests, toured before the start of their 1981 season. And then later that year we were graced by the presence of a truly outstanding Young West Indies side, which included six players – skipper Faoud Bacchus, Malcolm Marshall, Desmond Haynes, Gus Logie, Jeff Dujon and Harold Joseph – who had already been selected for the West Indies tour of Australia to follow immediately afterwards. Add in Wayne Daniel, Hartley Alleyne and Winston Davis and you can understand the strength and depth of their opposition.

But we learnt much from that tour and it was not just on the field that the West Indians impressed me. They were very approachable off the field and willing to offer advice. But it was the clarity of thinking in that advice which was most striking. One evening we asked Haynes and Marshall to come into our changing room to give us some pointers. They were more than willing to help, and it was then that I realized what class individuals they were. I never forgot that and when I later became coach of Western Province I immediately tried to sign Haynes as my overseas player. He was unable to come in my first season but fortunately could do so in my second and third seasons and it was thoroughly enjoyable working with him.

That evening in Harare, though, we spoke to him and asked how we might be able to cope should we reach the World Cup. We just did not know what to expect with bowlers of the pace of Michael Holding. 'Don't worry,' said Haynes. 'You've just faced the two fastest bowlers in the West Indies and done OK. Nothing will be worse than that.' For those of you wondering, he was referring to Marshall and Alleyne, even though others like Daniel and Davis were pretty quick, too.

We did win the ICC Trophy, beating Bermuda in the final, but the tournament was not a wholly enjoyable experience, as most of the other teams, even some of the hotel staff, treated us with a coldness bordering on ostracism. It was only a night out with the Fijian team, then alone in their friendliness towards us, that cleared up the riddle of this stand-offish attitude. They asked us why we had the capital letter R on our tracksuits and training gear. It stood for Rhythm – a popular South African clothing brand – but apparently the other teams thought it stood for Rhodesia and that we were diehard Rhodesians who wanted some recognition of our former country. All very strange, but at least we achieved our goal and qualified for the World Cup.

But the hard work had only just begun, not just on the playing field either. We had to raise a huge amount of money in order to afford this second trip to England, as otherwise the Zimbabwe Cricket Union would not have been able to send us. So we had to set about a programme of fundraising events with gusto. There were, among other things, large beer fests with all of us acting as barmen and stall-keepers, the selling of large numbers of signed miniature bats and the auctioning off of tobacco bales kindly donated by local farmers. Marina was instrumental in organizing all the wives to help out with other activities, such as many a cake sale, selling cuff-links, ties and other memorabilia to the general public when we played games against visiting sides. It did the team good to undertake such work, bringing them closer together

and appreciating the good times we had when we eventually
arrived in England.

On the playing side we sat down as a squad and agreed on
some basic principles. We obviously lacked experience at international level, with our batsmen having rarely faced top bowlers
and our bowling lacking the depth to trouble the better batting
line-ups. We knew that it would be difficult because of our full-
time jobs away from cricket but we vowed to train harder than
ever before.

We thought we could be genuinely competitive in two areas: fitness and fielding. We decided that we had to be the fittest side at
the World Cup and the best fielding side too. Those were areas
where sheer hard work would bring its reward, even if the other
sides were much more talented overall. And by the time we got
there I think we had succeeded. We were fitter than the rest and I
do not think there was a better fielding unit either.

The plan was also for the batsmen to ready themselves for the
quicker bowling, despite Haynes' confidence that we would be able
to cope, by employing two Springbok baseball pitchers, Arthur
Fulton and Kenny Doull, for net practices. They were instructed to
throw balls from 18 yards as hard as they could at all the batsmen.
They were obviously told not to beam us, but otherwise they could
pitch it wherever they liked. It was just a case of us trying to get
used to the pace, to become accustomed to having the ball fly past
our faces. It sharpened us up so much that when we then went into
the fast bowlers' net we had so much more time than we ever had
previously against bowlers like, say, Vince Hogg, who generally
terrorized us in the nets. Two guys, who had better remain nameless,
completely froze with fear and had to be taken out of the pitchers'
net, but otherwise it was a very interesting and beneficial exercise.

The plan for the bowlers was obviously more difficult and there
was no specific practice we could come up with other than ensuring
that they had sufficient control in their bowling.

My mantra as captain was that I would never make the players do anything which I was not prepared to do myself. That might sound rather clichéd and glib, but believe me, it is not always the case. We would have net practice for an hour and a half after we had all finished work, and then at 6.45 p.m. when dusk descended, the physical fitness would begin. Using the small amount of light coming from the clubhouse bar and veranda we would start with a series of shuttles – using the length of a cricket pitch in order to simulate running between the wickets – followed by some old-fashioned exercises, such as press-ups, sit-ups and burpees. Then it would be off for a 7 km run. Sometimes it might be around the Royal Harare golf course or on other occasions just round the streets of Harare. I preferred the golf course run because it granted me the opportunity to crack the whip with some of the more idle members of the squad. The final part of the run brings you around the Harare Sports Club ground, through a gate at the city end and across the cricket field back to the dressing rooms. As long as I finished in the leading group, which always included the likes of Hogg, John Traicos and a youthful Graeme Hick (whom we took to the World Cup as a seventeen-year-old), then I could wait near the changing rooms and keep a check on the stragglers. There were sometimes some who might even be tempted by a short cut across a couple of fairways of the golf course and round the back of the clubhouse.

That had happened before. Indeed temptation had once got the better of Barry Dudleston, the former Leicestershire and Gloucestershire batsman, now a first class umpire, who played for Rhodesia between 1976 and 1980. He did not finish the course by coming across the cricket pitch to the front of the clubhouse and I had to say to him: 'Look, Barry, you can bugger around and be lazy in England, but not here.' He naturally apologized. That sort of laziness really irritated me, and I would order any miscreants to do more shuttles and also to run up and down the steep stands at the ground. But it was very important that I would always do that extra training with them, so there could be no complaints. I would work some so hard that they felt really uncomfortable and were almost sick by the end of the session. Interestingly, when I toured Bangladesh with England in 2003 their board's chief executive was Macky Dudhia, a former Zimbabwe player and good character, and he recalled one of these sessions in conversation. 'You used to work us lazy ones hard,' he said, 'but you always did the extra training. That was one of the biggest reasons I respected you as a captain.'

So to the World Cup and probably my finest all-round moment as a player. It has been well documented that in our first game at Trent Bridge we beat Australia by 13 runs, and that I won the man of the match award for my 69 not out and 4-42. But do you know what? I do not reckon that Australian side was up to much.

And that was true for much of the eighties. In fact, I reckon that the misconception over their strength hampered English cricket for many years afterwards. Indeed, the influence of supposedly successful England players around this time very nearly wiped England off the cricketing map.

For it is assumed that the England side of the eighties was a very good one – after all, before 2005, they had been the last side to win the Ashes when Mike Gatting's team brought them home in 1987 – but even little Zimbabwe beat that poor Australian side. Yes, England had some very good players – there is no denying that when you consider the likes of Ian Botham and Graham Gooch – but it is interesting when you look at their ratio of success.

Thanks to the findings of the Cricket Reform Group – which, in showing great honesty, included a member of that side in Bob

Willis – it was revealed that the England Test team only won 19.23 per cent of its matches in the eighties. Only the forties (18.75 per cent) has a worse percentage. And it is no surprise that the nineties side, coached and supposedly inspired by the eighties generation, only managed a 24.30 per cent success rate. Compare that to the over 40 per cent (the 1950s, with 46.99 per cent, lead the way) enjoyed by the team so far in the new millennium. And I also find it interesting that someone like Graham Dilley, who is widely recognized as a very good English fast bowler, played twelve Test matches before he was on the winning side for England – and that in the freakish Headingley 1981 match – and was only a winner once more in his forty-one-match Test career.

More interesting is that between 1975 and 1990 England played the West Indies on thirty-three occasions and only beat them once in a Test, the last one of that period in 1990. When we lost 5–0 to Australia – one of the greatest sides ever – in 2006/7 it was the players from that era, that side, who were doing all the criticizing, reminding everyone of how they beat the Australians rather than recalling their abysmal record against the best side in the world then, the West Indies. There were two 5–0 whitewashes, one at home and one away, during that period. I never heard those mentioned during the 2006/7 Ashes. Our team had the class and ability to beat the best side in the world (at home in 2005). That lot did not. Also, if you can, have a look back at footage of the Test cricket played in England in the eighties. The matches were played to half-full stadia. These days you can barely get a ticket for the first three days of a Test.

Zimbabwe could also have beaten Australia the second time we played them in that 1983 tournament, at Southampton, falling 32 runs short of their 272. After being out for just 2 I remember sitting on the players' balcony with Kepler Wessels, twelfth man for Australia that day, as Davie Houghton and Kevin Curran set about a partnership which threatened to win us the match, and

Wessels said of his teammates: 'They're pooping themselves again. It's going to happen all over again.'

Sadly it did not and we also had near misses against India at Tunbridge Wells and the West Indies at Worcester. That Indian match is, of course, famous for a remarkable innings of 175 not out from Kapil Dev, hauling his side from the mire of 9–4 when he came to the wicket and later 78–7, to post 266, a total of which we only fell 31 runs short. As captain I copped a fair amount of flak after that match for my decision to replace opening bowler Peter Rawson after nine overs of his allocated twelve. Many felt that both he and Curran should have bowled their allocation uninterrupted because India were in such trouble. But Rawson actually came to me and said that he was knackered. And he was not the type to shirk hard work. He was a fine bowler – the best to whom I ever stood at slip – who went on to play for Natal with distinction. He knew what he was doing. As did young Curran, who was a cricketer for whom I also had a lot of time. He might have rubbed a few people up the wrong way in his career, but I liked his fearless attitude. It was just that Kapil played one of those innings about which we could do very little.

Nonetheless we could return home after that tournament with our heads held high. We had proved that we could compete with the best because we had also beaten Pakistan in a warm-up match at Uxbridge. That was very satisfying because I remember winning the toss and inviting them to bat. Their skipper, Imran Khan, looked at me in astonishment because that just was not the done thing in those days. He went back to tell his players and they all burst out laughing. Unfortunately for them there was only one team laughing at the end, as they were only able to muster 264, which we passed easily for the loss of only five wickets. That was sweet, but sadly for me that tournament was the high point of my playing career. My life was about to change.

2

Down South

I am a believer in fate and providence. I have to be. For evidence just consider this story. It is 1984 and I am considering my future, pondering a move to South Africa. My mother and all my brothers and my sister have left Zimbabwe, so I am the only Fletcher left. I am unsure how this new Zimbabwe is going to turn out; whether it will be a good place to live, and more importantly whether it will be the best place to bring up and educate two children. So I am sitting in my office, on the phone talking to my brother John, now living safely in Johannesburg. We are discussing a few things: I am grumbling about my uncertain future, and he is telling me that it is unfair to expect our sister Ann, with her young family, to look after our mother, who is in Durban with her. I suggest to him the possibility of taking a holiday and bringing my family down to South Africa to see him and his family. 'We can talk about things then,' I tell him. He thinks that is a great idea and we are both momentarily cheered. As I am walking away from my desk on the way to see the boss and ask for five days' leave, the phone rings. I dither about answering, but eventually pick it up. It is a chap from Cape Town offering me a job in computers. I have no idea who he is or how he got hold of me, but I listen to what he has to say and tell him that, by coincidence, I am just about to organize a family trip down to Johannesburg. 'We'll pay for you to fly on down to Cape Town for an interview,' he says, 'and then you can quickly rejoin your family.'

That very afternoon I am then playing golf at Chapman Golf Club. It is a weekly ritual that at 1.20 p.m. every Wednesday the 'famous four ball' get together. Clive Kluckow, Rob Davenport, Willie Armitage and myself. As I am walking up towards the clubhouse, with my clubs over my shoulder, a chap, whom I know vaguely, comes up to me. He says: 'Has Dave Parker [with whom I worked for many years in the Government Treasury Bureau] from Cape Town spoken to you, because he asked me for your number? Apparently there's a job down there which might interest you.' 'No, he hasn't called me,' I reply, 'but I did have a phone call earlier and that must be what that was about. Give me his number and I'll call him later tonight.'

I did call him. He knew nothing about the other job, and said there was a job offer in Cape Town – at the John Thompson engineering company – and so we arranged that we would meet for an interview at the same time as I was going down to South Africa for the other one. Two job offers from Cape Town in one day, both in computers and both using an NCR computer system with which I was familiar. And all this on the day that I had already arranged to go down to South Africa anyway. Weird.

After I'd visited my brother, I went to Cape Town and had the two interviews. The first job was the more glitzy and the second the more safe and down to earth. I chose the second. 'How typically conservative,' I can hear you say. The first company went bust within six months of my arriving in Cape Town.

So by late 1984 we were living in Cape Town. I cannot pretend that that was an easy period of my life. It had been a huge decision to leave Zimbabwe; a gamble which I only took on a gut feeling.

If we were going to leave it had to be then, because things might have worsened quickly and it would have been too late. As I mentioned, my children's future education prospects really concerned me. I thought they would need to go to university to progress in life, but at the time the University of Zimbabwe was not recognized around the world, so they would have to go to South Africa to attend university. And what I feared was that there might be a row between Zimbabwe and South Africa and that the borders might be closed, as had happened between Rhodesia and Zambia before Independence. In that case the only option would have been to send them to a university in the UK, something we would never have been able to afford.

Marina is part of a very close-knit family and what made the move harder was the fact that she was very ill at the time. And when we left Zimbabwe the monetary controls in place at the time meant that we were only allowed to leave the country with 4,000 Zimbabwe dollars, the equivalent of about 5,000 rand (£1,000 at that time). And all items we took with us – furniture, washing machine, tumble dryer and even my car – had to be four or more years old and you had to prove it. Luckily my Datsun Pulsar was five years old. That was what we had for the start of our new life.

When we arrived, Michael and Nicola both took time to settle in their new schooling, and I seemed to be working all the hours under the sun. You can imagine the stress and strain. Thank goodness Marina's parents Alex and Elisa, who had emigrated to Cape Town earlier, were there for us as a great help and huge source of support in those trying times.

After emigrating I have obviously been back to Zimbabwe, for cricketing reasons and also to see some of Marina's family. But family reunions have just not happened. That is the tragedy of Rhodesia, because families have ended up so diversely separated. When my brother Colin came to see me during the Ashes series of 2001 in England I scarcely recognized him. Christmas 2004 was the closest we have come to a full reunion when everyone bar Allan and his family converged on Durban for the Christmas Test. My complimentary ticket allocation had to be slightly extended for that match!

Until 2000 I had never been back to Carswell Farm. I had always wanted to, but never got round to it, so when the *Sunday Telegraph* cricket correspondent, Scyld Berry – a good man whom I respect, even if I am not sure from where he obtains some of his information – suggested making a feature piece out of a return there, I jumped at the opportunity.

I was amazed at how small everything looked. It was a strange sensation. I suppose you forget how small you were as a child and how big your surroundings were in comparison. The drive from the road, which is now the main national highway from Harare to Lusaka (in Zambia), to the farm used to look such a long way, but really it was less than 100 metres, and I could scarcely believe how close a big tree outside the farmhouse was to the building. As a kid I had always thought it to be a long way away. 'How did we used to play tennis there? The tree must have got in the way,' I thought.

One regret, though, was that the owner was not there. It was, before the war veterans began their supposed land reform campaign, a butchery, where they also bred crocodiles, whose skins were later used for shoes, handbags, etc. I was hoping to get into a Land Rover with him and go around the land, just to revive some more memories.

In Cape Town I earned some extra money by playing for Claremont (Constantia) Cricket Club as a professional and I attracted the interest of Western Province too. I was unsure whether I wanted to play first class cricket because I was thirty-six, of course. I spoke to Peter Kirsten and Garth Le Roux about it and they offered differing advice, Kirsten saying that I should probably wait until the following season, while Le Roux said I should just go for it. So I did. Well, sort of. At the end of January 1985 I played for Western Province B against Eastern Province B in a three-day match at Claremont, but did not score many runs nor take any wickets. And then I was selected to play for Western Province in a Benson & Hedges series (45 overs) match at the Green Point Stadium on an artificial pitch against the Impalas, who were a composite side made up of players who played in the SAB Castle Bowl, the junior first class competition beneath the Currie Cup – mainly provincial B teams but also including the likes of Boland and Griqualand West. Ironically I came up against two players from Glamorgan, the county with which I was later destined to have an association. They were Rodney Ontong, whom I actually dismissed, and Greg Thomas, who bowled extremely quickly. I got a duck, and never played for Western Province again, even though I was twelfth man in the Nissan Shield (55 overs) final against Transvaal at the Wanderers in Johannesburg, the selectors deciding to play an extra spinner, leggie Denys Hobson, in front of me. I was invited back to pre-season training the following season, but there seemed to be a strange negativity about the whole set-up. I did not like it and retired from first class cricket, vowing to concentrate on my business activities.

However, I continued to play for Claremont for another season, taking them from near the bottom of the table to near the top (remember what started at Alex), before deciding to retire from all cricket. But then a route back into cricket soon unexpectedly presented itself via the University of Cape Town (UCT), which, through a chap called Otto Langenegger, offered me a coaching role. I ended up doing the job for seven seasons and it was a thoroughly enjoyable experience, probably the most fun of my entire career in cricket, because the pressure was off.

I was working with some very good young players too, who

were always enthusiastic, and who, over time, achieved considerable success, winning not only the Cape Town League but the National Club Championships of South Africa too. Of my charges there the most famous is probably Gary Kirsten, who came to us as a number nine batsman who also bowled a bit of off spin. As I did to a number of other players whom I coached in Cape Town, I became something of a father figure to Kirsten. He needed guidance at the time, and I encouraged him to believe in himself more, not just to be content to live in the shadow of his brother, Peter. I told him that he could play for Western Province if he really believed. And it makes me proud that he often refers to a specific chat I had with him about this in his after-dinner speeches. He even mentioned it in his autobiography.

Eventually we were able to move him up the order to number four, and from there he gradually worked his way up to opening. The rest, as they say, is history, but he deserved all his success because I doubt whether I came across anyone in the game who worked harder, even if he could be rather mischievous at university. He was something of a loveable rogue. For instance he once turned up to an evening practice with John Commins, who later played three Tests for South Africa, after the pair had spent the day drinking in the pub. When those two, both of whom were outstanding fielders, missed a few straightforward catches, I knew something was up. It was a situation where you just wanted to laugh. I wish I could have done so, but had to keep a straight face in the name of discipline, sending them home to sober up not long after the practice had begun.

There were many other players who came through UCT and went on to first class cricket – including the Zimbabwean Test playing brothers Paul and Bryan Strang as well as the aforementioned Brian Murphy – but two of the most gifted players I coached there were wicketkeeper/batsman Adrian Plantema and all-rounder Tim Mitchell. Injury curtailed Plantema's career – he played only one first class match for Western Province – which was a shame, because it would have been mighty interesting to have seen how far he could have progressed, and Mitchell played a decent amount for Western Province without ever really kicking on.

But Plantema was an individual I spent much time with and when I had just become England coach he sent me this extremely touching letter:

This letter probably comes about eight years too late. However, on the other hand, eight years of reflection, during which time you could have easily faded from memory, has left as indelible a mark on my life as no other individual could ever have done.

Quite honestly, no other person has ever taught me so much about life, and secondary to that, cricket. My wife often thinks I am a bit touched when I chat about my days at UCT cricket and what you did for us as a team and as individuals. Whenever us chaps get together, an integral part of our conversation revolves around you and what influence you had, and still have on us to this day. The principles you taught us raw, immature young people will remain with me for life. Through the medium of cricket, it was you who taught me and gave me the grounding to understand what life is really about.

I often reflect on the wonderful times I had with you and Michael on a Sunday morning bowling in the nets at Claremont and the many times you, Marina, Michael and Nicks welcomed me into your house, fed me and were a family to me. When I think of those times, I always catch myself smiling.

Since leaving UCT, whether or not you know it, I have always followed your career very closely. I am incredibly proud of what you have achieved and how you have achieved it. What you have never been is a flashy guy. You have always been a fellow who produces the goods without ringing bells, blowing whistles or demanding public accolades. I honestly believe that whoever has had the privilege of spending time with the farm boy from Zim comes away a better individual.

When you were given the England job, I knew there was no better person in the world that could have got it. It is terrible to say, but I now actually find myself backing England as opposed to South Africa in the coming series – all because of a single individual. And I know my mate De Villiers is doing the same [son of former Springbok rugby player H. O. de Villiers].

I don't think you have the best side in the world. But cast your mind back to the late '80s when you coached a pretty piss-poor side to victory in the Premier League, took flak because the pundits said it was a stroke of luck and that we would embarrass WP at the National Club Championships, and promptly shoved those words right up their backsides when you led us to victory up here in Johannesburg. You have this amazing ability to extract the best from people. I know that under your guidance, England will be a changed team and even in the short time you have had with them, I know you will bring the best out of them.

Fletch, you have taught me what is right and wrong, you have taught me humility, courage and what it is to be part of a team. You have taught me to self-assess and to question whether or not my performance is really as good as I think it is. You have taught me the importance of honesty. You have given me a motivation in life to succeed in the right way. When I need help, more often than not I draw on the lessons I learnt on and around the cricket field at UCT.

Thank you for all you have done for me. Remember, you
have an individual in me that you can always rely on and who
will always be at your side in times of war.
Adrian

I was not sure that I would go any further than UCT with my
coaching, but again a strange sequence of events precipitated an
important change in my life. In 1993 the post of chief executive at
Western Province became available, and I applied. The computer
industry was getting on top of me and I could not see myself
making too much progress in it. I wanted to get back into top
level cricket and thought I could do it that way, by using the
experience I had gained in the world of commerce. But soon after,
Mike Minnaar, the convener of selectors at Western Province,
contacted me: 'I see that you've applied for the chief executive's
job. We would like you to withdraw that application, because we
have something else in mind for you.'

'What might that be?' I enquired.

'I can't tell you yet but I will phone you soon,' he replied. It
transpired that the then managing director of Orange Free State
Cricket, Arthur Turner, was being lined up as chief executive. He
had taken them from laughing stock to provincial champions for
many a season and was a good man with whom I later developed
an excellent relationship.

Instead, they wanted to offer me a coaching post. I was not too
sure about that, because I was not convinced that it would be well
enough paid. Coaching for me was a sideline and I had a comfortable enough living without taking a pay cut. The trend then
was for coaches to be paid peanuts: it was not a profession to be
entering if you wanted to earn decent money. But it was definitely
a job I wanted to do if I could broker the right deal. So I decided
to use H. O. de Villiers as my manager-cum-negotiator. That is
the famous H. O. de Villiers who was full back for South Africa in

the late 1960s and early 1970s. As mentioned above, his son was playing cricket at UCT and we had become friends. I told him to go in there and ask for a salary which might have been perceived as over the odds. I never expected them to accept, but they did. And in my opinion it was an important watershed for coaches in general because it was the first time anyone had been rewarded like this, pre-empting a shift away from 'jobs for the boys' to the hiring of more skilled and specialized coaches.

There was heavy irony in the fact that I was being lined up to replace Hylton Ackerman at Western Province. We had never seen eye to eye, even when we played against each other, and had clashed not long before – a confrontation that had been brewing for some time, but had its origins in a rather indiscreet remark I had made about Herschelle Gibbs. Gibbs had been selected for his first class debut at the tender age of just sixteen against Northern Transvaal, who included in their side the hostile fast bowler, Tertius Bosch, who tragically died in 2000 aged just thirty-three. I thought Gibbs had been exposed to this level of cricket too early, especially as the opposition included someone as quick as Bosch. So one day while watching my UCT side, an individual whom I knew – but not well – approached me. In casual conversation he asked me about Gibbs and I responded rather hastily: 'I think it was stupid that he was picked so soon.' What I did not know at the time was that this chap knew Ackerman very well.

All my time at UCT there had been a simmering conflict with Ackerman, because he, along with Robin Jackman, also ran the Western Province academy nets, to which many of my UCT play-ers were invited. But most of those players did not enjoy those academy nets – they preferred the fun we had at UCT – and Ackerman became rather envious of that, I think. Adrian Plantema once told me that Ackerman had come storming down the net to say to him: 'Listen, you might be taught that at UCT, but you're not doing that in my net.'

So at the end of season presentations for the local league, which UCT won that year, I was chatting with Fritz Bing, the president of Western Province Cricket, when Ackerman approached me. 'What's this about you having a go at us selectors about picking Gibbs? I've heard all about it,' he said. Things began to get quite heated and he fumed: 'You need to put your money where your mouth is. You haven't got the character to get involved and put yourself up to be criticized.'

On 1 August 1993 I began as director of cricket and coach at Western Province, and you know who my B team coach was? Hylton Ackerman! He had been demoted from his post as first team coach. As you can imagine, it was generally a rather uncomfortable arrangement which was doomed not to last, and, sure enough, within a year he moved to be a successful coach at Boland. But even more ironically his son, also Hylton but known as HD, then came under my charge at Western Province. Thankfully that worked out fine. In fact I've got nothing but praise for him and the manner in which he dealt with the situation. He recognized that there was a problem but never let it hinder our very good relationship as coach and player.

I have not mentioned this story in order to be seen to be 'having a go' at Ackerman senior, but rather to stress that I had learnt a crucial lesson. You had to be more careful about what you said. Too often unguarded comments can come back to bite you in many ways. It bit both of us – me and Ackerman – here. So there you go: perhaps another early reason for my always guarded stance.

The Western Province position charged me not only with coaching the senior side but formulating the whole cricketing structure for the Western Cape. That was a major task but just the sort I relished, and I'd like to think that by the time I left in 1999 there was a very workable structure in place. However, it might never have come to that because within four months of beginning this post I was asked to apply for the South African national coach's job. That was undoubtedly because we had had a flying start to the season at Western Province with three straight wins. The post was eventually handed to Bob Woolmer, a decision with which I had no quibble whatsoever as I had been in the provincial post so little time.

I needed to make sure that Western Province were a success during my time there. And I think they were. On two occasions we landed the old Currie Cup four-day competition: in 1995/6, when it was known as the Castle Cup, and then in my final season in 1998/9, when it was the Supersport Series and we overcame Border in the final (the first time there had been a five-day final since the 1989/90 season), having finished second to them in the round-robin part of the competition. That last win was extra special because it was a perfect ending for me with a typically gutsy display (opening bowler Alan Dawson scoring his maiden first class century after we were 84–7 on the first day) and it also coincided with the final game in the first class career of Eric Simons, a man for whom I have a lot of respect. I often call him 'the legend' not because he was that as a cricketer, but because of his character and personality. In that respect he is first rate and always will be. As a cricketer he was a fine all-rounder (even if he could barely hit the ball on the off side when I first encountered him); one who worked diligently and thought long and hard about his game. And as a result I always thought he would make a good coach and was pleased that he was appointed coach of South Africa in September 2002. However, I was equally surprised and saddened when he was relieved of his duties in 2004. As a fellow coach I had a good deal of sympathy for him because he did not have a bowling attack with which to work at the time.

Even with good one-day cricketers like Simons, though, one-day cup success eluded me at Western Province, although in the

1997/8 season we did finish top of the Standard Bank League. I will elaborate on this later, and you might find it hard to believe, given the manner in which I finished with England at the World Cup in 2007, but I have always maintained that I am a better coach of the one-day game than the longer game.

Invariably during my time at Western Province we were disappointingly knocked out of the Benson & Hedges series or Standard Bank Cup by regular winners Orange Free State, especially when Hansie Cronje and Allan Donald were in their side. I believe we were the best one-day side in South Africa at the time, because our record in the round-robin stages up until the semi-finals was regularly the best, even though generally we were missing more internationals than the other provincial sides. But then, strangely, when those internationals returned we struggled, especially if we then encountered Cronje and Donald. Both had an undeniable psychological hold over Western Province, which they were never afraid to exploit. If Cronje was away on national duty it was a different scenario, but when he came back we crumpled. Twice in my first two seasons Cronje scored match-winning centuries to break Capetonian hearts. And this despite having in our line-up one of the most destructive hitters of a cricket ball I have ever seen: Adrian Kuiper may have been well into the autumn of his career by then but he was as powerful then as Andrew Flintoff and Kevin Pietersen are now.

I probably should not have said that because my general rule is that comparisons are odious and useless, whether between eras or countries. Because when I first went to England it was a question on everyone's lips: 'What are the differences between South African and English cricket? Which is better?' I was always diplomatic with my replies. But one thing I do know and am very proud of is my record against English teams for Western Province. I never lost a game as coach.

Fifteen matches I make it, and all of them without at least four of my South African internationals in each game. Admittedly, many of those were against touring counties on their pre-season tours, and you can argue that they were rusty and unprepared, but my answer every time is that those matches always took place at the end of those tours (by when intensive practice should have made them ready for their season ahead) and often some time after the end of our domestic season. The Western Province players were certainly not in regular training then, and often those matches could be seen as the proverbial 'pain in the arse'. Two of those stick in my mind as being particularly telling, the first against Warwickshire's treble-winning side of 1994 when they toured the following spring, and the second against a strong Yorkshire side including the likes of Darren Gough, Michael Vaughan, Craig White and David Byas. Against the Tykes we batted second under lights at Newlands in dewy conditions which are usually devilishly difficult to conduct a chase. Sides just should not win batting in those circumstances but we won easily.

More important to me was the victory over England in the hastily arranged one-day match in early January 1996. It is a match often talked about because tour manager Raymond Illingworth organized it without skipper Michael Atherton's knowledge. But people forget that I was also missing my five internationals in Brian McMillan, Jacques Kallis, Gary Kirsten, Craig Matthews and Paul Adams, and still we won – in front of 15,000 delirious fans too. England were so miffed that they refused to shake our hands afterwards. The tradition I have always seen is that the losing coach and side always go across to shake hands with the winning coach and his men. I always made sure that happened with sides of mine. But when England did not do so here, we decided to go into their dressing room. England were in a mess then and I shall never forget seeing Illingworth in the corner with Atherton trying, on a scrap piece of paper, to indicate some field placings. It was quite sad.

As I mentioned earlier, Gary Kirsten was not the only cricketer I helped in his formative years. Jacques Kallis was at Wynberg Boys' High School (where he was also a formidable, big-kicking rugby fly-half) with my son Michael, so naturally I took an interest in him, recognizing early on what a talent he was. He was soon attending the Western Province nets and I decided to test him out. It is something I do to all young players, by pitting them against the best in the team.

So I asked Kallis to put his pads on and then armed Craig Matthews, our most potent seam bowler, with a new ball. Boy, did Kallis pass the test. He looked as if he had been playing first class cricket all his life. His batting technique, with his 'back and across' method (pressing on the front foot), has always been one which I hold up as being something near the model which I like to teach.

However, Kallis' debut aged eighteen for Western Province brought home to me the perennial problems I had with the selectors there and elsewhere, especially with England and also on the odd occasion with Glamorgan. It was a one-day game in the B&H series against Northern Transvaal and Kallis was down to bat at number six. Desmond Haynes made a brilliant hundred and as time was running out at the end of the innings I decided to drop Kallis down the order. I knew what he was like, because he still remains the same today to a certain extent, in that he needs time to get in. He is just not the type to go in and smash the ball around straight away, and to ask him to go in on his debut and score at seven/eight runs an over was clearly too much. So he eventually went in at number eight and got run out cheaply. It caused a real hoo-ha with the selectors berating me wildly for not giving the youngster a chance. But I knew him better than them and felt I was helping, not hindering him.

But that was nothing compared to the rumpus I caused as regards the selection of the team for a day/night match in Durban in 1996. It very nearly cost me my job. The first thing that I will confess is that I failed to hear fully the conclusions of a rushed meeting I had with the selectors prior to travelling for this match against Natal. I wish that I had been listening more intently, though. For, apparently, it was agreed that Faiek Davids, the Cape-coloured seam bowling all-rounder, must play, regardless of any other considerations. These were the early days of something approaching a quota system and this sort of thing was becoming common. However, they only picked the twelve for a match, and I, along with the rest of the management committee, chose the final eleven from that.

So we held our usual management team meeting the night before the game to discuss the side. Without my realizing what had been said the day before, it boiled down to a straight choice between Davids and Dave Rundle, an off-spinner. I was acutely aware that spin rarely plays a part in floodlit matches at Kingsmead, so was in favour of Davids, but the others wanted the experience of Rundle. So Rundle it was who played, and we won the match relatively comfortably.

But when we returned home, the acrimonious inquests began. The selectors were incensed about what they considered my utter disregard for their wishes. I was in great danger of being branded a racist. In fact, two of the Cape-coloured selectors went to the general manager of Western Province, another Cape-coloured chap called Peter Heeger, to ascertain my job description, hoping to discover that I had gone beyond my areas of responsibility so that they could press for my sacking. Thankfully Heeger stood strong and would not speak to them about this matter. And crucially, I had another important ally in Haynes, the great West Indian opening batsman, who spent three seasons playing at Newlands and whom I knew from that Young West Indies tour to Zimbabwe. As I said before, I was mightily impressed by him then and nothing he did while playing for Western Province changed that. He was a magnificent player and a fine man off the field. Fortunately for me he was in on that management meeting (himself strongly favouring Rundle) and he spoke up for me, saying that I had, in fact, wanted Davids to play, albeit not for the same reasons as the selectors on the Western Province Cricket Association Board.

There were plenty of young players I was keen to play. Herschelle Gibbs, especially after what I considered his premature exposure to first class cricket, was another whom I took under my wing. I advised him a great deal, not just about cricket but life in general. It was clear to me that, although an enormous talent, he had been misguided in his early days at Western Province and I can remember the very practice session when I reckon his cricketing life took a turn for the better. He had been enduring a wretched time with the bat, hardly able to score a run.

So when he came that day to attend a middle practice at Newlands, I told him to relax and just go out and play his shots – to forget about everything else that was cluttering his mind. He did just that. He smashed the ball everywhere, especially over cover where he is so strong, and a smile returned to his face. I went to him afterwards and said: 'Herschelle, that was a great knock. Would you like to open the batting? You can just go out and play like that.' He agreed and from that day on shed his middle order preference (until a return there later in his career) and was transformed into an opener. He has become known as a free scoring player, but I still believe that he could be freer in his game at times. And I always warned him not to be too cocky, because one day it might come back and haunt him – well, I think that day came in 1999 at Headingley in the World Cup match against Australia, when he supposedly dropped Steve Waugh when trying to celebrate the 'catch' a little too early. Although I do still believe that he had that ball under control and only dropped it in the process of celebration, so it should have stood.

Another young player to appear on the scene was Paul Adams,

the extraordinary left-arm Chinaman bowler. Much credit for his emergence must go to the late Eddie Barlow, then in charge of the academy at Western Province, who first thought that this unique action could be utilized at a higher level. Again I used my test. This time I asked Haynes to strap on his pads and face Adams. He came out with that familiar grin on his face: 'I can't read him at all,' he said, 'I think you should play him *now*.' So we did, handing him his debut against Northern Transvaal in early November 1995. He took eight wickets in the match, and just two days after the end of that match he was playing for South Africa A against the touring England side at Kimberley – another one of 'my' victories over the English.

This was my first time in charge of the A side, and I was well aware of the furore about Adams. No one had seen anything like it and everyone wanted to have a look at him. So when we had a middle practice the day before that England match, I was conscious of not allowing anyone from the touring England contingent a sneak preview of him. I posted two sentry guards to warn us if they saw anyone approaching so that we could immediately take Adams off and replace him with someone else. I was amazed that no one turned up. Mind you, it probably says everything about the previously mentioned lackadaisical lack of interest of the England management at the time.

Adams completely bamboozled England in that game, capturing nine wickets in a match which we won easily by six wickets, having forced England to follow on. My abiding memory is of Graham Thorpe, a quality player, being completely at sea against Adams, who dismissed him twice in the match. Three times in fact, we thought, obviously out on another occasion in the second innings, but benefiting from the generosity of the umpire before being sent on his unhappy way.

What was also interesting about Adams' immediate success was that I had encouraged him to utilize an unusual field. Because of his unorthodox action he often tended to drag at least one delivery an over down, presenting an inviting short ball which could easily be hit through the off side for a boundary by the batsman. So I said that he should have a normal spinner's field, but with a sweeper out on the off side to ensure that that bad ball only went for a single rather than a demoralizing four.

When I went with England to Pakistan in 2000/1 we encouraged leg spinner Ian Salisbury to do the same, something for which we were roundly chastised. Yet Mushtaq Ahmed, a quality Test bowler at the time, was doing the same thing for Pakistan and I did not hear anyone criticizing him. Nowadays many teams adopt this tactic. In fact, Shane Warne is probably unique among wrist spinners in that he is so accurate that he does not always require such cover.

I enjoyed being in charge of the South African A side, especially for the tour of England in 1996 which followed. It was a strong party we took there, including Adams, Herschelle Gibbs, Jacques Kallis, Lance Klusener and Nicky Boje. We thrashed most of the county sides we came up against, although it was a little disappointing to find them mostly fielding weakened sides and equally frustrating that we were not able to play an A Test match against England. Instead, we rounded off the tour with a match against a Test and County Cricket Board (TCCB) XI consisting of players whose counties were not otherwise engaged in county action at the time. That was actually the only game we lost all tour, on a sporty pitch at Durham, but otherwise the intensity of our cricket was too much for the English teams, who sometimes seemed intimidated by our aggression.

But I am not sure, as was suggested, that we always instigated any ill-feeling on the field. A case in point was the match against Nottinghamshire at Trent Bridge, where skipper John Commins, always a very quiet man on the field, became most upset when he was sledged rudely by left-arm spinner Andy Afford, after he had been dismissed in the first innings. We had some lively, sometimes irascible, characters in the likes of Klusener and the left armer Brett Schultz who thrived on this. So if their captain was being sledged, then they would take it out on the Nottinghamshire batsmen. And they did.

A. A. Jones was umpiring and was not impressed, and soon called me and Commins to his room. 'I've had enough of your guys with their sledging,' he said, 'and I would like John to go to the Notts dressing room and apologize.'

I told him what had happened and that Nottinghamshire had started it.

'If you tell the Nottinghamshire captain [Paul Johnson] to come and apologize to us first, then we will apologize to them,' I said. Of course that did not happen, and when we turned up at a cocktail party at the invitation of the Nottinghamshire committee, there were no Nottinghamshire players to be seen. I always believed in sticking up for my players in such situations, and, anyway, I did not feel that they had overstepped the mark on this occasion.

Something I did feel that needed modifying, though, was the amount the players were being paid for such trips and for representing South Africa A in general. For that trip to England the players received barely the equivalent of £1,000. Someone like Commins lost a lot of money by spending six weeks in England, because he had to employ somebody to run his company in his absence. The situation reached a head during late 1997 and early 1998 when I was coaching the side against West Indies A in South Africa. The players were receiving no match payments at all for that and with some animation I discussed the matter with Ali Bacher, the managing director of the United Cricket Board of South Africa as it was then. This was the latest chapter in a long-running saga with Bacher. He upset me on many occasions but probably no more so than when my UCT team won the National

Clubs Championship up in Johannesburg. In his congratulatory speech Bacher had said something along the lines of: 'It is good to see Duncan Fletcher doing so well as a coach. He wasn't that good a player but it gives heart to everyone when someone like him can succeed as a coach.' Thanks Ali.

My mood about the payment to the A team had not been improved when I discovered that the England A team, which toured Kenya and Sri Lanka in 1997/8 for the same period of time, received somewhere in the region of £15,000 per man for their six-week sojourn. I put that to Bacher but he was intransigent. I do not think he liked my plain-speaking entreaties on behalf of my team, and that contributed to the decision in 1998 to appoint Corrie Van Zyl, the former Orange Free State fast bowler, as assistant coach to Bob Woolmer for the tour of England. To my mind I had been overtaken in the pecking order, and no explanation was given, by Bacher or anyone else. The next time I spoke to Bacher was in 1999 while I was mulling over the England job. Previous to that I had received a couple of phone calls from South Africa, one of them from Arthur Turner, asking me if I wanted to coach South Africa. My reply to Turner was: 'Of course, I do, but why are you asking?' Arthur told me that there were a lot of people in positions of authority within cricket who were trying to persuade Bacher to speak to me about the possibility of taking over from Woolmer after the 1999 World Cup. Apparently they did not want to see me lost to South African cricket. Bacher eventually made the phone call, under duress so I have subsequently heard: 'Do you want to coach South Africa or not?' he said bluntly. 'It's OK you asking me that, Ali,' I said, 'but are you offering me the job? What are the financial implications?'

'You will receive 300,000 rand,' he said.

'Look, Ali,' I replied, 'I would like to do it but I'm already earning a lot more than that with my combined wage at Glamorgan and Western Province.'

'Oh, you're obviously not interested,' he replied gruffly, and put the phone down without even saying goodbye. It was not all about money but it was just that the difference between the two was so vast that I wanted to discuss it. Bacher gave me no chance to do that. He had not wanted to phone me and this would have been a good enough excuse for him to give to those other South African cricket officials who wanted me. I knew what I was going to do and I never looked back. But first we had better look back at how I initially became involved in the English (or more specifically Welsh) game.

3

Glammy

It was a chilly morning at London's Heathrow airport in April 1997. As I walked to collect my bags I turned to Marina and said, 'What the hell are we doing here? Why don't we just forget it and get on the next flight home to South Africa?'

Angst-ridden words indeed, and the only reason for this doubt and anxiety was the fact I was on my way to my first stint as coach of Glamorgan County Cricket Club: my first taste of county cricket and all its idiosyncrasies. It should not really have induced such feelings but I was just so nervous, so fearful of this unknown adventure.

I suppose a major factor was that we had left our children, Michael and Nicola, to look after our house in Cape Town at a time when violence was escalating in South Africa as a whole. But also it was the fact that I knew so little about county cricket and what it might be like. I will admit that I knew next to nothing about Glamorgan: I did not know who Matthew Maynard (their captain) was, I did not know who Steve Watkin (stalwart quick bowler of many seasons) was. In fact I knew none of their players. I had obviously had a few phone conversations with officials from the club but that was it. I just did not know what I was letting myself in for.

You might well ask why on earth I had accepted this job. But the initial contact had come the previous season in 1996 when I had been in England with the South African A side. We had played Glamorgan early in the tour and beat them convincingly by an innings, but I had not really taken any notice of their players – I later discovered that the MCC side we had played earlier had contained Hugh Morris and Robert Croft – because I was focused on our team and developing what was an outstanding set of players. I had liked the city of Cardiff though and do now recall on one of the match days seeing a chap pull up in the car park in a flashy Jaguar car. I had half a glance at the name on the side of it but it did not really register. When he got out he seemed to want to talk but I suppose I 'bagged' him – totally ignored him that is, the ultimate put down in the sporting vernacular. He, of course, turned out to be Matthew Maynard, who was resting for that game.

So I thought nothing further of Cardiff and Wales until we got to Worcester late in the tour and our team manager Goolam Rajah said that he had had a phone call from Hugh Davies, the chairman of cricket at Glamorgan, who had asked to come and see me. I was immediately impressed with Glamorgan's professionalism. They had gone about things in the correct manner in my view. They had used the right channels. So I spoke to Davies and arranged for him to come to Worcester. As soon as I put the phone down my mind was racing, and my immediate thought was: 'Yes, this sounds like a good idea.'

I had had one previous approach from a county – Warwickshire, who had been keen to employ me when Bob Woolmer took over as the coach of South Africa. Their chief executive Dennis Amiss phoned me and was so eager to engage my services that he offered me a retainer so that they would have first call should I become available. So uninterested in county cricket was I that I did not even think about accepting that. Maybe it was also the fact that Warwickshire were one of the best county teams at the time that swayed me. There would not have been a real challenge there for me.

So Davies, and Roger Davis, then a member of the Glamorgan committee, came to visit me and said that they wanted me to become the coach of Glamorgan. No figures were mentioned, just an outline of what they wanted and some basic background information. I said that I needed to go away and think about it.

I sought advice from many people, because it was such a big decision for me at the time. Naturally I had to speak to Arthur Turner at Western Province, who, as ever, was incredibly support-ive, stressing what a great opportunity it was and how it would inevitably help Western Province because of the experience I could gain in England – or rather Wales. Through a quirky turn of events Turner was until recently employed by Glamorgan as their senior sales and operations manager.

I remember phoning my brother John in Johannesburg and asking him what Welsh people were like. He just burst out laugh-ing and said: 'Remember that nursery rhyme Mum used to teach us – "Taffy was a Welshman, Taffy was a thief; Taffy came to our house, and stole a piece of beef."' There is, in fact, some Welsh blood on my maternal grandmother's side of the family – that is why one of my middle names is Gwynne. But more seriously John said that I had to go for it; especially as it seemed that Glamorgan was not a fashionable county at the time, not one of the high-fliers either. There was a challenge there. He was right.

So back to Heathrow and we did somehow summon up the courage to make the trek through customs to be met by Glam-organ's chief executive, Mike Fatkin. It was the start of a good friendship and smooth working relationship with him and also the start of what transpired to be a momentous year for Glamorgan with the capture of the County Championship title for the first time since 1969. Fatkin is a very skilled administrator, very professional and pragmatic in all his work and dealings. My negotiations with him were always very simple and quick: he would say what he was offering and usually that was it; I would accept.

I had spoken on the phone to Dean Conway, then Glamorgan's physiotherapist. It was a long call, mind you, because he had to repeat himself many times as I struggled to understand his Welsh accent – I still do even today! And I told him that I wanted all the players to be extremely fit when I arrived. I did not want to be wasting too much time getting them into shape. When he told me that there was nothing to worry about on that score because they were the fittest team around, I was sceptical. Maybe my experience with Barry Dudleston was clouding my judgement, but I had this impression that county cricketers in general were a little bit lazy and not as fit as their southern hemisphere counterparts.

Therefore, I was pleasantly surprised that Conway was right. These boys were indeed fit. They proved that to me when we went on a pre-season camp to Brecon, staying at Christ College. The cold weather had already got to me and I had a nasty bout of flu when we travelled up into mid Wales, but I was determined to stamp my mark on the trip, especially in terms of my fielding/fitness routines. They seemed to go down well and the players responded. And I was also grateful for the help I received from the second team coach, John Derrick, a very good operator for whom I wanted to arrange a reciprocal deal with Western Province, something which sadly never materialized. I was glad, too, for the assistance from the Glamorgan legends, Alan Jones and Don Shepherd, who always had a wise word or two.

When I had been finding out about Glamorgan much had been made of their fantastic team spirit, and while that was definitely there, I did get an early indication in Brecon that it was like any other sports team in that there are some members of the squad who are less liked than others. We played a round of golf, and when Robert Croft drew out wicketkeeper Colin Metson as his partner, the expression on his face said it all. Later during a game of football, one of the players clattered into Metson, leaving him sprawling on the ground, with no one seeming too bothered as to his well-being. It probably did not need Maynard to tell me that Metson was not the most popular member of the side.

I will admit that my initial insight into the mechanics of a county dressing room took me aback a little. There were things being said which made me think 'You shouldn't be saying that. Where I come from you get a smack on the chops if you dare say things like that.' I soon found this to be the way things were; that the humour was at times cutting and all too often brought people down to earth. I was told that it was all in jest but my philosophy is 'Where there is smoke, there is fire.' Having said that, I wouldn't want to paint the picture that the Glamorgan dressing room was a place in which I did not enjoy being. The genuinely humorous comments far outweighed those more caustic ones.

I felt Maynard was testing me out during those early weeks, just to see what I was like as a coach. I heard afterwards that he did not believe Glamorgan particularly needed a coach at the time – not that that was anything personal against me. He did not know me, after all, or maybe he remembered that incident in the Sophia Gardens car park!

I remember at one of my early practices that he asked me to give him some throw downs in the nets, and he enquired whether I'd seen anything untoward in his technique. I just said that it looked fine and that I wanted to have a good look at everyone before I passed too much comment. That was always my philosophy. A few days later Maynard invited me to his house and we had a few too many to drink – as you often do if you spend an evening with him – and talked cricket into the small hours. He mentioned that he had been impressed that I had not tried to show off during those throw downs by imparting my knowledge for the sake of it. From there on we got on famously.

I think my thoughts about Matthew Maynard are probably best summed up in part of the foreword I wrote for his auto-biography:

> During my career in cricket I have had the opportunity of playing with or being involved with an enormous number of cricketers. Some were ordinary, some were good, and there have been a small number whom I could only describe as outstanding. It is into this last category that I would place Matthew Maynard.
>
> His most important attributes are his all-round cricketing knowledge, his sound man-management and the ability he has to lead from the front. These combine to make him a natural leader . . . The instinct that Matthew displays is that of one of the shrewdest cricketing brains it has been my pleasure to encounter in cricket at any level.

That is why I wanted him as my assistant coach with England. We will come to that later. I do though have to put him straight on one thing he wrote in his autobiography. I do not often want to take credit and there is a hint of mischievousness involved here, but . . . It involves his description of a match against Kent at Canterbury in 1997. It was an evenly matched contest, poised on the third evening with Kent on 156–3 in pursuit of 319 to win. Alan Wells was well set on 84 not out. Maynard said in his book: 'That night, I had a chat with Dean Cosker. I wanted him to bowl over the wicket to Wells rather than round, not aiming at the footmarks outside leg stump, but bowling the ball across the bats-man. It worked at the start of the morning and Wells was caught at slip.'

I had been telling Maynard for weeks that Cosker had to bowl over the wicket! It was something we had been doing in South Africa for a long time, and even back in my Zimbabwe days where

I struggled to convince off-spinner John Traicos that the traditional theory of finger spinners always bowling around the wicket
when turning the ball away from the bat was ill-conceived. Traicos
just would not bowl over the wicket to left handers, but obviously
left-arm spinner Ashley Giles was later more receptive to my ideas
when playing for England. It is not that I think they should do
this all the time, but it is definitely very effective on pitches that
are not turning much and especially dangerous early on when the
batsman is unsure of where his off stump is. If you bowl around
the wicket the batsman can easily use his pad as the first line of
defence in these circumstances.

I thought that one of Maynard's finest moments that season
came at Liverpool where we faced Lancashire in a match affected
by almost incessant rain. Thankfully, though, the weather relented
enough on the last day for there to be the possibility of some
cricket. Naturally Maynard was keen to engineer a positive result.
He came to me and the rest of the management team (which con-
sisted of Steve Watkin, Hugh Morris and Tony Cottey) and said he
was thinking of setting Lancashire 273 in sixty overs. We all
thought that was too generous a declaration given the ease with
which we had scored runs on the first day before the rain. But
Maynard was adamant, so I just said to him: 'If you think that is
reasonable, go for it. I will back you all the way.'

It was a brave decision but how it worked. Lancashire were dismissed in just 14 overs for 51, Waqar Younis taking 7–25 with
some devastating swing bowling. He had one hat-trick and might
have had another if Neil Fairbrother had been adjudged leg-before
first ball as we all thought he should have been.

That was the day I realized that I was dealing with a side that
might be something special. I had also been worried before arriving about how Waqar would react to me. He was a legend in the
game and I was a guy who had played no Test cricket. But I need
not have fretted.

That Liverpool trip was also memorable for other reasons. Firstly because, due to the weather, we got a chance to visit Anfield, the home of Liverpool FC, the team I have supported for many years. That was special. As was one of the nights in the hotel bar, when we knew that there was no chance of play the next day. I am not usually in favour of too much drinking during a match but this turned out to be a never-to-be-forgotten night. I went out for a meal with Mike Fatkin (a fanatical Arsenal fan by the way), Maynard and a couple of other players before returning to the hotel bar where most of the team were. One drink led to another and before I knew it I was teaching Waqar the rudiments of a rugby scrummage and Morris, not known for his overindulgence, kept appearing sitting on the floor of the hotel lift as it opened and closed in the lobby, unable in his inebriated state to stand up and reach the button required to take him to the floor where his room was.

That was rare for me as I normally know when I have had enough to drink and the right time to leave. But the next morning I was in a bad way. I still maintain to this day that it must have been something we ate, but we have all said that at sometime or other have we not? There seemed little chance of play and the forecast was dire, but the rain had actually stopped sufficiently for us to be able to warm up. As we did so I kept looking across at the nearby portable toilets, contemplating whether I should rush to them to be sick. 'The boys will hear me, though,' I kept thinking. Fortunately the rain soon arrived to save me. Meyrick Pringle and Alan Dawson, two of my Western Province players playing club cricket in the area, also arrived soon afterwards to see me, disbelieving of the state I was in.

Another night which sticks in my memory bank is one at Leicester, sadly the one on which Princess Diana died, but we knew nothing of that when we were enjoying a team meal at a local restaurant. I like team meals and what they do for the team ethos. And by that I do not necessarily mean just getting drunk, but having a couple of drinks, relaxing and enjoying each other's company. Well, that is what we did on that particular night, but then the singing began. And how. My first initiation to the joys of Welsh singing had come in June when I had been to the inaugural match at the partially completed Millennium Stadium, watching Wales overcome South Africa (and, yes, they are the international rugby team I support) for the only time in their history. The atmosphere was electric. As it was back in Leicester as the boys began their repertoire, which rather surprisingly was not exclusively Welsh. In fact it centred more around being a tribute to the Drifters, a band for whom I'd not had a lot of time before then. That night clearly had an effect, for I still have a Drifters CD in my car now.

Quite how much effect I had upon Glamorgan during their Championship-winning year is difficult to say. I obviously did not have enough time to make huge technical changes to the players because of the already full schedule. For instance, I knew that young left-arm spinner Dean Cosker had a problem with his action which needed to be remedied, but could do little about it mid-season.

Cosker and Darren Thomas were two youngsters I enjoyed working with. I thought Thomas had the ability to become a genuine all-rounder with his natural talent and I spent much time working with him on his bowling, paying dividends when he produced a spell of 5–38 on the final day at Taunton when we clinched the County Championship. His problem is that he struggles to cope when the red mist descends upon him; he needs to stay in 'the zone' when that happens, but otherwise I thought he had many admirable qualities.

There was, though, one important disciplinary decision which I felt I had to make during that season. It involved a left-arm spinner called Phil North, who was called up for our annual pilgrimage north to Colwyn Bay. Cosker was selected for the England U19 team and we could not secure his release, so, as we desperately needed a second spinner for this most placid of strips, Maynard suggested North, a good friend of his who had been on the Glamorgan staff previously, but was then playing league cricket as well as turning out for the Wales minor counties team. It was a huge risk to pick him because there were so many people against it. So I did not expect North to behave the way he did – by partying late after the first day's play was washed out and then disturbing his room-mate Hugh Morris when he eventually stumbled in.

We could see Morris was seething at breakfast, because he really wanted to score runs that day, and we coaxed the story out of him. Even worse, North then did not appear at the ground on time. I just turned to Maynard and said, 'I'm sorry. Friend or no friend, he cannot play.'

Maynard was reluctant to leave him out, but I stressed that there was no way an individual could behave like that. And to be fair to Maynard he told North himself. I had offered to, but it showed good character that Maynard wanted to.

I was never afraid to make tough decisions like that. Once as skipper during a club match in Zimbabwe I sent one of my players off the field after he was involved in an incident with a colleague. It was when I was at the Alex and the person concerned was called Cecil Grimmer. He did not want to go, but I said to the umpires, 'Get this man off the field,' and we played with ten men.

I also once disciplined Grant Paterson, a member of the Zimbabwe squad. He was a talented batsman and a funny individual, but at the time was more concerned with larking around when we were trying to instil a work ethic among the national squad. So when I caught him chatting with some friends on the veranda at the Harare Sports Club while the rest of us were netting, I made him run around the field – something like fifteen

times in order to finish him off. Then as I was running in to bowl
I noticed that one of the batsmen was laughing uncontrollably.
Paterson was making faces behind my back. More laps followed
for him – with me accompanying him – and then when he did
something similar at a later practice, that was it for him. I single-
handedly threw him out of the Zimbabwe squad. Matters were
patched up after a couple of weeks and we have been very good
friends since, but I think I made my point.

As I think I did after the one moment of controversy that year
at Glamorgan, involving some ill-chosen words and actions by the
Surrey captain, Adam Hollioake, and coach, Dave Gilbert, after
our match at the Oval. The match ended in a draw after we
declined to chase 254 in 46 overs on a pitch by then taking considerable turn.

Hollioake showed his displeasure by hurling the ball away when
the draw came and Gilbert described our decision as 'outrageous'.
I do not usually get involved in such situations but this one really
irked me. They were calling us negative but, in fact, they were the
ones who were being negative. It had been a tight match which
had ebbed and flowed. We seemed to be in control until Graham
Thorpe responded with a very good double hundred in Surrey's
second innings. When he was eighth out they should have
declared, but they went on to make another 31 and used up too
much time. They desperately needed to win, and we did not, but
the bottom line was that we had no chance of scoring those runs
on that pitch. They had two international spinners in Saqlain
Mushtaq and Ian Salisbury, and we had our number three, Adrian
Dale, unable to bat because of a back spasm and opener Steve
James struggling with a dislocated finger. The draw effectively
put them out of the Championship race, probably the reason
for their silly remarks which included them saying that they would
do us no favours because they were playing Kent, our nearest
rivals, in the last match. I did not say anything immediately but

later commented: 'Glamorgan play with their hearts. Sadly, there is another team in the competition who seem to play with their mouths.'

I thought Matthew Maynard came into his own during the Championship run-in. It has been said to me that he always cracked under the pressure at international level, but he did not convey that impression to me with some of the innings he played towards the end of that season. The most remarkable was at Taunton where he reached his century without one single. He came good when we needed him.

The basis of our success that season was the opening pair of Hugh Morris and Steve James, who invariably got us off to a good start in our quest to make sure we had runs on the board. But someone whose contribution should not be overlooked is Steve Watkin. He was the ultimate professional, whose seamers could always be relied on. And Tony Cottey too. He didn't have a very good year with the bat, despite the long hours I spent with him practising, but his contribution in the dressing room was enormous.

Winning the Championship at Taunton was made all the more memorable for me by the special presentation which Maynard made to me after the game. After a short speech he gave me a Wales rugby shirt from the team as a way of saying thanks. There had been some good-natured ribbing ever since that Wales/South Africa game, but this was them saying that I was now one of them. I have still got that shirt today.

The celebrations took a bizarre twist when I ended up standing in front of everyone in my Wales shirt, with Waqar next to me in a Nelson Mandela mask. To reuse an earlier phrase that was one hell of a night.

However, when I returned to the hotel with a couple of players I was a little surprised to see Robert Croft sitting in the hotel bar with some friends from his home village. That disappointed me. I thought he should have been with the team. Only he will know what his motives were, and whether it was a genuine case of becoming separated from the group, but I thought it showed a rather selfish side to his character.

Croft and I had had a small spat earlier in the season, which has since, for whatever reason, become public knowledge. He played a practical joke on me at Abergavenny, snipping my socks, which I just did not find funny. I was angry, not so much with him but with the fact that none of the other players challenged him. They should have known that it was wrong and told him so.

Croft actually changed my perception of right-arm finger spinners that season. I had come over from South Africa with the idea that their presence at first class level was redundant, but he bowled so well in 1997 that he forced me to alter that view. Some of it was down to the way many county batsmen play spin – in other words by letting spinners bowl at them instead of using the sweep and sweep/slog more regularly – but that must take nothing away from Croft's skill. He is a very smart cricketer; one who knows his game and knows others' too. I think that he could become a good coach one day. However, he may need to brush up on his man-management skills if he is to become the complete package in that field.

As I was still doing the Western Province job, I was too weary to return to Glamorgan in 1998, but was delighted to do so in 1999. I found things to be very different from 1997. The team had changed and we found ourselves without our overseas professional (Jacques Kallis) for much of the season. And, of course, there was the small matter of the England coaching job, which I took during the season, to cloud the issue.

My first official approach about it came during Glamorgan's opening Championship match of the 1999 season, away at Derby. But it was a match I more recall for an unscheduled meeting with the club chairman, Gerard Elias, and chairman of cricket, Hugh Davies, because that reintroduced me to the sort of selection problems I had had at Western Province, where I felt that the committee was interfering unnecessarily.

During that pre-season I thought I had seen something special in the young fast bowler David Harrison. I had watched him bowl in a friendly against Somerset and said to Maynard – who, incidentally, always had the final say in selection – that we must look to play him as soon as possible. When we handed him his first class debut in that first match it put some more experienced players' noses out of joint and extraordinarily resulted in Elias and Davies coming up to Derby. They told us that in future they wanted to have previous warning about any major changes in selection policy. I could not believe what I was hearing and eventually just walked out of the meeting. They seemed to have forgotten that the last time Maynard and I had worked together, we had won the County Championship, and here they were questioning our ability to make decisions.

I just knew that it was not going to be Glamorgan's season when in the next game Maynard broke his finger badly, and soon Steve James joined him on the injury list. If you add in the absence of Hugh Morris, who had retired after the 1997 triumph, and first Kallis' involvement in the World Cup and then a stomach injury, then no side could really have coped with that. But it was also obvious to me that the team had not moved on since 1997. Everything was the same, from net practice to attitude. There was a reluctance to innovate. For instance, when Kallis belatedly arrived he faced the spin of Croft and Cosker in his first net session. He continually lofted the ball straight back over their heads, quite often into the stands. 'What's he doing?' asked many of the Glamorgan players. They rarely practised that sort of positive approach in the nets.

Another example was the fact that I had been keen in 1997 for

James to bat in the middle order in one-day cricket. We had tried it and it had worked, but then when it failed for a few games, we reverted to him opening. It was the same in 1999. There seemed to be no taking up of the challenge from James or the team. It made me laugh a couple of years later when Glamorgan had some success in one-day cricket, with James in the middle order.

The only experience I had of the two-divisional structure in county cricket was in that 1999 season when the CGU National League tasted promotion and relegation for the first time, but it is no secret that I think too much county cricket is played. There is little doubt in my mind that there must be a reduction in the number of county matches, because, at the moment, a high level of intensity is missing for too much of the time. There is little desire to practise and learn new things about one's game. It is just play, travel, play, travel and so on. There is just no time to take one's game forward.

So, as a result, I have got an idea of how I would structure the County Championship. What also worries me about the current format of two divisions, aside from the volume of cricket, is that some sides do not play others, sometimes for many seasons. Some derby games have been lost for too many consecutive years because sides are in different divisions. And it is not as if a real elite division has been created. My proposal would hopefully create plenty of cross-pollination and also, more importantly, allow there to be more control over the number of Championship matches played in a season. For I still think that the current number of sixteen is too many.

What I would do would be to list the counties from one to eighteen as they finish in the season, and then take the odd numbers to play in one division and the evens in the other. They would play each other once, making eight games. From there you could then tinker around with the remaining number of games to be played in order to find the optimum number. Say if you wanted eleven matches then you could take the top two from each division and play them against each other once, three extra matches making a total of eleven, to come up with an eventual champion. You would then go down the two divisions taking the next two from each to provide another three games for everyone and giving small amounts of prize money all the way down in order to maintain interest and competition. At the end of all this you again have an order from one to eighteen from which you start all over again the following season. If you did want a bit more cricket you could then take the first three from each division, and so forth down the divisions, to create five more matches each.

But it was not too much cricket or the fact that Glamorgan were doing badly in 1999 that persuaded me to take the England job. It was just that for me it was, and always will be, the ultimate coaching post. I was appointed in June and with the benefit of hindsight I should have left Glamorgan immediately. That was the course of action many people were advocating, especially as England were faring badly against New Zealand at the time. But it was loyalty that made me stay at Glamorgan for the remainder of the season. I just did not want to let them down. It goes back to those Prince Edward schooldays. But things were difficult. I admit that my mind was not fully on the Glamorgan job, but I never felt that I let them down.

Things must have been bad, because I even had a row with Matthew Maynard. It was during Glamorgan's match at Headingley against Yorkshire. They were undecided about their overseas professional for the 2000 season, and Maynard called a management meeting to discuss this issue. However, he failed to invite me and conducted the meeting in one corner of the hotel bar while I sat like a lemon in another. I was furious. Surely I could have added some input to that meeting. It was as if Maynard thought I was betraying him by taking the England job.

But he had been one of the most enthusiastic of those urging me to take it in the first place. Maybe he now felt isolated because I was also taking Dean Conway with me to the England job. The three of us were very close friends and maybe Maynard's natural reaction was to distance himself from me and Conway. Whatever, we are all still close. But at the time I could not let this lie. As soon as the meeting broke up, I called Maynard over. 'Take a seat, Matt,' I said. I proceeded to tell him how hurt I was, and spoke in quite strong terms which I think shocked him a little, but by the end he knew he was wrong. He came to me the next day and said: 'Nobody has spoken to me like that for years, but you were right. Thank you.'

No, no: thank you, Glamorgan, for two wonderful seasons.

4

Hello, Dav

'Hello, Dav,' said Simon Pack, the ECB international team's director, as I arrived at the London offices of Lord MacLaurin on 15 June 1999. Of course, he was confusing me with Dav Whatmore, later to coach Sri Lanka and Bangladesh, who was another interviewee, along with Leicestershire's Jack Birkenshaw, for the position of coach of England. But it did not bother me. There cannot be a person alive who has not, at some time or another, addressed someone by an incorrect name, and I later came to find Pack a good man, despite the widespread criticism he attracted. But there was another important factor in my carefree attitude: as prestigious as it was I was not even sure whether I wanted the job.

I had first heard (not directly, of course) that I might be under consideration to be coach of England when I was with Glamorgan in Cape Town on their 1999 pre-season tour. The opening match of the tour was at the Stellenbosch Farmers' Winery ground and both captain Matthew Maynard and physiotherapist Dean Conway mentioned to me that there was talk that I was in the frame for the job. It was news to me and I even wondered whether they were pulling my leg. Then Eddie Bevan, the BBC Wales cricket correspondent, came to me at a two-day match at the

University of Cape Town and said that his office had been on the phone asking about it because it was hot news in the UK.

That shocked me but it did set me thinking, even though I was more concerned about how the match was going because it was an interesting one for me personally, being played in a format which I had been keen to develop. It is a limited overs match played over two days where you could bat twice. Each team has 110 overs and you use them accordingly, being able to declare at any stage, with the overs remaining being used in the second innings. I reckon it makes for some exciting cricket and certainly makes the captain think about how the game might progress, for example how to make sure that your overs are used by your best batsmen. And thankfully here it also produced a thrilling finish. This game could be used in any format, over three or four days, even up to Test match level, taking a draw out of the equation and even stopping such negativity as the use of nightwatchmen.

All the rumour did have some substance though, and, as I have said, my first official approach about the England job came during Glamorgan's opening Championship match of the 1999 season, away at a damp and dull Derby, when Pack phoned me to ask if I was interested. I said I was, even though I knew that I had a lot of thinking and investigating to do. The interview was duly arranged for the aforementioned day in June, the first day of Glamorgan's County Championship match against Kent at Canterbury.

Interestingly, any doubts I had about the job – I was happy with my dual role with Glamorgan and Western Province – had only been exacerbated two games previously when Glamorgan played at Leicester. I had had a confidential whisper that Brian Bolus, the chairman of the England management advisory committee, was in favour of appointing Birkenshaw as coach, with his county colleague James Whitaker as his manager. So when I knocked on a door upstairs to inadvertently find those three together talking, I thought to myself: 'I've got no price.'

But all this doubt might not have been a bad thing going into the interview. Indeed, it may well be a useful tip for prospective interviewees, because I did not approach it with the attitude of 'I really need this job.' I did not have to say, 'My life depends on this.' I think this made me more confident and relaxed, able to talk without any hint of desperation. And there came a point in the interview when I suddenly realized that I was making progress. We were seated at a round table, seven of us – myself, Pack, Bolus, Lord MacLaurin, Dennis Amiss the Warwickshire chief executive, David Acfield the chairman of Essex and Hugh Morris, by now the ECB's technical director. MacLaurin was on my immediate right and as I spoke he made a point of turning his chair to face me, crossing his legs in the process. 'He seems very interested and he really wants to listen to this,' I thought.

I told them that if I got the job I would want my own structure in place, whereby everyone involved in the off-field management team reported to me, including the manager, whom I saw as being more of an operations manager. I told them that the relationship with the captain was crucial, albeit a delicate one because cricket is different from all other team sports, where managers can dictate from off the field. Cricket is the only one where the captain is the true leader. I also made it clear that I would finish the season with Glamorgan regardless of what happened. As mentioned, my sense of loyalty would see to that. And I finished by saying: 'Gentlemen, I have to tell you that these are my current earning capacities in my dual role with Glamorgan and Western Province. This is what I want.'

I left and made my way philosophically back to Canterbury. I worried how they had taken my wage demands. I knew that I had one ally in Morris but as for the rest, I had no clue. I was soon to find out. That very afternoon Pack called. 'I want to come and see you,' he said. 'We are offering you the job.'

I had expected them to deliberate for a few days. Surely that was what happened in these sorts of things. But no, I was being offered the post of coach of England. I was shocked. 'Come on now, Fletcher, you are going to have to think about this,' I said to myself.

Pack duly arrived the following day, surreptitiously meeting me at the back of the Canterbury pavilion. The offer was what I wanted and the only condition I was keen to implement was that Glamorgan's physiotherapist, Dean Conway, came with me. I was actually a little surprised that the ECB were so ready to accede to that request, but it later transpired that they were trying to replace Wayne Morton, their physio at the time, and my request was a convenient excuse. Conway's decision that he wanted to join me was very important, for without it I might not have taken the job. I probably would have felt too isolated. In fact, Conway saying that he would love to do it gave me more confidence in my decision.

Conway was, and still is, a very, very good friend, who became the main shoulder I could lean on during my time with England. I reckon I am a pretty good man-manager but he eats me alive when it comes to that facet of management. He is as good as anyone I have ever seen at handling people. Of course, first and foremost he is also very good at his job as a physio, but for me he was so good at looking at the bigger picture when I could become blinkered within the team environment. What is more he was always immensely popular with the players, whether at Glamorgan or with England. He later reduced his workload to being with the one-day squad only (finishing as I did after the 2007 World Cup), and the biggest compliment I can pay him is to say that, while it often took a few days for the one-day players to gel again when they met up with the Test boys on tour, Conway was the only one who could just walk in and make it seem as if he had been there all along. There is no doubt he will be a great loss to England cricket because characters of this nature are so important in the make-up of an international side and also very hard to find.

Pack had no problem with Conway joining me, but I could sense some urgency in his desire for me to accept immediately. But I was still not sure, so I used the excuse of needing to speak to my wife first. 'Give me five days,' I said to Pack. After the match finished at Canterbury I went back to Cardiff to Marina and my son, Michael, who was staying with us, and deliberated. And boy, did I deliberate.

Sometimes people exaggerate and say they have had sleepless nights fretting over a problem. But I literally did have nights where I did not sleep. I remember reading a letter in the *Daily Telegraph* some time after I had been appointed, ironically from a chap in Llandaff Road, Cardiff, of all places, saying something along the lines of: 'How can Fletcher arrogantly walk into this job? Does he realize what it entails?' If only he had known the anguish and uncertainty I went through during that time.

Pack called me after five days but still I was not ready. 'Give me three more days,' I told him. I needed to do some more investigation. Glamorgan, and in particular their chief executive, Mike Fatkin, were being incredibly supportive, saying that I could always return to Glamorgan at a later date.

So I sought the advice of many people there about the job and more especially about the England players with whom I might be working. All the feedback was positive, except for that from one person: Robert Croft, who had just been involved in the 1999 World Cup, where things had not gone smoothly. I spoke to him in Southampton, where we were preparing for a NatWest Trophy match against the Hampshire Board XI, the night before I had to make the decision, and he said: 'You'd be mad to take that job.' He also intimated that I would not be able to handle the characters involved. That confused me. I spoke to Marina again and she just said: 'It's up to you.'

I mulled it over all night – another truly sleepless night – and then phoned Pack the next morning. 'OK, I'll take it, but I only want a two-year contract,' I said. The original offer had been for a term of three years but I thought that after two years I would know whether I could do the job or not. I did not want to let anyone down. I would like to think that I was acting responsibly towards the ECB.

The contract was constructed in such a way that if things had not been going well and the ECB had wanted to get rid of me, they would have had to pay off my contract in full. So I could have just taken that and to hell with how good I was. But I did not. I went back to Cardiff and rather apprehensively told Marina and Michael of my decision. I was not sure what their reaction might be, but they soon let me know, whooping, cheering and clapping excitedly. 'We are so glad,' Marina said. 'We discussed it at length last night and decided you just had to do it. We were going to phone you but we decided against it because we did not want to influence you unduly.' That was a wonderful response, so typical of my family, and from that moment I thought, 'Right, I'm on my way here.'

Pack had been keen for me to commit quickly because the issue of the next England captain had to be determined before the Test series against New Zealand commenced. I had been asked about this appointment, but had just replied that I felt I could work with anyone. Some people had said that I might struggle to work with Nasser Hussain, but I just wanted to go into things with an open mind. It was suggested that I wanted Matthew Maynard as my captain, but I can honestly say that it never once crossed my mind.

Hussain it was and we were both unveiled to the press at Lord's on Friday, 25 June. This meant a fraught train journey up from Wales that morning, with doubts and anxieties again filling my mind. I had never met Hussain before so I made sure that I grabbed a quick, private chat with him before the formal proceedings. I outlined my philosophy to him, about the structure I would like to use, and emphasized how important I thought the body language of the skipper was. I told him that the eyes of the world are always on you as captain and that at all times you must be seen to be enjoying the game and exuding a positive attitude. We then met the press and you know what? Hussain mentioned to them about the body language. I immediately thought: 'This boy listens.' I knew then that we could foster a relationship as coach and captain. He led the way when it came to the time for photographs. I had no idea what to expect but barely two flashbulbs had gone and he said: 'Right, that's enough.' He was not very tolerant of the media then but became more so and handled them very well in later years. Maybe that is one lesson I should have learnt from him.

I put together the rest of my backup team by deciding to go for Phil Neale as my team manager ahead of Whitaker, who I felt might be comparing me with Birkenshaw if I had appointed him. I knew Neale reasonably well and everything I had heard about his character and efficiency proved to be correct. He has become an important cog in the wheel which has driven English cricket forward. So, too, Nigel Stockill, whom I was very fortunate to have as my physiologist, a very knowledgeable man in his field and another who fitted in exceptionally well.

As I alluded to at the start of this chapter, I also thought that Simon Pack did a good job as the international team's director, a post no longer directly filled. The reason he copped so much flak was because his military background prevented him from understanding how sportspeople think. His dictatorial attitude was fine in the army but could often rub people up the wrong way in the cricketing world, as he sometimes talked down to them. But in a way his straight talking was good for the ECB at the time.

Thus I thought it ill-advised that they almost had to alter their structure in order to get rid of him, resulting in the wrong structure ever since. I remember going to Tim Lamb, the ECB chief executive, to say this; that I thought it wrong that the England team itself was not going to have a department of its own within the ECB. After all the England team is the department which earns the money.

Pack was someone I could talk to sensibly about the central contracts, which were already being put in place when I was appointed. He listened and understood my feelings on the subject, but too many others did not. There was meeting after meeting on this subject and I kept thinking: 'This is an absolute joke.' The ECB were trying to reinvent the wheel. Their problem is that they have a deep-seated belief that cricket in England is unique and cannot be like that in other countries.

Yes, it does have its differences but there are areas where there is an unfathomable resistance to change. For instance, from the start of my tenure I told the ECB that there was no reason why England could not play away series in the English summer – every other country does it. For example, you can play series away in the West Indies and Zimbabwe in April and May. Initially, there was astonishment at this idea but it was refreshing to see that in 2004, four years after my suggestion (it always took a while for them to sink in!), we played in the West Indies while the county season was taking place in England.

So, with regard to central contracts, I felt that there was no reason why we could not just replicate what was already happening in other countries; but no, the central contracts review group set up under Don Trangmar, the Sussex chairman and former Marks & Spencer executive, wanted to make them so complicated. Thankfully the contracts were eventually greatly simplified.

I found myself in a rather awkward situation, not having actually taken up my post, and so kept my counsel most of the time, but I did feel moved to speak up when the thorny issue of compensation due to the counties arose. This was the first time I saw at first hand the debilitating effect of the self-interest of so many counties. It staggered me that so many people were more interested in the welfare of their own county than that of the national team. They were saying that they wanted compensation for those players that they had developed and were then going to be awarded central contracts. But I was arguing that if that was the case then England should be recompensated when the players returned to their counties as much better cricketers. For that is what happens all over the world – international cricket improves cricketers.

The confusion over primacy – county or country? – was brought home to me in a letter I once received from Peter Walker, the former Glamorgan and England cricketer, whom I knew well from my times in Wales. He was corresponding in his role as a trustee and vice-president of the Professional Cricketers' Association: 'As you're well aware the county game has, and is, taking a constant and systematic pounding in the UK media,' he wrote. 'The county game could do with a lift when and wherever possible. This is not by pretending nothing's wrong with it, but by supporting its existence and development role for you in the process of suggesting ways of improvement. Unless our national side is more caring of its parent, the former will soon become a single child and eventually an orphan to boot in a world that could not care less!' Now this is not a personal attack on Walker, but the final statement is indicative of the addled thinking which pervades the county game. It is the England team which looks after the county game. Without its revenue most counties would not survive.

It is, though, a pertinent question to be asked as to whether central contracts have, overall, been a success. Sometimes I have not been sure myself of the answer to that, but what I do know is that they have, in general, given the players much more confidence; a psychological boost that the selectors are backing them over a longer period of time, rather than just for a one-off game.

And one of the major benefits of central contracts which I pushed hard for was the payment to the captain. Previously he was given an allowance which did no more than buy a round of drinks at the bar for his players. But I insisted that the captain be compensated considerably because of the two huge roles he has to fulfil – first as a player and then as a captain, the latter obviously carrying huge off-field responsibilities and on its own deserving nearly as much as another player. England captains present and future please take note and be thankful for your impressive salary. You are lucky I am not requesting a cut!

However, the aspect of these contracts which caused most controversy and ire among the counties was my pulling of players out of county matches when England were not in action. My take on it is that, if people really did their homework, they would realize that players did not get pulled out of that many county matches in a season. What happened was that a whole group of players was pulled out of one round of matches and it made the situation look a lot worse than it actually was. I would be surprised if a player was pulled out of more than two Championship matches in any one season.

One of my main justifications is that I never considered the English summer to be any different from a winter tour. If I selected a player in every single match of a long winter tour I would be accused of overly exerting him. Common sense suggests that he will need a rest at some stage. So why should the English season be any different? In fact, more cricket is played than when on tour, with seven Tests as compared to the usual six on tour. England players spend so little of the English summer at home, with all the travelling required in between matches. Another is that there is a good deal of hypocrisy among the counties. When I went to see the county chairmen at the start of the season to explain the situation, they agreed with me wholeheartedly because there was no pressure on them then in terms of results. Come the end of the season when promotion and relegation issues were to be decided, then it was a different matter. There was one chairman of a county who said to me on two occasions: 'Duncan, I agree with what you are doing, but there is no way I could say that in front of my constituency.'

Many of the county coaches were the same. In private they would agree with me but in public it was different, especially when their chairmen were at hand. The only occasion I can remember getting public support from the coaches was at Edgbaston in 2003 when I arranged a meeting with them all, and John Carr, then the ECB's director of cricket operations, stood up and asked at the end of my discussion with the coaches: 'Can I have a show of hands as to whether we are playing too much cricket?' Every coach there raised his hand, including Graham Gooch, who, two years earlier when not a coach, had criticized me publicly for saying we played too much cricket.

As I mentioned earlier, that has always been my criticism of county cricket – that too much cricket is played. I have never criticized it in any other way. I might be a forward thinking sort of chap but I am also a great believer in tradition. I took my cap off every time I walked through the Long Room at Lord's, and so would never say that there should be fewer counties or anything of that nature.

The issue of players being pulled out of county cricket reached its nadir in 2003 when, with England 1–0 down in the series against South Africa, Geoffrey Boycott wrote a scathing piece in the *Daily Telegraph* in which he accused me of 'destroying county cricket'. He said that I was 'wrapping James Anderson in cotton wool' and went on to say cantankerously: 'He simply doesn't care about county cricket; he never played in it and he has no empathy with it . . . county cricket doesn't mean a damn to him.'

I will make a point about that immediately. Boycott probably does not remember a plane journey from Johannesburg to Cape Town during England's tour in the winter of 2004/5 when he was sitting just in front of me and Matthew Maynard. But I do, and so does Maynard. When I went to the toilet Boycott engaged

Maynard in conversation and Maynard asked him how much
county cricket he watched. His reply suggested it was not exactly
top of his fixture list.

Anyway, Boycott continued his article:

People make the point that everything is dependent on Test
cricket. Of course it is, but by resting England's players too
much and putting county cricket down you're going to get
lesser players emerging . . .

Fletcher has been brainwashing former captain Nasser
Hussain . . . and a number of players on central contracts
into believing they need play hardly any county cricket.
They are always resting and I think that's wrong.

The argument on resting doesn't work. Take Anderson,
of Lancashire. He has been rested between Tests apparently
because he's a kid of 19. Great seam bowlers such as
Trueman, Statham and Bedser didn't rest – they bowled
themselves into form and fitness . . .

Fletcher is the invisible man. He gets all the plaudits
when England do well . . . but he doesn't bat or bowl for
them . . .

He should have been fronting-up to help the captain and
his team. Coaches are supposed to help and be seen to
help . . .

They're using Troy Cooley, an Australian. How many
Test wickets did he take, I wonder? I've looked in Wisden
and I can't find his name anywhere.

Where is the batting coach? A real top-notcher with
8,000 Test runs such as [Graham] Gooch or myself. We're
not using one.

It was just the start of a litany of scornful stuff from Boycott.
And it did annoy me, not so much the personal side of things at

that time (although that changed as he became more vitriolic) but the fact that I thought he had his facts wrong and did not understand what I was doing. So when the *Daily Telegraph* offered me the right of reply I took the unusual step of accepting it. I collaborated with Mark Hodgson, then a media relations officer at the ECB, to produce this:

Geoffrey Boycott made some strong comments about myself and my management style in Monday's Telegraph. He was a fine player and is now a respected commentator, but I think his accusations were a combination of the curious and the unfair.

The crux of his argument was that I do not respect county cricket and he suggested that I withdraw England players from playing county cricket because I don't care about the county game. He based his arguments around James Anderson, saying that he is rested too much and should be bowling more. He said it was normal for the Australians to play their Tests and then return to state cricket.

This is untrue. In the Australian four-day state competition last season, the Pura Cup, Jason Gillespie and Glenn McGrath did not play a game for their respective states, Ricky Ponting played once while Brett Lee and Shane Warne played just twice.

Compare this with Anderson, who this year played non-stop county cricket up to the first Test against Zimbabwe, including four county championship matches for Lancashire. Since then there have been just two matches in which he could have played, but from which he was withdrawn. The first was against Kent which was scheduled to finish just two days before the start of the second Zimbabwe Test.

Up to then he had bowled a lot in the season and, had he appeared, he could have been playing a total of nine days out of 11 which I thought was too much. With the volume of cricket coming up, he needed time to rest and recuperate.

The second county match he could have played in started on July 15, three days after the NatWest Series final. By then, he had played and travelled solidly between June 5–July 12 and I felt he needed a rest, especially with a tightly-packed Test Match series against South Africa coming up, including two sets of physically tough back-to-back Tests.

I made this decision purely on the basis of what, in my opinion, was best for James's development and for the best interests of the England team. I strongly refute any suggestions that this was because of any lack of respect for county cricket.

Let's not forget that I did coach Glamorgan for two seasons, which I really enjoyed. It is because of the enjoyment and respect I have for the county system that I have always said I would like to eventually go back to coach Glamorgan or another county.

I am fully aware that county cricket produces some highly-talented cricketers and I appreciate the major role county cricket and county coaches play in the development of our best players. Indeed I specifically asked for a one-year extension to my England contract, precisely because I could see the potential in the exciting players coming through the system.

The international programme has expanded hugely since Boycott's day, with England players committed to 10 one-day internationals and seven Test Matches each home summer and multiple series abroad in the winter. In my opinion, if we want to avoid injury and burn-out as much as possible among our players, we need to regulate the amount of cricket they play carefully.

The suggestion that I have been brainwashing Nasser Hussain is strange. Hussain is a strong-minded individual and perfectly capable of making his own mind up in cricketing matters. In fact I think Nasser brainwashes me at times!

Boycott also criticised my management style, suggesting that I am not 'fronting up' or being 'seen to help'. Like it or not, I do not seek the limelight – this is not my style. I do not seek to be high-profile, whether we win or lose, but prefer an active, thoughtful and level-headed behind-the-scenes management role. This is not going to change. In fact my management structure seems to have been copied in other sports.

The argument about using specialist coaches who have played at international level is again odd. Some of the world's best coaches have never played international sport. Great players don't necessarily make great coaches. I never saw Troy Cooley bowl, but I know he is a fine bowling coach and he came highly recommended by Rod Marsh who has played a lot of Test cricket.

As for a batting coach, I like to think I have made an impact here. I certainly feel we are now generally a more consistent batting side than in the past and players have certainly improved their success rate against the world's best spinners.

Of course, everyone is entitled to their opinions and if others do not like my management style then so be it. I feel we are continuing to make progress as a team. Throughout the whole of the 1990s, before I took over in 1999, the England team won seven Test series. Since the South Africa tour in 1999, when I took over, we have won six series and suffered four series defeats. Two of those were against Australia, acclaimed as one of the best sides in history, and one against India away. The team have remained a close-knit and well-disciplined unit throughout my time as coach, even during a number of tough winter tours.

I am not suggesting we are the finished article. We have a long way to go, but we are steadily progressing and our most immediate priority, starting tomorrow, is to get back on level terms with South Africa.

At least we did get back on level terms, eventually drawing that series 2–2. But even though Boycott said in his article: 'I have no personal animosity toward Duncan Fletcher,' I always felt there was something personal in his criticisms. There always seemed to be – he went strangely quiet when we were doing well and could not bring himself to give me any praise for that success – and this became especially obvious after the Ashes win of 2005. For it was then that Boycott tried to contact me at home in Cape Town. He has a house at an elite golf estate in the Western Cape and was out there when he somehow got hold of my home phone number. I was not in when he phoned but he spoke to Marina. He wanted to play a round of golf with me and Bob Woolmer. He was having a laugh. Why should I even want to talk to him after the way he had been treating me? I did not even return the call. However, about a week later I was at home one evening and the phone rang. Marina said that it was Boycott. I hesitated whether I should speak to him.

As soon as he mentioned his intentions I had a feeling I knew what he was after. More than likely he wanted to be able to say in one of his articles that he had played golf with the coaches of both the England and Pakistan teams before the series about to start that November. He was looking for information and looking to make a good story.

I could hold back no longer. I tore into him, asking him how he had the audacity to phone me when he had so maliciously criticized me on a regular basis. It had been unwarranted and continual, so much so that it really upset my wife and family. I have to be honest and say that I was quite rude to the man.

But what was so pleasing was that, after I had let him know what I thought of him, his tone changed remarkably. He suddenly became different. It was the classic case of the biter bitten. He now said: 'Shall we rather meet for a cup of tea somewhere?' To which my answer was: 'I do not want to be involved with you in any manner. Thanks very much.' And I put the phone down.

And immediately I began thinking, 'Fletcher, you've made a mistake here.' Marina mentioned this straight away and I did a lot of thinking about it, so much so that I even phoned Nasser Hussain for his advice. He told me that it might be best to go and have that cup of tea. But I just could not do it. I had to stick to my principles.

But, of course, it did mean that Boycott's articles would become more and more venomous. And they did, leading to his call for me to go as coach even before we had begun the disastrous 5–0 Ashes beating Down Under.

I spoke to BBC's *Test Match Special* commentator Jonathan Agnew, with whom I had once played at the Alexandra club in Harare, some time after this and he mentioned that Boycott had said that I had been aggressive towards him. 'Yes, but at least I did so on the telephone and not so that everyone could see it in the media,' I said.

Of all the people I have met in cricket many have had harsh words for Boycott, even if they did have respect for some of his batting exploits.

This mutual dislike between us had begun as soon as I took the England job. Boycott had said that I should never have got it because I had never played Test cricket. That was a common criticism at the time and I will deal with it briefly by saying that I obviously would have played Test cricket if Zimbabwe had been granted Test status earlier and I reckon that some guys who have not played it actually appreciate it more, and as a result study it more intensely because they do not take it for granted. I also think that I played at a high enough level for sufficient time (for Rhodesia and Zimbabwe) not to take too long to adjust to the demands of Test cricket. I think what irked Boycott most was that I never asked him to help with the England team. Some people thought he would not actually help the team.

But do you know what really made me laugh? That Boycott, like so many other commentators, was so contradictory in his opinions. In an interview he did just before our tour of the West Indies in early 2004, he was asked why he thought there were so many injuries to the modern day cricketer. His response? There were two factors: first today's way of life is different, the children are a lot more sedentary, and secondly – that there is too much cricket and too little rest! He continued the theme in his column of 10 August that year when we played four Tests at home against the West Indies: 'With the Oval game following straight after this one [Old Trafford] that will be four Tests in five weeks and that is plain stupid. Administrators want their heads testing for agreeing to so many games in such a short space of time. It gets worse in the winter with three Tests in a row in South Africa at Port Elizabeth, Durban and Cape Town and I despair of people who come up with schedules like that. You'd find more brains in a pork pie.'

Those Tests in South Africa in the winter of 2004/5 did, indeed, create a lot of talk about burn out. That made me chuckle because that is exactly what county players do week in, week out. So during the Test in Cape Town I thought I would tackle Mike Soper, the ECB deputy chairman, who was staying in the team hotel and had just then chaired the domestic structure interim working party, about it. 'What do you reckon to these back-to-back Tests, Mike?' I asked. 'Oh, they're ridiculous,' he said. 'Just too much – you shouldn't be playing them.'

'Thanks very much,' I replied. 'That's exactly what they are doing in county cricket all the time.' I had snared him, reminding him that his working party had said we were not playing too much cricket.

Often the English press would think they had snared me. But mostly it was because my comments were misinterpreted. No wonder I never said too much in public. For instance, my comments about England needing to play more international one-day cricket. Some critics immediately pounced on this and said I was contradicting myself because I was constantly preaching the need for less cricket. What I was saying was that there should be less Test cricket in order to accommodate these extra one-day matches. If in the English summer one less Test was played (and England do seem to play much more Test cricket than the other countries) and you included the two practice days required for that, that is seven days which could be freed up. England could play three one-day internationals in that time.

I also think that domestic one-day cricket should be played in one window during the season, because it is nigh on impossible for the players to keep chopping and changing between formats. As a batsman you receive a ball which you play a one-day shot to, for example, running it down to third man, and then all of a sudden you realize that it is a four-day game and there are three slips behind you. Tests and one-dayers are not mixed up at international level, so why should it be done at county level?

People say that they do not think that the extended rest and practice time will improve standards. I know it will. I will tell you why. In 1993/4 something big happened in international cricket and England got left behind. I know because I was at Western Province in South Africa at the time and was involved. Up until then the cricketers of South Africa and Australia had been amateurs playing as professionals. Yes, they were being paid to play cricket but not sufficiently so that they could live on that salary alone. They had to have another job. They had to work during the day and then fit in their training and practice around that – that is what I did when I played for Rhodesia and Zimbabwe. And even though England had a fully professional set-up, South Africa and Australia still dominated series against them.

But then in 1993/4 those countries decided to pay their players more so that they did not have to go to work during the day. And the key was that that extra time was then used for practice. Extra games were not organized to fill that time – in neither country do they still play more than ten first class games in a season – but they worked on their play. And England, where it had already been proved that playing more games does not necessarily make you better, got left further behind, especially in the one-day game.

At Western Province we had many, many middle practices where players could develop and experiment. The old-timers say that you learn by playing matches in the middle, but how can you try things in a game situation? If you are a batsman and you try a new shot, you cannot be called back if you are out. There is actually evidence in South Africa to enhance my argument of less cricket. When I started at Western Province there were only seven and then eight (with the introduction of Boland) provinces, but Ali Bacher decided that he wanted to bring in other provinces into the top tier.

I disagreed vehemently with that, as did my chief executive at Newlands, Arthur Turner; so much so that at one point Bacher, on holiday in Cape Town, arranged to speak to us and demanded that we desist from our criticism of his policy. But lo and behold, what has happened? South Africa endured a relatively unsuccessful period where the provincial coaches were complaining that there was too much cricket (with eleven teams in a complicated system involving a Super Six competition but where no team played more than eleven matches) and that the standard was too diluted. So in 2004/5 they went back to having just six teams. QED.

But back to the England job. Having been pleasantly surprised by my first impressions of Nasser Hussain, I did not see him again until we met to pick the squad for the winter tour of South Africa and Zimbabwe. It was an awkward situation, what with England faring so poorly against New Zealand and my choosing to remain at Glamorgan.

But I think Hussain appreciated my loyalty. I made sure that I spoke to him before each Test and wished him and the team good luck. From the outside I could see that the team was really struggling but the gravity of the situation was emphasized to me when I made a furtive trip up to Old Trafford for the third Test. During this trip, which had been arranged in order to formulate a future policy for when I took over, I was glad of the professionalism of Brian Murgatroyd, then the ECB's liaison officer. I had heard good things about Murgatroyd from Dean Conway – two Welshmen sticking together! – and these were substantiated as I was whisked in through the rear of the Old Trafford pavilion and then, when there was a whisper that a photographer had caught a glimpse of me in the dressing room, back out again to the hotel, where we had dinner that night.

I did think, 'What have I let myself in for?' while I was in that dressing room. It was blatantly obvious that this was a team who had lost their way. Hussain was out with a broken finger and Mark Butcher was captaining England for the only time in his career. I saw him taking a contemplative smoke at the back of the dressing room and I have scarcely seen someone so despondent. Graham Gooch, then a selector, was in temporary charge and he said to David Graveney, the chairman of selectors: 'We need to sort this mess out. The only solution is for Duncan to take over straight away.' I could not.

If the stark situation at the ground was not enough, then the discussions over dinner that night really began to worry me. We began talking about selection for the winter tour of South Africa and, in their panic at the situation, people like Brian Bolus were saying that youth was the only way forward. He immediately wanted to end the careers of the likes of Mike Atherton, Alec Stewart, Phil Tufnell and Andrew Caddick. But I thought that the older generation could play a part, a very important part, even though for most of the discussion I just sat and listened. For I was mindful that I did not know enough about many of the players to make considered judgements.

Bolus was particularly anti-Atherton, probably because of Atherton's rows in the past with Ray Illingworth, but I knew that I had to have a spine of experience down the team, and that included Atherton as opener. I had already spoken to him when he scored 268 not out for Lancashire against Glamorgan at Blackpool and I knew that he was keen to play a part in the future, despite having been out for some time with a back injury.

Stewart was top quality, end of story, and I also thought that Caddick was a world class bowler, who had been mismanaged. I knew he could form a potent partnership with Darren Gough. The one I did agree with them about was Tufnell. I did not want him to go to South Africa, because I did not think he offered enough – he could not bat or field and even his bowling was limited in my view (how eerily reminiscent of the Monty Panesar scenario later). He may have been able to flight the ball nicely but that is not enough these days. You need to be able to put some serious revolutions on the ball as a finger spinner, something Panesar can do. But he did make the trip because Hussain was adamant that he had to go. I wish I had been stronger on that because I had done my investigations and spoken at length to Bob Woolmer at Warwickshire about Ashley Giles, whom I concluded was a good all-round package who could play an important role.

When the team was eventually selected, my one demand was that Michael Vaughan was included. I had seen him only briefly but liked what I saw, so I was happy that the tour party was extended to seventeen from the originally intended sixteen in order to accommodate him. Otherwise, it concerned me that the tour was being seen as something of a trial. So many players were being tried out that it had the look of a development trip rather than a full-blown Test tour.

But it was an early indication for me as to how difficult selection could be. I sent out a questionnaire to all the county captains and coaches asking them to select twenty-five players (not including any from their own county so as to exclude the obvious bias) whom they thought could take England forward in the following two or three years, and in doing so describe to me their strengths and weaknesses. But no common factors really came out of that, so that I never did it again.

Selection was a huge problem for me because I had to rely on others to give me the correct information. Now and then I would try to get to games if England were not playing, but it must be remembered that one cannot watch cricket properly all day, every day. Everyone needs a break sometime and I am no different. My wife probably does not agree with that though, because often I would sit at home on a day off glued to the TV if there was a player involved whom I wanted to see. For me TV was the best place to watch when I wanted to scrutinize a player, because of the increased technology these days.

Going to a county ground could be a suffocating, fruitless experience, because if people knew I was there, they would often want to talk to me. You would have administrators wanting me to have lunch with them, and telling me how good their own players were. I just could not watch the cricket properly in those circumstances, so often I would just go to county games unannounced, and either sit with Marina or alone.

I remember once seeing Paul Collingwood at Bristol, where he was playing for Durham, while sitting up in the stand with Marina. But then David Graveney phoned to ask where I was and he happened to be at the ground too. The locals soon recognized him, and then me as well, so that was the end of my scrutiny for the day.

It is quite a skill to be able to identify players and just because you have been a great player does not necessarily mean that you can do it. Take Ian Botham. I thought I would ask his advice before the South Africa trip. 'Get rid of all the guys like [Mike] Atherton, [Andy] Caddick and [Phil] Tufnell,' he told me.

'Why?' I asked.

'Because they're too old, rather go with youth,' he replied.

'Who then?' I asked.

'Graeme Hick and Robin Smith,' he said.

'But hold on, they are the same age,' I replied in exasperation.

His reply I could not then believe. 'But they are different,' he said.

That was the last time I used Botham for selectorial advice. Just like with Geoff Boycott, it was a complete sea change of opinion and it confused me, because Botham's opinion is so influential in England. Indeed, at times I think it swayed Graveney.

So I struggled throughout my time as England coach to find consistent observers. Jack Birkenshaw was quite good but the most reliable was Matthew Maynard while he was still playing, whom I could always phone to see what his experiences had been of a certain player. When Maynard joined me in the England set-up I started to use Warwickshire's Nick Knight on a regular basis.

This problem was further illustrated by my early experiences with Marcus Trescothick. It is fairly well known now that he first came to my attention during a superb hundred for Somerset against Glamorgan at Taunton in that 1999 season, but there were two other interesting aspects to that game. The first, less importantly, was the heckling I received from some of the local supporters, who were keen for their wicketkeeper Rob Turner to be included in the England winter tour party.

One chap in front of the pavilion continually sang a song along the lines of: 'Jump now, Fletcher, before you're pushed.' I had not even started the job! But it amused most of the Glamorgan players, especially Steve James, who was quick to tell me: 'Good luck with your new job.' I did not say anything but inside part of me was agreeing with that singer.

Second, and much more critical, was the chat I had with Somerset's coach, Dermot Reeve, during that match about Trescothick. He clearly did not rate his player – probably why he had been batting him so low in the order and encouraging him to bowl – and said to me: 'He's got a problem. If you just set a ring of fielders to him, he will get frustrated and edge one soon enough.' I could not believe it, because he should just have been put at the top of the order and told to get on with it.

But I did make sure that he was selected for the A tour of Bangladesh and New Zealand that winter. Even then tour manager Mike Gatting returned to tell me: 'I'm not sure about this Trescothick.' But Gatting was certain about leg-spinner Chris Schofield – whom I had pushed to be included on that A tour because we needed to have a look at him in our desperate search for a spinner. Gatting said he was the future of England cricket. As a result we offered him a central contract in 2000; it was the gravest of errors.

So to the South African tour. English cricket was at such a low ebb that encouragement was a bit thin on the ground, so I will always remember the thoughtfulness of the late Lord Colin Cowdrey, who phoned me at our hotel at Heathrow airport to wish me luck. That meant a lot to me. This was a true legend of the game – that word is too often misused these days in cricketing terms. To me a legend is a man who on and off the field has common decency and is very humble in acknowledging what he has done. Lord Cowdrey was one, as was Sir Donald Bradman, so too now Mike Procter and Graeme Pollock. Too often the word is now applied to ex-players who are more interested in massaging their own egos.

At Heathrow I was indebted to the help of Phil Neale, who had to stand by my side as the players arrived, just to make sure that I recognized them all. There were one or two whom I had not met before and I did not really want to be making an embarrassing faux pas like my friend Mr Pack.

It took just one net of that tour, though, for me to realize that we were in for a tough time. It was glaringly obvious that we had no depth in either batting or bowling, with certain individuals standing out as not being good enough to play Test cricket. Vaughan, though, shone like a beacon for me with his technique far superior to the other newcomers. The way he played Caddick in practice, riding the bounce with soft hands, indicated that he had what it required. I immediately went to Nasser Hussain and said: 'We might be about to create something of a controversy here, but Michael Vaughan must play in the first Test.' As the add-on of the tour party he had not been earmarked for a Test spot, and Hussain gave me a perplexed look. 'Are you sure?' he said. I most certainly was.

My confidence in Vaughan was vindicated by the calm manner in which he went about his maiden Test innings in the first Test in Johannesburg, arriving at the wicket with the score at 2–2, that rapidly becoming 2–4. He only scored 33 but considering that we were 122 all out and both the poor conditions and the high standard of the bowling, it was a remarkable effort.

Which brings me on to the conditions and my first rant of this book at the ICC. There was no way that we should have started when we did at Johannesburg that day. Common sense should have prevailed and the start been delayed, because it was so obvious that the weather was going to clear and a lot of time could have been made up with the provision for an extra hour each day. The pitch was so wet and the light so bad that it was embarrassing. Winning the toss in any match usually brings with it a considerable advantage but here it was tantamount to winning the match. What chance did our inexperienced batsmen have with Allan Donald and Shaun Pollock – both at their top of their games – steaming in? Any side batting first on that pitch could have been shot out for fifty. Is that good for cricket? I do not think so. The match referee – Barry Jarman of Australia in this case – should have done something about it. But he did not.

I soon came to realize what it is like to deal with the ICC. It is like being in a Communist country: if you say decent things about them you are a good boy and are rewarded; if you criticize them, then you are immediately sent to the Siberian salt mines. What irks me most is the way they sometimes consider themselves so superior to the players. A good example of this is a meeting we had with them in 2002 during our tour of New Zealand. They had arranged it in order to get to know the players better. The time was fixed for 10 a.m. and, as I am a stickler for punctuality, I made sure all the players were there ready for the three ICC representatives – the then president Malcolm Gray, the chief executive officer Malcolm Speed and cricket general manager Dave Richardson. It was knocking on for 10.15 a.m. when I said to the players: 'If they are not here in two minutes we are off.' The players knew what I was like: we did not hang around for anybody. Then the three of them walked in. There was not one word of apology. It was so rude. Speed spoke first and then handed over to Gray, who proceeded to go through the new fines system which they were implementing. Some way of getting to know the players, by telling them how much they were going to have to fork out if (or it seemed to be 'when' in the eyes of these chaps) they misbehaved, ironic given that they had shown ill discipline in turning up late.

I had two proposals I wanted to outline to them. The first was the function of the match referee, which was a bugbear of mine from that first Test in Johannesburg – indeed throughout my England coaching career. My stance is that I think every international tour should be seen as the opening up of a business venture in that country. So someone should be sent ahead to check things out, just as you would in business. And that man should be the match referee, and he should be responsible for the whole venture. Everyone should report to him – whether they be umpires, coaches, captains, groundsmen or local officials. He should be in charge of the net facilities and the match pitches that are prepared, including those for the warm-up matches. For instance, South Africa should have had an official warning from the match referee for the wholly unsuitable pitch they provided for us at Potchefstroom for the warm-up match against South Africa A in 2004.

People always thought that we were being niggly whenever we complained about the nets on tour, but they should have remembered that international cricketers surely deserve at least three decent nets with net bowlers provided, and a bowling machine too. Complaints of this nature should be made to the match referee, but as things stand, they are not.

Instead, I was often dealing with local officials – the likes of the chairman of the Bombay Cricket Association – about such matters, creating unnecessary tension which could be easily avoided by the presence of a third party. And the match referee should be able to make decisions like the one never made at the Oval in 2005 when we won the Ashes.

For there at 5.59 p.m. Australia took the offer for bad light and the game was effectively over, but because of cricket's arcane regulations we had to wait until 6.15 p.m. until it was officially called off. Match referee Ranjan Mudagalle should have been able to use his walkie-talkie to talk to the umpires at 5.59 p.m. and tell them it was off. England's players could have left the field knowing they had won the Ashes. Instead everyone had to wait that little bit longer.

My second proposal to the ICC representatives was the idea of umpire referrals. In a nutshell I thought that the fielding side should be permitted three referrals an innings to challenge the umpires' decisions. I thought it a good way of utilizing the technology available and also reducing some of the pressure on umpires, which is becoming ever more onerous. I thought these two proposals were valid and this meeting with the ICC was the right occasion to voice them. But when we returned from that tour I was summoned by Tim Lamb, who told me he had received a call from Speed, accusing me of 'grandstanding' in front of the players. I was apoplectic, and immediately demanded a meeting with Speed. But I soon calmed down and realized I would be wasting my breath. For that is what you are doing if you try to talk to the ICC.

The referrals system was considered by the ICC in 2006 but rejected because they felt that it went against the spirit of the game. But at least the ECB decided to trial it in domestic one-day cricket in 2007 (how long did that take again?), albeit only using two referrals and not the complete implementation that I would have liked, with full use of the technology available. One recommendation they left out was the definite recognition of a time span in which the referral must be made after the on-field umpire has made his decision. I think the TV umpire should hit a red light after no more than ten seconds to say that no referral can then be made. Instead it is still rather wishy-washy with the wording saying 'without undue delay'.

The introduction of this referral system actually helped in my eventual resignation from the England job. I was already feeling that the ECB was showing me no support during the World Cup in 2007 but it really miffed me that nobody spoke to me about this system. It was my idea after all, and nothing had changed since I first thought of it at Western Province in 1995.

Alan Fordham, the ECB's first class operations manager, did phone me but it was only after the system had been drawn up. It was just a courtesy call and I was disappointed they had not used me more.

That first Test of mine in charge at Johannesburg was an eye-opener in many other ways too. For a start it made me realize how mischievous – even malicious – the press can sometimes be. Ours was naturally a very sombre dressing room on that first day as we were shot out by the rampant South Africans. Mike Atherton was undone for a duck by an absolute beauty of an in-swinger from his old adversary Allan Donald and I remember seeing him sitting there close to tears. There was an eerie, depressing silence about the place as we succumbed.

But then Alan Mullally went out to bat at number eleven. He is a real character, who often said the most funny things at the most unexpected moments. So when he fortuitously top edged Donald for six, and his face, racked with fear, appeared on the TV screen on the viewing balcony, it was a natural reaction for us all to have a chuckle. It was black humour which relieved the tension of a morbid day. But, of course, some overeager photographers had caught the moment and as a result the story splashed across many of the papers the next day was that of the England side laughing and not caring that they were being heavily beaten. It was irresponsible reporting, and that was only the beginning.

I had had an inkling as to the rough ride I could expect as coach after the very first game of the tour, where we had been embarrassingly beaten by the scratch Nicky Oppenheimer XI. The assembled press corps were very aggressive towards me after that, with Colin Bateman of the *Daily Express* especially so, asking me: 'Do you realize that we are very proud as Englishmen and want to win?' Of course I did, but I found that question strange and, as the years have passed by, more and more ironic, because I have often wondered whether some members of the media actually enjoy England winning. Indeed, one year at the annual Vodafone dinner it came to my attention that a leading broadsheet correspondent had stated openly that their job was easier when England lost.

I was still naive to the ways of the press, when, in the build-up to the first Test, I asked Dean Conway to organize a team night out in Johannesburg as a means of team bonding. We had often had these during my times at Western Province and Glamorgan and I thought nothing of extending them to my time with England. So off we went to the Butcher Shop and Grill for a meal which became more and more raucous as the evening went on, culminating in Chris Read being vociferously urged to stand on the table and sing. The guys were so excitable that Phil Tufnell, of all people, was trying to exert some calm on the proceedings. Unbeknown to us, though, the press were dining in the restaurant next door and heard the commotion, coming inside to see what it was all about. Maybe things had got a little out of hand but I can recall seeing the team leaving the restaurant that night, and how happy they were; the old guard mixing easily with the young, the tour underway with a unified squad. Of course, the press had a story staring them in the face but in fairness they declined to write it, although there was a sense of them saying: 'You owe us one for this.'

It did not stop them handing out some withering criticism after the Johannesburg Test, which ended before lunch on the fourth day. They became very excited when they discovered that we were planning a trip to Sun City. This had been planned all along because we had had a lengthy build-up to that Test, with three four-day matches in Cape Town, Bloemfontein and Pretoria (one draw and two wins for us), so I thought it was the right time to relax briefly. I have never believed in 'naughty boy nets', but thought we should have a good, hard net before we left and then off to unwind with some golf. But the press thought this ill considered. They thought we should have been in the nets all the time. But I think I won some respect from the players because I stood by my beliefs and did not bow to media pressure.

The next Test in Port Elizabeth only brings back memories of some shocking umpiring by Rudi Koertzen. Thankfully we managed to overcome this – he made at least five awful decisions – to salvage a draw, but as I shook the hand of the South African captain, Hansie Cronje, afterwards I said: 'I'd like to see how you fill that umpire's report in, Hansie.' Taken aback he blithely replied: 'You can see it if you want.' He had known what he was doing in the closing session, appealing excessively – even bowling himself – at Koertzen's end. It was as bad a display of umpiring as I have ever seen – at least until I went to Sri Lanka and New Zealand in 2002 – but I kept quiet in public, instead phoning Lord MacLaurin to ask his advice.

We had noticed that Koertzen was allocated to umpire us again in the series and we felt uneasy about that. MacLaurin suggested I speak to Ali Bacher, but I knew that would not be too profitable given our already strained relationship. At the very beginning of the tour Bacher had rebuffed me at the welcoming press conference in Sandton. Phil Neale had spoken to him beforehand and said: 'Duncan is in charge of this tour.' But Bacher could not accept that and made me sit on the end of the table, with Neale in the more prominent position next to him, when we were introduced to the press along with the captains.

My remarks to Cronje clearly hit a nerve. Our first match of the Standard Bank triangular one-day series (Zimbabwe being the third team), which followed the Test series, was at Bloemfontein against the hosts. We had restricted them to just 184 when I walked into the lunch room during the break. As I did so, I could see Cronje staring at me, his gaze not deflecting from me for a second. He had just had a rough decision – caught behind off Darren Gough – but what that had to do with me I was not sure. As I was getting my food, I discovered. He came up behind me and said: 'I want to see your umpires' report for this match.' I just replied: 'Hansie, they're your umpires' and made my way to sit down. The funny thing is that I never had to fill in umpires' match reports anyway.

As it was, our next match after the Port Elizabeth Test was at Alice, a town 100 km north-west of East London where Bacher had arranged a one-day match to spread the gospel amongst the black majority. I understood Bacher's motives and welcomed them, but still that match should not have been played on that ground. It was patently unfit for international cricketers. Yes, we were able to rest some of the Test players but not all of them, and if someone had got injured – which they could easily have done on the bumpy outfield and uneven pitch – I would have been livid. But it was not for that reason that I approached Bacher for a word. I said: 'Ali, we were not happy with the umpiring at Port Elizabeth.' He barely let me finish before he retorted: 'It has got nothing to do with you. It is not your duty to approach me about such matters.' And off he walked. If I did not already know, I knew then: if you get on the wrong side of Ali Bacher, expect short shrift.

What is interesting is that after that match at Port Elizabeth Koertzen developed into an excellent umpire whom we were more than happy to have officiating our matches. But even good umpires can have bad days and Koertzen still made two more poor umpiring decisions against England which cost us dear. The first was when he gave Rahul Dravid not out in the second Test against India at Trent Bridge in 2002. It was an obvious nick behind, with Dravid barely established at the crease, but he went on to save the game with 115. We had just crushed them at Lord's and should have been 2–0 up but for this. And the second was in the ICC Champions Trophy final against the West Indies at the Oval in 2004 during the match-winning partnership between Ian Bradshaw and Courtney Browne, when a seemingly plumb lbw was turned down. Oh, for a referral system then. And how different things might have been for us in one-day cricket if we had won that tournament.

Just as frustrating was the Durban Test of that trip where we made the South Africans follow on, but could not force victory. This was the type of game for which Phil Tufnell had been selected, yet he could not handle the pressure and finished with just 1 wicket from 55 overs; 45 of those, wicketless, in the vital second innings.

I was losing patience with him, not helped by an incident during an earlier fielding practice. I thought the team in general had taken well to my routines, even though the older ones still did not see the full benefits of strenuous exercise. In fact, Tufnell was often lax in his attitude. I always welcomed all sorts of characters into my set-up – funny ones, naughty ones – but there was one thing everyone had to do and that was work hard. Tufnell would not do that. For the most part he would complain of a sore shoulder in order to attempt to skip fielding practice, but in this one instance he made a fool of himself by revealing that there was little wrong with his shoulder after all. I was conducting my favourite 'ten catches' routine; a simple but often lung-bursting exercise where I hit ten catches of varying height and distance. The players are made to run long and hard with very few of the catches being simple skyers. But the cardinal rule is: you must catch ten, no matter how many you drop. So on this particular occasion Tufnell was having a difficult time of it, not catching many, but what was funny was that as he got crosser he was throwing the ball in harder (no sore arm now), often trying to throw it over my head in the vain hope that I might run out of balls and end the torture. But there was no way I was giving up until he caught ten. He eventually did and I walked away. To his credit Tufnell did come to me the next day and apologize. I just said to him: 'It doesn't matter who you are, you've got to put the work in.'

Rather sadly, that first tour of mine with England is now recalled for one thing above all else – the infamous Pretoria Test which we now know was tainted by the match-fixing of Hansie Cronje. But at the time, the heavy rain aside, it was like most of my then short Test match coaching career full of disagreement between myself and the match referee. This time the row with Barry Jarman centred on the bowlers' run-ups. On the first day, on which South Africa struggled to 155–6, the bowlers were complaining that the grass was too thick in their delivery stride and that they were slipping as a result. So at lunchtime I ran out on to the field to have a quick look, before going over to the groundsman to voice my concerns and ask him to cut it. This brought immediate rebuke from Jarman, who told me I was not allowed on the playing arena during the hours of play under any circumstances. Petty and officious are the words that spring to mind.

Of course, we won as well, and that allowed Dean Conway another opportunity to organize a raucous team night out – that night in Johannesburg had not deterred me from having these nights, I was just more careful about where and when they were held. And I could always rely on Conway to come up with something weird and wonderful – this time a farmyard-themed evening (do not ask me why because I am not sure even Conway knows!). There were live chickens in the team room, one pig's head and two sheep's heads on silver salvers – with cigarettes in their mouths! – on the top table, where Conway and Ashley Giles sat as chairmen of the fines evening. Little did we know then as we laughed and celebrated as to what had actually happened at Centurion.

My take on the dodgy declaration is that I still think it was a reasonably difficult target to chase. I thought 249 in 76 overs was certainly no gimme. OK, you can say that the pitch was not worn because there had been no play at all on days two, three and four, but South Africa had laboured with the bat on day one and their bowlers were obviously fresh after four days' rest. I still thought it a very good win at the time. I will admit that I was a little surprised that Cronje wanted to make a game of it, but at the time there was a vibe going around Test cricket that everyone wanted to make it more interesting. So I thought his positivity was just an extension of this. When the truth eventually emerged I did think: 'Yes, there was a desperation on his part to make sure there was a game.' I took part in some of the negotiations with Graham Ford, their coach, at the back of the dressing room, as captain Nasser Hussain was out on the field and it did seem that whatever we wanted we could get. There was certainly no hard fight on the figures. But at the time I just took that to be overconfidence on their part.

I do not want to say too much about Cronje because that has been done in detail elsewhere and he has now passed away, but there was always something about his make-up which puzzled me. I remember during my dealings with him while I was at Western Province that I mentioned to Eric Simons, one of my players: 'I can't put my finger on it but there is something strange about Hansie.' When the story then erupted Simons phoned me to say: 'You were right.' It was not that I necessarily suspected match-fixing, just some odd characteristic. What I will say, though, is that I admired him enormously as a cricketer and a leader. I used to watch him working in the nets with his team and he reminded me of Mike Procter when he captained me, and led marvellously from the front, in Rhodesia. From that point of view it would have been a pleasure to have played under Cronje.

5

The Consultant

'Right, guys, this is the deal: you have a million-pound job, but the only snag is that you can only get to work each day by bus. And there is only one bus. It arrives punctually every day at eight o'clock. If you are late for work, you lose your job. So you have a decision to make: do you get to the bus stop early, on time, or late?'

That is how I have always begun my talk to players about using the forward press, which, for the uninitiated, is a trigger movement used by batsmen to balance and ready themselves before the ball is bowled. It is one of my better known coaching principles, and a good place to begin a chapter in which I will attempt, without wishing to become immersed in some coaching manual-type thesis, to explain some of the fundamental theories which have influenced my coaching philosophies and sadly have been all too regularly misinterpreted by the media.

The answer, obviously, to the above question is that you get to the bus stop early. Ideally you want to be on time, but by doing that you run the risk of being late. It is, therefore, best to get there early, because if you are late, there is nothing you can do about it – it is all over. The analogy is that in cricket you have got one ball coming at you, and you have a decision to make. The bus stop is the pitch of the ball – do you want to get there early, on time or late?

And that is the basis of my theory about using the forward press; why not get into position early if you can? Why leave yourself to make a bigger movement when you can already be in position to make a shorter one? The old-fashioned coaches might argue that a batsman should stand still before delivery, but that is tosh – you cannot do that against the pace of bowler generally encountered today and to do so would mean making a decision about where the ball is going to pitch almost at the same time as the ball is leaving the bowler's hand. And if you do that, you do not know if the ball is going to swing. But if you press, then you only have a small final movement to make to get to the pitch of the ball, so you can make your decision much later.

And anyway one of my major philosophies about batting is that the more movement you make, the greater the chance of error content. I favour a reasonably wide stance for a batsman, so that his press and then final movement do not have to be too large. I also always emphasize that a batsman must make sure that his technique can look after him when he has made an error. That is what happens with the great batsmen. Their excellence is manifested in their technique getting them out of trouble when they make an error of judgement, rather than them playing shots more perfectly than others.

But, as we shall see, it is not just against the pacemen that I advocate the forward press; in fact, I think it is more important against spin. The key thing about the press is that it is not just a lunge forward, as some people see it. Many batsmen do that and they are clearly not balanced. It is what its name suggests – a press on the front foot with one's weight and balance slightly behind, but not over, the front foot.

If your weight is over the front foot, then you have lunged, and you are stuck. 'What about back foot play?' I hear you ask. Well, anyone who has tried the press will know that it is simple and effective then to press off the front foot to play off the back foot. In fact, I advocate that batsmen, when facing spinners, score most of their runs off the back foot. The press gets them into a position to take advantage if the ball is overpitched but they can then rock back if the ball is shorter – sometimes so because the bowler has thought that the batsman is coming down the pitch because of his press movement. The key is, though, that you must press all the time. A good example is Nasser Hussain. I taught him the press and he used it to good effect. However, he found that Shane Warne always seemed to know when he was coming down the wicket at him. The reason? Whenever Hussain was going to charge down the wicket, he did not press first. Warne might not have known that, but I bet that something sub-conscious told him so, and he reacted accordingly.

The press is not just a lunge forward because sometimes it also involves a corresponding back foot movement to ensure that the batsman is aligned properly in a position to hit the ball back where it comes from. It is probably best to use Michael Vaughan as an example, because he was my most well-known convert to the press. Before I worked with Vaughan his trigger movement was just a simple move of his front foot across the crease (if it had been straight down the wicket that would have been OK) without a complementary back foot movement, meaning his balance was askew and he was falling over towards the off side. He came to me before the Ashes tour of 2002/3 – and I think Hussain also had some input on this – with the problem and we worked hard at it, with pleasing results when Vaughan did so well on that trip. It is important to get the timing of those initial movements right. You can, in fact, make them too early – as in the bus stop analogy, you would fall asleep and miss the bus – but more likely is that you make them too late – and that is when it looks as if you are lunging.

Commentators will say that a certain batsman is lunging on to the front foot too early, when in reality he is making the movement too late, and has no time to make the next one. When Vaughan was struggling a little on the South African tour of 2004/5 it was because his timing of those trigger movements was slightly out. Allied to that, like many batsmen who are short of runs and therefore nervous, in his overeagerness to get bat on ball, he was making a small third trigger movement which was giving the impression that he was not moving his feet. Of course, when an England captain is not scoring too many runs, it leads to all sorts of enquiries and inquests among the pundits, but it did make me wonder when one of them (OK, it was Barry Richards) said on TV during that series: 'Michael Vaughan should go back to what he was doing in Australia a couple of winters ago – standing still before the ball is bowled.' Um, he had obviously been watching carefully! There was no way Vaughan was standing still in Australia. He was doing exactly the same in South Africa. What I will say about Vaughan, though, is that during that period and throughout his career, he has always worked his socks off in practice, ever-willing to organize one-on-one practices with me when the others in the squad were resting on tour.

Those were the practices I enjoyed most, spending quality time with an individual to work on specific areas of his game. Sadly there was often too little time for those in the congested modern international programme – or in the bulging county calendar for that matter. I remember when Jacques Kallis was a youngster at Western Province how I once spent an hour and a half bowling off breaks at him – just the two of us – because he had a slight problem against spin bowling (a common fault among schoolboys because they have never encountered quality spin), going down the net every few balls to discuss various points. Those sorts of practices have always brought me real satisfaction and enjoyment.

Which brings me on to the playing of spin bowling. One of the reasons why I recommend the forward press against spin is because of my allied preference for the sweep (usually played behind square along the floor) and slog/sweep (played in front of square, mostly in the air) shots. I think those two shots are vital against top quality spin, especially when playing in the subcontinent where the pitches obviously turn more than anywhere else in the world. Often that has attracted its fair share of criticism, none more so than in Sri Lanka in 2001, after defeat in the first Test at Galle, when Christopher Martin-Jenkins of *The Times* wrote: 'The England coach and captain now have to be more flexible . . . England were rather too obsessed with the sweep.' This comment was the culmination of a building theme within the media, suggesting that the Sri Lankans were playing spin differently and we had got our theory wrong. Martin-Jenkins also threw in some other criticisms, saying that we had been wrong to select Graeme Hick in front of Vaughan for Galle, and also we should not have downsized a three-day match between the Galle and Kandy Tests to a one-dayer. Two of those three points he made really annoyed me because it showed that he was not thinking further than the next day about what I was trying to do.

The selection issue did not bother me, because that was his opinion and it was debatable, but the other two did, and I was especially pleased to be vindicated about the downsizing of that match, because we went on to win the subsequent Test in Kandy. The players were tired and who knows whether they might have managed to win if they had had to slog their way through a three-day match with all the attendant travelling which it entailed? On the sweeping issue, I felt strongly enough to go and see him in his room, armed with some figures I had obtained from our analyst back in England. In that match in Galle we had faced 198 overs of spin and played seventy-eight sweeps, while the Sri Lankans had faced 84 overs of spin and played forty-five sweeps. It does not take a mathematical genius to work out that if the Sri Lankans had faced as many overs of spin as we had, they would have played more sweeps. 'I'm sorry. I didn't realize,' was his gobsmacked response, as I proceeded to espouse to him my theories on playing spin. The evening ended rather bizarrely by his asking me if I would be willing to coach his son how to play spin. I am sorry, but I had other rather more pressing matters in hand.

I had touched the right chord though. This is what Martin-Jenkins, backtracking hastily, wrote the following day: 'They [England] are lucky to have in Duncan Fletcher a coach who has thought deeply about the best way to tackle one of the greatest spin bowlers in the game's history. If anyone can help the England players to work him [Muttiah Muralitharan] out, Fletcher can . . . The sweep can be both a productive and a dangerous shot. It has to be played to the right ball, but Fletcher is convinced that, without it, Muralitharan cannot be successfully countered.' Full credit must go to Martin-Jenkins for admitting that he was wrong – not many journalists do that.

I have watched the great Sachin Tendulkar bat against Sri Lanka on a turning pitch in Sharjah, and he employed the sweep and sweep/slog all day in making a big score. They were shots I played a lot of when I batted and I believe can be safe and profitable, if played well. Playing the shot well is, of course, the most important thing, as with any cricket shot. There are, of course, always exceptions to the rule and there are certain spinners you might not be advised to sweep. One of those is India's leg spinner, Anil Kumble, whom we always mentioned in England's team meetings as being someone not to sweep, especially early on in one's innings, because he can easily get under the bat with his skidding deliveries.

The two types of sweep shot are much easier to play if the forward press is adopted because you have already eliminated most of the movement required – all you have to do is squat to play the shot, because the sweep is probably the only shot which does not require you to get your foot to the pitch of the ball. The press is also beneficial when defending against spin with close catchers around the bat, because a shorter movement is required, therefore creating less momentum into the shot – which is usually the reason why batsmen end up popping up a catch to either short leg or silly point. I believe all but the very, very best spinners must be attacked as soon as they come on to bowl, so that they are not allowed to settle. Some might argue that the best way to do that is to hit them over the top, using a straight bat rather than the horizontal blade of the sweep or slog/sweep. I am not advising against hitting over the top – in fact I actively encourage it once a batsman has settled against a spinner or on a good pitch which is not turning – but my first option would always be the sweep.

For evidence, consider this comparison: when you are playing a spinner, there are three things you have to determine as a batsman. First, how much is the ball going to spin? That can be taken out of the equation by the sweep because you smother it. If you are coming down the pitch to hit over the top you do not know how much it is going to turn, which can lead to problems. Secondly, how much is the ball going to bounce? That can again be dealt with by the sweep, but not so by the hit over the top – thus why you should sweep on unpredictable pitches, and hit over the top on more predictable ones. And thirdly, how fast is the ball travelling? That judgement has to be made whichever shot you play. The sweep has negated two out of three judgements. It looks like the better option to me.

Despite what they often say, most spinners do not enjoy being swept, because it disrupts their sense of which length to bowl. Sometimes you hear them saying: 'I love it when a batsman sweeps me.' That is just reverse-psychology in my book. Muralitharan is one who often says that, but I have watched him closely when he has been swept early on in his spell. His walk back to his mark has always been a very timid one in that instance; the walk of a man who does not like what he is seeing.

A quick word on going down the pitch to a spinner. First, my view that most batsmen do not realize that when playing spin they have to move faster than when playing quicker bowlers. I suspect that most of their minds go into 'slow down' mode as soon as the spinner comes on – that is probably why most of the better players of spin have been those whose movements are quicker than you think, like Jonty Rhodes and Mohammad Azharuddin. Secondly, I tear my hair out when I see so many of the English players advancing down the pitch using the old *MCC Coaching Manual* advice of crossing over their feet as they do so. By this I mean that the back foot actually comes behind the front leg rather than just alongside it, having a tendency to close the batsman off so that he can only play on the off side and defying all the rules of alignment which I preach.

There is another aspect to playing spin, which I consider most important: the batsman should crouch low in his stance so that he is looking underneath the ball in order to see the loop. Now, this again might seem to be going against traditional thinking in that young spinners are always told to flight the ball high enough so that it is above the batsman's eyes. But hopefully I have answers to back up my theory. In fact, one should always have answers to back up one's theories. My philosophy stems from my time working in the manufacturing industry, where I encountered the Japanese 'just in time' system. It is a manufacturing management method developed in the 1970s, which was a little complicated but very logical, and revolutionized industry at the time. Basically it was designed to produce the desired component 'just in time' to be added to the next component of the product, rather than way in advance, and in doing so eliminate the manufacturing waste which accrues because of overstocking. In doing this they were naturally looking to continually improve their systems, but they had one important maxim when considering change: you had to ask the question 'why?' five times, and receive five decent answers, in order for change to be implemented. If not you kept things the same. That struck a chord with me, because it is wholly applicable to cricket. The players are always striving to improve their techniques, but they should always ask their coach why three times (I have modified the number), and receive three good answers, before they agree to work on an alteration in technique. Too often, when questioned, a coach will say: 'Just try it and see what happens.' That coach has obviously not thought things out. So I also apply that to my coaching techniques: I always ensure that I can answer the question 'why?' three times.

I had begun thinking about staying low when batting while playing for Zimbabwe with Barry Dudleston, who once said to me: 'Duncan, I've noticed one thing about you: you always seem to pick up the length of the ball very well. Why is that?' I did not have an immediate answer, but I knew that I stood tall to the seamers and then crouched when the spinners came on. I did not have the reasoning behind it though, so was always reluctant to pass that information on. I did eventually find out why – with the help of a woman who has become rather famous for her work as an eye coach.

Her name is Sherylle Calder, once a South African hockey player, but now probably best known for having worked with the England rugby squad before their World Cup triumph of 2003. She has also worked with, among others, the Australian cricket team and the All Blacks rugby squad. She also worked with the England cricket squad during the South Africa tour in 2004/5 but I kept that quiet, because I have never believed in boasting about such things. But I had first met her when I was at Western Province in 1996 and arranged for her to do some work with the players there. She also helped my son, Michael, with an eye problem. He was having problems studying, unable to read properly, which really worried me, so I asked Calder to take a look at him. She asked him: 'Have you got a computer?'

'Yes,' he replied.

'Where is it?' she asked. It so happened that the computer was positioned to one side of his desk, and consequently one of his eyes was getting lazy. She prescribed him a set of eye exercises – and moved his computer to face him straight on – which cured the problem within a couple of weeks.

But when I asked Calder about my theory of staying low and looking up at the flight of the ball, she did not have an answer. 'I will think about it,' she said. She did not need to, because during her very next session with the Western Province players, she gave me the answer without even knowing. She was giving them an exercise to do in order to show them how weak the muscles are around the eyes. 'I want you to keep your head still and look forward, then without moving your head get your eyes to look upwards,' she told them. 'Now when you look up,' she continued, 'you should notice that your vision becomes slightly blurred . . .' I had got it. That was it. Because batsmen had always been coached to stand upright and, while keeping their heads still, look up at the flighted ball, they were sometimes getting their eyes into an area where their vision became slightly blurred. So, if you crouch low, you do not have to move your eyes, because you are always underneath the ball and you can watch its curve accurately by picking up its reference points along the way. That is why short players generally play spin well, because they can judge the length better. If you think about it, when a catch is hit flat at, say, cover, it is often difficult to judge the flight because there are no points of reference to go on. The same, too, if a catch is hit straight up – and I mean straight up, for example those often taken by the wicketkeeper – it is equally easy to misjudge for the same reasons; whereas the reference points of normal catches are easy to pick up. Obviously when you are facing quicker bowlers you can stand taller at the crease because you can look down for your points of reference, but it also went some way to explaining why the bouncers of shorter bowlers, like Robin Jackman and Malcolm Marshall, were difficult for me to pick up. It is because their trajectory was flatter and, therefore, their points of reference were difficult to determine. I think that theory holds for all batsmen. Certainly on the West Indies tour of 2004, all the England batsmen found the bouncers of the relatively small Tino Best difficult to pick up. But, of course, bouncers from taller bowlers, although you might be able to pick them up easier, are generally more difficult to play. From that day on, though, I knew that I could impart that coaching technique to my players, because I knew that I could answer those questions 'why?'

However, no theory is all-encompassing. There are always exceptions, and some players do exceedingly well despite not adhering to what you might think best. Therefore, as a coach you need to be very wary of changing a player. Sometimes even if you answer those three questions, the player might be reluctant to alter. And sometimes who can blame him? One of my main coaching maxims, of which I have always had to constantly remind myself, is that it is far easier to destroy a player than it is to make one. So I always make a concerted effort not to go rushing in and suggest change for the sake of it. You must observe the individual and his mechanisms for a decent length of time before you consider change.

When I first took the England job I just stood back and watched – as I did at Glamorgan too (Western Province was slightly different in that I knew many of the players and their games already) – and I know this must have caused players to think: 'We've got a coach here who doesn't want to pass any information on.' Indeed, some time after I had been at Glamorgan, Matthew Maynard said that his initial reaction to me was that he feared he had signed a mute. But, as I have mentioned, I needed to observe, not show off with my knowledge, which some coaches on an ego trip can do.

The easiest thing for a coach to do is identify the problem a player might be having, but the real skill lies in being able to identify the cause of that problem. I always use the analogy of the dominoes. You have a long line of dominoes. You push the first one and all the dominoes fall, bar the last one. Somewhere along the line one of the dominoes is out of place, but can you work out which one? That is the skill which makes a coach stand out as being a class above the others. It is crucial not to panic. A player may come up to you and profess a problem, but unless you are totally certain of the cause, it is best just to say: 'I can't see anything.' And then when you do know, speak to the individual.

But when do you speak to a player about a technical problem? That is the biggest conundrum for any coach. If you asked me to give you a definitive answer as to when to do it, there is no way I could. It varies from player to player, and generally the decision has to come from a gut feeling. It is the same as in any sphere of life; it boils down to the fact that those who are most successful are those who make the greatest number of correct decisions. What is very, very important is that coaches do not just blithely assume that they understand how an individual's body works. I have studied the biomechanics of cricket closely and know that they can work in different ways for different individuals. For instance some players' genetic traits mean that they can only bat, bowl and field in a certain way, leading to technical faults which cannot be rectified. As a coach you must be aware of that, and not try to change them in those circumstances.

If you look at all the top players in the world, many of them have quite noticeable technical flaws, but what makes them very good players is that they are lucky to have a huge mental toughness, which is strong enough to overcome those technical shortcomings. The example I always use is that of Gary Kirsten, who was limited technically but more than made up for it with hard work and mental fortitude.

But having said that, there are faults which can be rectified, and it comes back to the age-old question of whether you tackle these when a player is doing well or when he is struggling. I was going to say 'when a player is in form or out of it' but resisted, because I have a slightly different take on that. I believe that all cricketers go through windows of good fortune and windows of bad fortune. Anyone who has played knows that as a batsman, say, you can be in great form but get out cheaply and then, sometimes inexplicably, be in shocking form but still eke out runs. A bowler often bowls a heap of tripe and gets a hatful of wickets. Other days he bowls well and does not pick up wickets. Sometimes it just comes down to fortune rather than form, but class will always out.

It can be difficult to judge whether a technical alteration you have made is not working or whether the player has entered a window of bad fortune. For instance, during the South Africa tour of 2004/5 Andrew Strauss was having a magnificent series (he deservedly received the man of the series award for his 656 runs), but I was noticing technical difficulties which I knew would catch up with him later on. If I had mentioned them to him, and then his runs dried up, how would I have been able to tell whether it was my change or just him going into a window of bad fortune? I left him as he was.

Also during that tour I noticed a problem with Robert Key's technique. It was during pre-match net practice for the Cape Town Test, for which he had been drafted in late because of an injury to Mark Butcher. It was his stance which was worrying me. Now, I have always insisted that, as a batsman, the period up until the bowler lets the ball go is the only time in which you are in total control. That is the time, in your grip, stance, pick up and trigger movements, where you should be able to get everything 100 per cent correct. Once the ball is delivered, then things are out of your control. What was concerning me was Key's head position in his stance. I first noticed it before he had batted in that game, where he got a first innings duck. It is a common fault in that, because he was worried about covering his off stump, he was almost getting too side-on. His chin was tucked into his left shoulder, creating a lot of tension (which should always be eliminated in a batsman) and as a result his neck was stiff, eventually meaning that his eyes were not parallel to the ground – an absolute necessity for any batsman, along with their head being still, at the moment of delivery. Because he had not been in the Test side I had not always been at his net sessions during the tour, so I was a little bit unsure as to whether this fault had been occurring all tour. The problem was highlighted when a local left-arm seamer bowled at him, because for him he had the perfect stance, opening up just enough. And just to prove to him without actually telling him, I asked Paul Collingwood to bowl some of his right-arm swingers from around the wicket. Again Key opened up perfectly. I decided to leave it, though, until at least after the match. Thankfully, he scored some runs in the second innings (41), while still batting with a poor stance. So I seized my moment and spoke to him about it. 'You know what,' Key replied, 'I was getting cramp in my shoulder towards the end of that innings and wondered why.' The next time he went to the nets he rectified the problem, and announced himself much happier.

That was one of the more easy problems to eliminate. I remember that in one of Marcus Trescothick's early games for England he was in the middle of a golden spell with the bat. He was batting at Lord's and I turned to Nasser Hussain, who was sitting beside me. 'Tres has got a real problem with his technique you know,' I said, 'It will really catch up with him at some stage.'

Hussain laughed and blurted out: 'What do you mean? He's scoring loads of runs!'

What was happening was that Trescothick was standing very upright at the crease, with a predetermined back lift, but he also had a duck in his stance just as the ball was about to be delivered.

'What will happen,' I said to Hussain, 'is that he will come into one of those windows of bad fortune and his timing will go awry. He will duck too late and his eyes will be moving as the ball is bowled.'

A rather flummoxed Hussain replied: 'Well, that's up to you to sort out.' And sure enough at a stage some time later, I had to, with the added complication that Trescothick was hiding his bat behind his body when picking up, rather than having his bat come down from the position of first slip as a left hander should. But fortunately Trescothick is a good worker and a good listener too. He cops a lot of flak for his lack of footwork but that never bothered me overmuch. It is more to do with balance than anything else with Trescothick, and if that is right, the bowlers can watch out. His record proves what a fine player he is.

Geometry also plays a huge role in batting. 'Angles, angles,' I keep reminding players in order to align themselves to hit the ball back where it comes from. That is often a fairly simple philosophy to follow, but it can become more complex. Imagine, for example, that you were the left-handed Graham Thorpe facing Muttiah Muralitharan in Sri Lanka in 2001. The Sri Lankan was mostly bowling over the wicket, because that is what he generally prefers. Which brings me on to another point which I have to get off my chest briefly. Why is it that he, and all the other subcontinental off-spinners, are allowed to bowl over the wicket at left handers without censure, while, when Ashley Giles bowled his left-arm spin for England over the wicket to right handers, he was berated wildly? There is no difference between the angles, with both looking to bowl a leg stump line, and Muralitharan obviously turns the ball much more than Giles, so he should be the one going around the wicket! Giles had a very crossed natural action – in other words his right leg went across his body, closing him off – making it difficult for him to be effective from around the wicket because he would need to turn the ball very sharply indeed to negate the angle caused by his action. Anyway, back to Thorpe versus Muralitharan. Thorpe's initial theory, based on previous advice, was that he needed to close himself off in his stance and look to hit the ball through the off side, even though, as we said, Muralitharan was pitching the ball on or outside the leg stump. I told him to think about how he could hit the ball back where it spins from, hitting a straight ball with a straight bat. The answer was to open up his stance and hit the ball to the leg side with a straight bat. That might seem like hitting against the spin to the old-timers, but the laws of geometry will back me up to prove that he was, in fact, playing a straight ball.

Remarkably Thorpe then got himself in a tizz against the innocuous off spin of Graeme Smith in South Africa in 2004/5. It got so bad that Smith would bring himself on to bowl almost as soon as Thorpe reached the wicket. He was all at sea because he was getting confused about his angles. He was trying to play him like he was Muralitharan, but there was clearly a huge difference. For one thing Smith was bowling around the wicket. For another he was pitching on the off stump. And, of course, he was not turning it half as much either. Now was his opportunity to play the ball on the off side as he had previously been advised.

Angles are also very important to the bowlers. Over the years I have had much work to do with a succession of right-arm seam bowlers who have struggled to bowl around the wicket at left handers. From Alan Dawson and Eric Simons at Western Province to Matthew Hoggard and Steve Harmison with England, with many others in between, I have had to explain the simple laws of geometry in order to help them with, what was becoming for them, a mountainous task. What happened with all these bowlers was that, when bowling around the wicket to left handers, they were not moving their bowling marker (where they commence their run-up) far enough across to their right. If you do not run in from wide enough there is only one thing that can enable the ball to land

somewhere near where you want it to – a change of action. And
that can spell all sorts of problems, including serious injury. Simons
was the one who benefited most from the advice; becoming
Western Province's specialist bowler at left handers. Before that he
hated bowling at them. In fact, in the 1998/9 Supersport Series
final against Border, who had a number of left handers in their line-
up, it was written on the board before the game: 'Left handers –
bring on Eric.' Harmison took some time to get the angle of his
run correct, but for a period had it spot on – he leaves his mark in
line with the far right-hand edge of the cut strip as he looks at it –
opposing groundsmen please do not get any clever ideas!

When I took the England job I presumed that I would be just
putting the roof on the house that is most players' techniques, but
sadly discovered that in many cases I was digging large founda-
tions, especially in one-day cricket. Andrew Caddick was well into
his thirties and we were teaching him how to bowl a slower ball,
and here is another story of a bowler, which illustrates the naivety
I often encountered. He shall remain nameless because he has
since made great strides in his career– probably due to awakening
his cricketing brain a bit.

It occurred during the Headingley Test of 2002 against India, a
match I still cannot believe we lost. India won the toss and surprisingly batted first on a day made for English-type swing and
seam bowlers, yet somehow managed to score 628-8 declared.
They should have been dismissed for 160, but we bowled atro-
ciously, not thinking about what we were doing, bowling our
same old, programmed length when a different, fuller one was
required in these conditions. The ball was swinging around corners on the first morning but only one wicket came in that first
session. So this bowler came to me at lunch, perplexed because his
booming out-swingers from over the wicket to the right hander
were almost swinging too much to sufficiently trouble the batsmen. It was obvious what he had to do: begin his run-up from

wider and bowl wide of the crease in order to reduce the swing on the batsman and make him play more often.

'OK,' he said knowingly, and marched back out on to the field to put his bowling marker wider. You know what he then did? He began his run-up there but halfway through he joined up with his old run and ended up delivering from exactly the same place, with all the same attendant problems! At tea time I now went to see him. I explained that the theory was to be bowling wider of the crease, which he was not doing. I didn't have much time and really should have found a blackboard and shown him exactly what I meant. But I did not, so what did he do now? He went out and bowled from wide of the crease, but using his original run-up, so that he had to change his action. Result? Most of his deliveries passed harmlessly down the leg side. It was one of my most frustrating days as England coach, so that by the end of it I just had to find a blackboard or something similar to make my point.

I found it in a room used by the Leeds Rhinos rugby league side. In there were two whiteboards on which I drew a series of diagrams to illustrate my point. In fact, I simplified matters by realizing that he began his run-up on one of the NPower adverts on the outfield, so I pinpointed the side of the N from where I thought he should begin it. The next day he did it and bowled much better. Mind you, I am not sure that the rugby league guys do too much in that room, because the next year I went in there to show another bowler something else and the same stuff was still there! A rather annoying postscript to this story was that before the next Test the bowler arrived at practice and immediately threw down a video tape on the table. 'I've spoken with my county coach and we've sorted it,' he said. 'He told me to place my bowling marker to the left of where it normally is.' And to think that is what I had been trying to tell him!

Even though throughout my England stint there was a full-time bowling coach present and I focused more on the batsmen,

I did enjoy working with the bowlers from time to time. On the one-day tour to Namibia in 2004, which preceded the controversial Zimbabwe trip, I spoke to fast bowler Simon Jones about his grip on the ball, because I felt his fingers were too close together and their angle on the seam was slightly out. He altered that and soon announced: 'I feel like I've got more direction now' because his hand position behind the ball felt much more solid. I also talked to him about not trying to bowl flat out all the time; to keep his quickest ball as his variation. In other words, say bowl consistently at 140 kph, then suddenly throw in (not literally, of course!) one at 149 kph bang on the stumps. This goes back to what I was talking about at the beginning of this chapter, about the forward press and a batsman being late, because if he is late there is nothing he can do about it – he cannot speed up his bat all of a sudden.

I also once did some interesting work with Darren Gough, who was having problems with falling over in his bowling action. I used a principle involving visualization, which I had picked up from golf. It is thought that if you visualize the finish of your swing, the brain is so powerful that it can put everything in place in order to reach that finishing point. Using that principle I told Gough to try to hit his left armpit as hard as he could with his right arm when finishing his action. In other words, just run up and bowl, and only worry about the follow through, because his body and brain would do the rest to ensure he reached that point. He did that, and did not fall over.

As the title of this chapter suggests, I consider myself the consultant in the mechanics of a cricket team and its backup staff. I advise players, but leave the decision up to them whether they take that advice. Admittedly, some points I make with more forcefulness than others, but in general I leave the final decision up to the player. They must take responsibility for their own game. My idea of being the consultant is derived from my business background.

Every team I have been involved in has had the same team management structure. The captain is always the boss, the managing director. I discovered that must be the case when I became skipper of Zimbabwe. Being an all-rounder, I was worried that I might not be able to spend as much time on my own game as I wanted, so I asked for a coach to be appointed above me. So in came Peter Carlstein, the former Rhodesian batsman who played eight Tests for South Africa, but within five or six net sessions I realized that there was a serious problem, because nobody knew who was really in charge. In no sport can the players have two bosses and that was how the Zimbabwe team suddenly felt. It was an important lesson.

Below the captain is a middle management team, which is consulted for advice on all major team decisions. This usually consists of three or four players from different parts of the squad – e.g. a batsman, a bowler and a youngster – who can give the captain and coach a feel of the mood in the camp. They are the equivalents of your floor managers, sales managers and works managers in business. I use them because some players might feel uncomfortable speaking directly to the captain or coach about a certain issue, so instead they can confide in a member of the management team, who can then relay the message to the captain and coach. I think that this arrangement covers all the bases in leadership terms, because it usually ensures that the correct decisions are made. I have been involved in teams with an average leader but strong management team, which have prospered, and also those with an outstanding leader backed up with an average management team, which have not been successful. Ideally, of course, you obviously want an outstanding captain backed up by an outstanding management team.

Players usually responded well to being invited on to the management team, considering it an honour and in some cases altering how they behaved. Graham Thorpe is a good example. Apparently in the past he had been something of a rebel, not particularly bothering about punctuality or dress code, but once on the management team that all changed.

Of course, this does not mean that the rest of the team were excluded because of this group. At the first practice before a Test – usually on the Tuesday afternoon after we had convened on the Monday evening – I liked to sit the team down on the square, near the pitch on which they were to be playing. We would talk. As we did so, the players could familiarize themselves with the ground on which they were to play. But in that chat, I would often tell those on the team management group to keep quiet, otherwise they might end up dominating the discussion. That way we would get to hear everyone's opinion over the course of time. That created a joint team effort, where everyone was involved in that decision-making process. It is no use if you have a team sitting around waiting for one person to make a decision. Then it is easy for the team to use that person's judgement as a crutch should they fail. 'I was told to do that,' they might say. Not with this method.

Every England player also had a copy of this poem:

The Guy in the Glass

When you get what you want in your struggle for pelf
And the world makes you King for a day,
Then go to the mirror and look at yourself,
And see what that guy has to say.

For it isn't your Father, or Mother, or Wife,
Who judgement upon you must pass.
The feller whose verdict counts most in your life
Is the guy staring back from the glass.

He's the feller to please, never mind all the rest,
For he's with you clear up to the end,

And you've passed your most dangerous, difficult test
If the guy in the glass is your friend.

You may be like Jack Horner and 'chisel' a plum
And think you're a wonderful guy,
But the man in the glass says you're only a bum
If you can't look him straight in the eye.

You can fool the whole world down the pathway of
　　years,
And get pats on the back as you pass,
But your final reward will be heartaches and tears
If you've cheated the guy in the glass.

　　　　　　　　　　　　Dale Wimbrow (1895–1954)

It was a vital part of England's approach to cricket under me. 'Look in the mirror' could often be heard when someone was complaining. I quoted this poem in the book *Ashes Regained* I wrote about the 2005 Ashes triumph and was astonished by the response. I was even asked to read it out on Radio Five Live.

But there were also times when an outsider was brought in to provide extra motivation. For example, at Lord's before the first Test of the 2005 Ashes we invited Alan Chambers to speak to the team. Chambers was a Royal Marine commando; he and colleague Charlie Paton had in 2000 become the first Britons to reach the geographic North Pole without support, dragging their 550 kilo sledges 800 kilometres across the ice from Canada. They had lost two others from their party on the way and run out of food before the end of their remarkable journey.

It was an incredible story he had to tell. It moved us all. Throughout the Ashes series that summer you would often hear calls of 'Remember the Iceman' when the going got tough. And Chambers was a source of great inspiration during the rematch

Down Under in 2006/7. While all the flak was flying it was the e-mail correspondence I received from him which helped me most. He was the most positive person I communicated with during that time. And I told the press so at the end of the tour – after we'd won the Commonwealth Bank Trophy – giving them a quote Chambers had given me from Mother Theresa, saying that when you are successful you win some unfaithful friends and some genuine enemies. It was a perfect quote for me, reflecting what I thought of my many critics. Many of them had been jealous of the Ashes win and had wasted no time in sticking the knife in once we began to struggle.

6

Winners

I coach cricket teams to win. All that deep thinking about the
game, all that planning, the meetings, the one-on-ones, the worry,
the problems of dealing with the media, the inadvertent ignoring
of my wife because my mind is wandering to how to get a certain
batsman out in the next game; all that and much, much more is
done for one sole reason – to win cricket matches. So when I look
back, I suppose that the summer of 2000 represented a watershed
for English cricket, certainly for the team under my coaching; for
it signified the time when we began to win. Win regularly, that is.
In fact, it was the start of a four-series winning streak.

However, at the start of that summer such good fortune seemed
little more than a pipe dream. I returned from the South African
tour of the previous winter having made up my mind that many
of the new players we had taken there were just not up to Test
cricket. They were mostly good guys but just not technically proficient enough to grow at the highest level. It was a time for strong
decisions because central contracts were making their first tentative appearance in England. But tentative is an apt adjective
because what disappointed me at this juncture was that only
twelve contracts were awarded. I was under the impression that

there might be at least twenty. I thought it a typically half-hearted gesture from the ECB, losing its real effectiveness and only allowing me the opportunity to rest the odd player at a given time.

This was the start of a rather uneasy relationship with the ECB over certain matters during my tenure. I soon realized that they were dealing with many issues in an old-fashioned and blinkered manner, signalling the start of a huge mission on my part to convert them; to banish their short-sightedness and to get them to think only of making decisions which would help England win cricket matches. This was no better illustrated than in an early-season meeting with chief executive Tim Lamb. I went to him to ask for a full-time assistant coach. Bob Cottam had come to South Africa as bowling coach, but I did not foresee him being employed on a full-time basis. The only trouble was that I did not know who might be able to occupy the position; my lack of knowledge of the coaching talent available in England posed a similar dilemma to the one presented to me in the selection of players. So I asked Lamb. His response staggered me. 'I've got someone for you,' he said. 'Don Bennett has just retired from Middlesex. He would be a good man for you.' As I did not know Lamb too well at the time I could not be too forthright, but, amid some astonishment, my reply was: 'Sorry, but I think I need someone a lot younger than that.' With all due respect to Bennett, a fine servant to his county, he was well into his sixties then. He was palpably not the man I needed, or wanted, demonstrating beyond doubt to me that there were those within the ECB hierarchy who did not have their finger on the pulse of international cricket and the way it was moving forward. In fact, from then on my search for the ideal assistant – or assistants – continued unsolved for some time, until I had Troy Cooley and Matthew Maynard on board together late in 2004.

There were two other issues with which I was soon to be in disagreement with the ECB, with the governing body further showing their dated thinking. First there was the future international one-day schedule for England. My thoughts on its volume are well known and recorded elsewhere in these pages, but what was annoying me most was the misguided intransigence of the ECB, who kept insisting that the marketing department dictated the schedule. I said: 'The best way to market cricket in England is if the England team are winning.'

We needed a programme which suited us, not the marketeers, or indeed the opposition, who were often overly accommodated, especially where pitches were concerned. That was my second gripe. When you go to the subcontinent they prepare pitches to suit their teams, which is fair enough, but that was not always the case in England then. The turning pitch at the Oval for the Sri Lankans in 1998 still rankled with many of the players who had been involved and was a good example of the ECB's prevailing mood on the matter. It was almost as if we could not be seen to be trying too hard to win.

The first home Test of 2000 was against Zimbabwe, at Lord's. A stroll in the park, you might think. But, remarkably, I walked into the England dressing room to find a mood of tension and apprehension. The Zimbabweans, who did have some decent cricketers then in the likes of the Flower brothers, Murray Goodwin, Neil Johnson and Heath Streak, had a bit of a hold over the team because of some recent one-day results, and it was something I had to rid them of quickly. 'Come on, guys,' I said, 'you've got to think positively here. If you play properly you should walk all over this lot.'

There was also a problem over selection. I was very keen for Steve Harmison, who had been introduced to the squad for the first time, to play. Sure, he was raw but every fast bowler is at that stage of his career and I could not believe that we were leaving him out of the equation. But, as I was still new to the job, I bowed to Nasser Hussain's insistence that Ed Giddins should play.

Hussain's thinking was that the ball always swings at Lord's and it was a 'horses for courses' selection. I have never believed in that nonsense and it took me about another year to bring Hussain around to my line of thinking. I believe that you pick the bowlers whom you think are the best, and that they will then learn to run on all courses. I was worried that Giddins would do well at Lord's and we would then be forced to pick him again. I feared that might come back to haunt us. Sure enough, Giddins took 7-42 in the match, claiming the man of the match award, and he had to play the next two Tests – against Zimbabwe at Trent Bridge and then the first of the West Indies series, inevitably faring poorly. Harmison was to wait another two years to make his Test debut.

I am not making excuses but that Trent Bridge Test against Zimbabwe was remarkable. Rarely, if ever again, have I seen a situation where the climatic conditions so favoured the opposition at every stage of the match. When Zimbabwe bowled, their canny medium pacers were helped by overcast, muggy conditions. When we bowled, the sun came out. And so on. In the end we were grateful to escape with a draw. We then got whipped by an innings and 93 runs in the first Test at Edgbaston against the West Indies.

I can hear you saying: 'Hang on, this chapter is entitled "Winners" and so far we've had one facile win against very mediocre opposition, a scratchy draw against the same opponents and one absolute hammering.' Your scepticism is not without foundation. Indeed, things could have been so different if we had not managed to win the next Test at Lord's – something we only just did. I often sit back and wonder what might have been if we had lost this Test. It is one of sport's, indeed life's, great clichés that there is a fine line between success and failure, and this match, if any, clearly defined that. We scraped home on the Saturday evening by two wickets, Dominic Cork hitting the winning runs in a low-scoring, topsy-turvy match. It really was an incredible

Test, so nerve-racking that even my placid, even-keeled demeanour was in danger of cracking while we were eking out those 191 to win. Of course, we had been placed in that position because of some world-class bowling from Andrew Caddick, whose 5–16 from 13 overs instigated the West Indians' demise for just 54. He and Darren Gough were magnificent in that series; Caddick amply demonstrating what he was capable of when things were going well for him.

But at Lord's the Somerset paceman also inadvertently revealed a side to his character which did not always endear him to teammates. At times Caddick tended to say things in the wrong tone, the words often not coming out as he might have intended. I do not think he was ever malicious (he was a popular and helpful member of the dressing room), just a bit clumsy in his timing. He and Gough were a tremendous partnership, feeding off each other with their competitiveness, but, being very different characters, there was always a chance that their rivalry could spill over.

And during this game it very nearly did. They were no different from any other bowlers who play a Test at Lord's; they wanted to get their names on the honours board by taking five wickets in an innings. Neither had achieved it before, and Gough had come close in the first innings with 4–72. So when Caddick returned to the dressing room after his five-wicket haul he carelessly boasted: 'I've got my name on the board!' right in front of Gough, who, for once, was speechless. I was viewing all this through the corner of my eye, as I always tried to with these dressing-room confrontations and conflicts, but was mighty glad that Gough did not react. He was clearly upset, and could easily have railed at Caddick, which might have caused an almighty furore.

I, too, sensed that this was not the time to intervene. I bided my time, and at some stage later in the Test – I cannot recall exactly when – I took Caddick out on to the balcony and gave him a good talking-to. I finished by saying: 'If you've got any character about you, you will go and apologize to Goughy. Don't do it immediately because it will be too obvious, but make sure you do it at some stage.'

And all credit to him, he did. I think that was a seminal moment for those two, when they both realized that that maybe they had been at each other a bit too much. In the past maybe both would have considered themselves too macho to have apologized, but Gough accepted the apology in good part and from there on their relationship was fantastic, Caddick finishing the series with 22 wickets at just under 20 apiece, with Gough grabbing 25 at just over 20 each. We should not forget Cork either who took 20 wickets at 12.25 as we waltzed the fourth and fifth Tests to win the Wisden Trophy, which the West Indians had held for twenty-seven years. We were winners now.

Not so much so in one-day cricket though, even if we had beaten Zimbabwe in the NatWest series final earlier in the summer, because October 2000 gave us a rude awakening when we travelled to Kenya for what was then called the ICC Knockout. For a start our attitude leading up to that tournament was all wrong; from the ECB all way down to the players, it was considered something of a Mickey-Mouse competition, which was just a gentle warm-up before the real stuff began in Pakistan later on in the winter.

When we arrived we soon got a wake-up call, as we saw how seriously the likes of the Australians and South Africans were taking it. They were there to win it; we were there to take part. I vowed that we would not make that mistake again. But more than that, I was scared – yes, scared – by what I saw of the England one-day team. Our naivety and rawness in the international one-day arena was all too glaringly obvious. I was seeing cricketers who did not realize where one-day cricket was heading and what was required of them as players. The quarter-final against South Africa (we had beaten Bangladesh in the first round) confirmed this and much, much more. We won the toss at the Gymkhana ground and batted. After eight overs our score was five. Five!! Opening the batting were Marcus Trescothick and Alec Stewart. I was sitting there thinking: 'Surely they have assessed the situation and realized that they have got to do something – improvise somehow.' But, no.

We eventually stuttered to 182 and got smashed by eight wickets. It brought home to me how desperate our need was to play more international one-day cricket. I am not intending to castigate either Stewart or Trescothick, two very fine cricketers for whom I always had the utmost respect, but their problems were indicative of England's at the time. Stewart was actually playing in his 134th one-day international but the problem was, like that with so many other England players at the time, that they had not been 134 consecutive matches – he might have played ten, then been dropped, then reinstated, then dropped again. And England's one-day matches then were spread out so thinly (remember that they only used to play three in any one summer) that any experience gained almost became ineffectual. In the time since Stewart's one-day debut in 1989 a comparable Indian or Pakistani would have probably played 400 or more one-day internationals.

It also reminded me of what the step up to the highest level entails for a batsman – something these two very good players had forgotten momentarily. What usually happens when a batsman moves up to international level is that he suddenly does not understand what a bad ball is. At domestic level, he gets his quota of half volleys which he dispatches with ease to the boundary. Now up a level, he does not get any half volleys – or very few anyway – and has to try and score off the ball pitched slightly further back. That is why it is often great to see an international player return to the domestic game and dominate like never before, because he is looking to score off balls which he had not been previously. It is a shift in the understanding of what is required, and exactly what was not happening in Nairobi. Trescothick and Stewart were waiting for the half volley which never came.

Just as I was waiting for the brickbats when we went to Pakistan. I knew that my honeymoon period as England coach was over and that from now on I would be looked at in a much more harsh, critical manner. The press might have been a little aggressive towards me after that very first match of mine in charge in Randjesfontein when the Nicky Oppenheimer XI had humbled us but since then they had been reasonably sympathetic. 'This might be a little different' I thought, as we headed for a tour which was always going to be politically sensitive, being the first excursion to Pakistan since Mike Gatting's famous contretemps with umpire Shakoor Rana thirteen years previously. I thought it showed great confidence in me and my management team that the ECB allowed us to run that tour without any external assistance, made even more pleasing when it passed off without incident.

On the field the tour had been deemed mission impossible in many quarters, because England's batsmen had such a hang-up about playing spin. Shane Warne had been tormenting them for years, and the devastation Muttiah Muralitharan had wreaked in that match at the Oval in 1998 still loomed large in most of their memories.

It was time for me to introduce my theories on playing spin. That was never going to be a simple, or readily complete, process, because there were some older heads who had been playing a certain way for a long time. But I would like to think I got there eventually. The forward press and the crouching to the spinners was adopted by nearly everyone, and with success too. Mike Atherton told me that he was suddenly judging the length much better, relating how he had naturally stooped low to spinners as a youngster, but how his bad back had made him stand taller of late. What helped me put all this into place was the standard of net pitches provided in Pakistan. They were exceptional – as, to be fair, they had been in Nairobi earlier. They put to shame the facilities we were then providing at home. Lord's was as bad as anywhere. Here was the home of cricket unable to provide decent practice facilities. In fact, it took a threat to move our practices away from there for the MCC to wise up their act.

It came about after a closed practice, which we had arranged for a few of the contracted players at the Middlesex academy at Finchley, went so well that I thought it might be better to practise there before Lord's Test matches. They really laid it on for us when we went there; the surface was outstanding and a lavish lunch was provided. 'This is what we want,' I thought, 'instead of players moaning about how poor the nets are, and how their techniques are being ruined.' There had been occasions at Lord's where we could not even use the nets because there were no covers to protect them from the elements. But my Finchley threat woke everyone up, and I am happy to report that the nets at Lord's after that were fantastic. So they should be. Some of the English venues have some catching up to do, but in general the facilities in England are much improved.

In Pakistan the groundsmen were so helpful. Graham Thorpe suggested that we scuff up the nets in order to replicate the worn surfaces on which we would have to encounter spin, and there was never a problem in doing that. The net bowlers provided were pretty good too. So much for Pakistan being a nightmare place to tour. It was my first visit, and I was already really enjoying it. It was different, yes – going to Peshawar was like entering the Wild West with its horse-drawn carts – but eye-opening and also very humbling when one considered the poverty on view. I was even enjoying it despite succumbing to the inevitable tummy-bug. We began the tour in Karachi, where the captain and I spent one of the early practices sitting under a tree in the shade, while the others sweated in the sun. I rarely missed practice, but was just too ill to do anything. I was soon cheered, though, when we won the first one-day international, thrillingly scoring 306 to win, with Andrew Flintoff blasting 84 from 60 balls. For that he quite rightly received the man of the match award, the prize for which was a brand-new car. A very, very small new car though, and Flintoff was expected to get into it – some feat given his enormous frame – and not only that, but drive it for a small distance around the outfield. Now, that was a laugh.

Not so the millions (or so it seemed, anyway) of tiny midges which filled the air, plaguing that match and the following two one-dayers, which we lost. Pakistan had won the toss and batted in that first match, but quickly realized their folly, winning the next two tosses and fielding, recognizing that the conditions were damn near impossible to bowl in once the lights kicked in later in the evening. Not only was there heavy dew on the ground but the swarms of insects were so bad that the bowlers had to run in with their mouths shut.

That was something Nasser Hussain did very well to do when he received an absolutely shocking lbw decision in the third match at Rawalpindi, umpire Mian Aslam granting Wasim Akram the decision even though the ball clearly pitched well outside leg stump. But once off the field Hussain could hide his frustration no longer and smashed the door of the dressing-room fridge with his bat. That was all it was, frustration, but no, our friend Barry Jarman, the match referee, had to get involved. He called Hussain to a disciplinary meeting, and I went with him. 'I don't want you here,' Jarman said to me, 'I want the England team manager.'

'I am the manager,' I retorted.

'No, you are not, Phil Neale is,' he argued.

'I am in charge of this tour and Phil Neale reports to me,' I said.

But Jarman was insistent, even though Hussain tried to explain too that, even though my title was head coach, I was still in charge of the tour. He still wanted Neale there. I snapped. 'Right, OK then, I will get Phil Neale in here, but I will instruct him that every time you ask him a question, he leaves the room and consults me.' That might seem a little petty now, but it was the only way to get Jarman to see sense. It was yet another example of a match referee irritatingly attempting to impose his authority in the wrong sphere.

Jarman left after the one-dayers to be replaced by the Sri Lankan Ranjan Madugalle, whom I consider, along with Mike Procter, to be one of the better match referees. His presence, along with the ice-cool umpiring of Steve Bucknor, was much needed in the final, absorbing Test in Karachi – as good a Test match as I was involved in. It will always be remembered as the Test which finished in the dark, but the way the Pakistanis behaved in that final session, with us chasing 176 in a minimum of 44 overs, was abysmal. All credit to Bucknor, who told them he was going to stay on the field until the result was determined, and Madugalle, who warned them at teatime about their antics, but the time-wasting was ludicrous, as the Pakistanis vainly attempted to deny us the victory we deserved. They tried all manner of things to do this; altering the field almost every delivery, with fielders being moved from such far-removed positions as long on to backward square leg – and they were walking slowly – when there was a left-hand/right-hand combination at the wicket. The Pakistanis were desperate. They had never lost a Test in Karachi in thirty-five matches and had been widely favoured to win the series comfortably.

They had a good side, with the likes of Wasim, Waqar Younis, Saeed Anwar, Inzamam-ul-Haq, skipper Moin Khan and Saqlain Mushtaq, but their plan was clearly to unseat us with spin. Thus I was delighted that we played the leg spinner Mushtaq Ahmed so well that his 52 overs in the first Test only yielded a single wicket, leading to him being replaced by the debutant Danish Kaneria. We also played Saqlain so well that he had to bowl a mountain of overs so that by the second and third Tests he was a very tired man. But I think that their policy of preparing the pitches to suit the spinners backfired. They took as much grass off as they could, but the squares in Pakistan – as opposed to those in Sri Lanka, which often break up alarmingly – are so well grassed that the root system still remained in place, meaning that the pitches did not disintegrate as they hoped.

The pitches were slow and difficult to score on, but they lasted the distance, and that suited us because we were in the middle of a process of consolidation in our Test cricket; attempting to ensure that we ground out the first innings scores of 400 or 500 which all the best teams need to control Test matches. It had been a constant failing of recent England sides. Making 200 had been an achievement.

But this new resolve resulted in our drawing the first two Tests, which further increased the pressure on the home team. We knew that if we could hang in there, we might have a chance. Thus Mike Atherton's first innings century at Karachi, which took over nine hours and wrongly attracted much criticism, was vital.

There was also some humour during that tense, last day in Karachi. While Pakistan were dawdling along in their second innings in their attempt to draw the match, Waqar, whom I knew well from my time at Glamorgan, came into our dressing room to speak to me and Dean Conway. I always found him a humorous guy and it was typical that he joked: 'You don't really think you are going to win this do you?'

'Yes' I replied.

'You've got no chance,' he laughed. Moments later a couple of quick wickets had fallen, and Waqar suddenly realized he had to go and pad up. 'You might now!' he quipped as he left. Another wicket fell almost immediately and Waqar was in. But he was not ready. As luck would have it, Conway had been summoned on to the field to attend to an injury. He was leaving the field as Waqar was shuffling out to bat, still adjusting his hastily donned kit. Conway could scarcely control his laughter, with Waqar only able to mutter 'Don't say a word!' as they passed each other. Sadly for Waqar (but not for us!) he was run out second ball, and even worse for him, Conway was again called out on to the field. So now they passed each other going in opposite directions, with Conway laughing even more, if that was possible, than he had been a couple of minutes earlier. Waqar's was more of a rueful smile this time.

Hussain had warned me that this England team had a history of bottling small run chases such as this one, so I was constantly breaking it down into simple one-day scenarios to relax them before they went out to bat. We altered the order slightly, moving Alec Stewart up to number three and dropping Hussain down to six, but it was Thorpe who was our match winner with his calm 64 not out, not forgetting Graeme Hick's quickfire 40 either. No one panicked and it was a fantastic effort; England's first Test win in Pakistan for thirty-nine years and a third successive series win.

There were still those critics who considered that something of a fluke, which only served to increase the heat ahead of our next series, which was in Sri Lanka, after a well-deserved break at home for everyone at Christmas. This was another sensitive tour, given that there was much ill-feeling lingering between the sides since a rancorous one-day match in Adelaide in January 1999, and so it proved. It will probably not surprise you to learn that I also had the odd problem with the match referee. This time it was Hanumant Singh from India. He passed away in November 2006, but I will never forget him, simply because I cannot. That is because I have got a wooden elephant named after him. It sits halfway up the stairs in my Cape Town home, and was bought by my wife, Marina, who, along with my daughter Nicola, had joined me on an overseas tour for the first time. In recognition of my many dealings with him on this tour I just had to name it after him. Even now he is still the match referee of my house, and every night we all respectfully have to say goodnight to him in the hope that he will look after us as dutifully as he did the two teams during this series.

The saga began as soon as he was announced as match referee for the series. Some of the players remembered him from the tour to Zimbabwe in 1996, the occasion when a somewhat more garrulous England coach than me, David Lloyd, uttered the famous words: 'We flippin' murdered them' after a draw in Bulawayo. There was a feeling that Singh was anti-England, as well as meddlesomely intrusive, during that tour. So when there was a pre-Test series meeting we knew we were in for a hard time when Singh looked straight at me and Hussain, saying: 'I am going to be very strong in this series, and I don't want any trouble.' He did not seem to be directing it at the Sri Lankans. He was always looking at Hussain and me when pointing out certain areas of discipline he was concerned about. I shall also never forget Sri Lanka's coach, Dav Whatmore, saying in an aggressive manner at the same press conference: 'We can't wait to get stuck into the Poms.' Added to this, the net facilities which were provided for us were hopeless. So the pot was simmering nicely already. Little was I to know that, even before the Test series began, it would be close to boiling over.

First was a two-day game against a Sri Lankan Colts XI. The very fact that it was only a two-day game caused some controversy, but I thought that a decent idea and I see that some other countries have copied it since. My thinking is that an opening game, like that, is nothing but a glorified net, so why not just spend one day in the field to get the necessary mileage in the legs, and then bat for the other, in which time you should be able to get most of the top batsmen a knock? The result of the match is irrelevant, and for the host country it is a good opportunity to blood some previously untried youngsters. But the detractors could not see that at the time, and never could when we organized similar matches during my England tenure. The match duly provided some good practice, but its mood offered a telling precursor to what was to come.

Darren Gough had been a central figure in that stormy Adelaide encounter, and the ill feeling clearly lingered within him. It was going to take very little to rile him, and it came in the form of a couple of the young Sri Lankans sniggering at him when he was given out at the end of our innings. That would have enraged anyone, and as Gough walked off he sounded a loud warning to his giggling antagonists: 'I'll see you when you bat,' he chided. It was nothing really, but the Sri Lankans made a real fuss about it, their coach making a formal complaint.

Coincidentally this chap was coach again when we played a four-day match against the Sri Lanka Board President's XI in Matara. This was a fixture we had expressed some displeasure about, because we had taken advice from Dean Conway who had toured Sri Lanka with the England A team in 1998, and he had warned us how taxing the daily bus journey from the Lighthouse Hotel in Galle to Matara was. He was not wrong. The journey took over an hour and a half each way, but not only that, the quality of bus left much to be desired, with its seats more like benches, which inevitably led to existing back problems of some players being exacerbated. Once we had become accustomed to the hair-raising driving methods of the Sri Lankans – some say they are the worst drivers in the world but I reckon they are the best, judging by the tiny gaps they manage to squeeze their vehicles through – the tedium of the journey was such that myself and Bob Cottam took to counting the number of dogs we saw on the side of the road. That kept us busy, mind, because there were plenty of them (if my memory serves on one particular day it was eighty-eight one way); many of them in the middle of the road too, but not once did we see one which had succumbed to injury.

Before the end of the game, though, there was something much more weighty to occupy our minds. It involved the behaviour of the opposition's excitable left-arm fast bowler, Ruchira Perera. He was later to achieve greater infamy for being at the centre of a throwing controversy at Lord's in 2002, but this could easily have been the much bigger story. It revolved around the remarks he made to Craig White, who was playing wonderfully well for his 85 not out, driving and pulling as he did at his best. The thing was that these were not just any old sledging words. They were racial. Perera completely lost his head and told White what he thought of the 'white' race, if you will excuse the pun. White was upset and, when he told the rest of the team about it, they were incensed. They wanted something done about it. The gist of their umbrage was what they perceived as double standards. They reckoned that if any of them had said only half of what Perera had uttered, they would have been on the next flight home, amid an international incident. The matter concerned me deeply, because I was well aware of its sensitivity. It was my first proper test of credibility as a manager of an England tour; the first time the players were looking to me for a strong lead. But being a Zimbabwean, a nationality to which racism is all too easily tagged, I was wary of making accusations without solid foundation.

I needed to gather some strong evidence. I spoke to White again, and the non-striker, Robert Croft. I felt that I had sufficient proof. So a meeting was called with the umpires, the opposition coach and a local official who was acting as a sort of match referee. I was very, very nervous about this. I knew that it was what the players wanted, but was worried about the outcome if things went wrong. 'Where would it lead?' I was asking myself. It was one of those unknowns with the media.

I began by saying that I wanted something done about the 'racial sledging' of one of my players. As I said this, their coach leant forward aggressively: 'What are you accusing my team of?' he said.

'Racial sledging,' I replied very nervously.

'No, there wasn't,' he retorted angrily.

This was the moment of truth for me. I had to lay all my cards on the table. I turned to the umpire who had been officiating at that end. 'Was there racial sledging?' I asked. To his eternal credit, the umpire said that there had been. You will struggle to find a more relieved man than I was at that moment. That umpire was a very, very courageous man. All I could think was: 'Imagine if he had said no, and the press had got hold of it. What would happen to me then?' With that confirmation, the match official said that he would take the matter further.

I went back to the team to tell the players, but still they were not sufficiently placated. They wanted Perera to be punished in the same manner they thought they would be if they were found similarly guilty. A call was made to Tim Lamb back in England in the hope that he would ensure that. What also irked us was that the press had got hold of this but were treating it as a minor story. Again the players were asking; 'What if it had been one of us?' Eventually on the very last journey back from Matara to Galle, I received a phone call. It was from Lamb: 'Don't worry, it has all been sorted. Perera has been told to write a letter of apology.' A letter of apology! You can imagine the reaction of the players when I told them this. Mine was not one of satisfaction either – I had put my job on the line here.

A meeting was hastily convened when we returned to Galle, where there were some extremely irate players. Three or four of them were especially vociferous and I could understand their frustration. Everyone, myself included, was annoyed with Lamb's submissive stance and the way the ECB seemed more concerned with appeasing the opposition rather than looking after their own players. But I decided the only way out of this was some considered discussion. I let everyone have their say, and gradually as time went on, the feeling mellowed. Croft stood up and said: 'I think we should leave this decision to Duncan.' Slowly it was grudgingly decided to leave the matter. And we did eventually receive that letter from Perera.

This was not a tour I enjoyed overall. There was just too much happening off the field, too much unnecessary antagonism for it to be a trip I look back on with great affection. At one stage I thought: 'I'm not actually doing much coaching here.' But before we deal more with the playing acrimony, I think we should talk about a rather different incident which will live with me for ever.

There are certain happenings in everyone's lives where calamity or tragedy are so narrowly avoided that you often cannot prevent flashbacks of them occurring from time to time. Waking up in a cold sweat is probably an exaggeration of one's reaction, but the recollection always brings the question: 'My God, what if . . . ?'

Aside from the Rhodesian war times, there was one such incident when my son Michael was inches away from being run down by a car in Cape Town, but here in Colombo was another, which, although conceived as a bit of fun, could on reflection have easily ended in trouble. For once I will lay the blame at the feet of Dean Conway, who has already earnt enough lavish praise in this book anyway. As I have mentioned, Conway was brilliant at arranging team parties, but on this occasion his imagination might have got the better of him. We were staying at the Taj Samudra hotel near the seafront in Colombo, and Conway decided that the team, and management, should have a Le Mans-style race in the tuk-tuks which are widely used as taxis in the Sri Lankan capital. These are three-wheeled auto-rickshaws, which can go surprisingly fast – with their drivers as fearless and quick-witted as all the other drivers in the country – but they are notoriously dangerous, as Zimbabwe's Heath Streak will testify after damaging his shoulder in an accident while going shopping.

So it was two to a tuk-tuk and there were twenty-two of us lined up outside the hotel, waiting for the start call, at which point we would shout the name of our allocated driver. It all sounded great fun at the time, with the two losers facing the indignity of having to wait on the rest of the team for an hour afterwards, serving drinks and snacks in specially appointed aprons. Even more funny was the fact that Conway had attempted to rig it so that Hussain and Atherton, who had been paired together, would be in the tuk-tuk whose driver had been 'bribed' to come last. Sadly that did not materialize as some confusion led to scorer Malcolm Ashton and media relations manager Andrew Walpole suffering that fate.

The 'racetrack' was the main seafront road – it was night time, remember, too – involving the circumnavigation of two unlit roundabouts where no one obeys the rules of the road. My partner was Croft and I very quickly realized that this was the most stupid thing we had ever done as an England team. Croft was urging our driver to go faster, as all the vehicles weaved and swerved about the road, some even going up over the pavement. But panic was beginning to hit me. 'What if someone gets badly injured here? What if six or seven get badly injured . . . ?' It could easily have been so, such was the utter determination of the drivers, who had been well paid, of course, to win. Thankfully nothing untoward happened, but I went to Conway afterwards and said: 'Dean, that was very, very stupid.'

'What do you mean?' replied my great friend, the Welsh physio. 'It was good fun wasn't it?'

It was good fun, yes, but nobody cared, amid the laughing and shouting, about the possible consequences. They would not have had to take responsibility if the tour party had been decimated by this dangerous escapade. I would.

We lost the first Test in Galle, but I thought it a courageous effort. The guys never gave up in smouldering heat, faced with umpiring which can only be described as shocking. Marcus Trescothick made his maiden Test century, sweeping superbly – vindicating my theories I thought, but not according to the press, among whom, as I have already mentioned, Christopher Martin-Jenkins was most strident. My thinking though, was, confirmed when Mike Atherton said to me: 'We've got to sweep more here, Duncan.' He had been a little reluctant to use the ploy too often, but he realized how productive it had been for Trescothick and that he and the rest of the batsmen had to follow suit if they were to succeed in this alien environment.

Mind you, some of the batsmen could do little about their downfalls. Graeme Hick was wrongly given out caught behind, and momentarily dithered to portray his disappointment. That was all it was, yet Mr Singh went out of his way to intervene and handed Hick a one-match suspended ban. I recall thinking at the time: 'If they are worrying about such minor things, then this sport has got a real problem.' It hit Hick hard because he felt very insulted that he was now considered a miscreant. It is not in his character to be like that and it affected him, so much so that, as we shall see, by the third Test he had lost his place in the side – a blow to us really because we had hoped that his powerful hitting would be a key factor at number six in this series.

There was, though, one very humorous light-hearted moment which emerged from this plethora of poor umpiring decisions. It involved Robert Croft. Like many others he had just received a terrible umpiring decision. It was so hot that we were all sitting inside the dressing room, with the air-conditioning on and the glass door shut. So Croft climbed the stairs to the room, in obvious anger, and as he opened the door gave it a fearful smack with his bat, shattering glass everywhere. As he walked past me, I said brusquely: 'Is that bloody necessary, Croft?' He went through to the dressing room and took off his gloves, but there he found a broom. Within a minute, in his impish Welsh humour, he bashfully came back out and began sweeping all the glass up, still with his pads on. If I had been angry with him seconds earlier, it immediately dissipated as I burst out laughing. Not even the fact that I then saw a piece of glass in my leg, with blood pouring from it, could detract from this excellent off-the-cuff humour.

Croft was hauled before Mr Singh for that. But I had been to so many of these meetings by then that I was beginning to take them with a pinch of salt. 'Come on, Crofty, let's see what trouble you're in,' I said to him with an air of indifference as we set off for it. So when Mr Singh asked Croft if he had read his charge, I interjected: 'No, he hasn't read it – it doesn't matter.'

'Hang on here, I'm the man being charged,' Croft then blurted out, rather astonished, and quite rightly so – something we often joked about afterwards. But at least we were then so aggressive in our defence that he ended up walking off scot-free from yet another of those damn disciplinary hearings.

And at least Mr Singh acted to curb some of the Sri Lankans' more intimidating on-field behaviour, fining four of them, Muttiah Muralitharan, Mahela Jayawardene, Russel Arnold and Kumar Sangakkara, 25 per cent of their match fee for running towards the umpire when appealing. But there was another matter which I felt he ducked; a very serious one too. On the fourth morning I walked out on to the playing arena with Nasser Hussain. As we did so, I spotted Mr Singh and went over to speak to him about a couple of other issues – one that some of the Sri Lankans had been scuffing up the pitch by running down the middle of it when batting, and the other that I felt one of the Sri Lankan batsmen had shown similar supposed dissent as Hick, but had not been punished. But as I did so, Hussain called me over. He was clearly agitated. 'What do you know about pitches?' he asked. I could not believe what I saw. Every morning the pitch is supposed to be brushed clear of debris by the groundsmen, but all they had done here was brush it into two areas, one at each end where the two spinners likely to do all the bowling that day – Muralitharan and Sanath Jayasuriya – would land the ball. I immediately shouted: 'Mr Singh, please come over here.' He knew immediately. He knew that something untoward had taken place. He called one of the groundsmen. 'Get this off from here,' he ordered, and smartly walked away.

'But Mr Singh,' I pleaded as he turned away. He did not answer. An official reprimand was the least that should have followed. But, sadly, nothing.

My curiosity about the antics of the Sri Lankan groundsmen was further heightened by a note which was pushed under the door of my hotel room during that match. The veracity is doubtful but it was interesting nonetheless, certainly at the time, but maybe less so to me now that I have seen how so many cricketing fanatics around the world can behave. It was addressed to Phil Neale, Nasser Hussain, Hanumant Singh and myself. It read, in broken English:

SECRET OF WINNING TEST MATCHES BY SRI LANKAN IN SRI LANKA.

ONCE THE WICKET HANDOVER TO UMPIRES, ALL SRI LANKAN CURATORS AND THEIR STAFF GET TOGETHER AT MIDNIGHT AND DAMAGE THE WICKET BY WATERING, ROLLING AND HAMMERING WITH HAMMER HEADS. THIS HAPPENED EVERY TIME BUT NO ONE TRACED SO FAR. SO TRY TO GET HOLD THESE FELLOWS THIS TIME BY KEEPING YOUR SECURITY MEN RIGHT ROUND THE GROUNDS (GALLE, ASGIRIYA AND SSC). BCCSL PRESIDENT, COACH WHATMORE AND ALL PLAYERS KNOW ABOUT THIS. AND SRI LANKAN UMPIRES AS WELL.

There was also the brouhaha surrounding the fixture against the Sri Lankan Colts XI between the Galle and Kandy Tests. It was scheduled to be a three-day match but I managed to get it reduced to a one-dayer. The travelling back and forth to Matara had convinced me that this had to be the case, especially as there would have been similar journeys involved to Kurunegala where this match was played. The Sri Lankan authorities were, for once, very obliging and credit to them for that. But I know coach Dav Whatmore was livid, because he clearly viewed it as further opportunity to debilitate a beaten side.

But we were having none of that, as we bounced back courageously to win the second Test at Kandy, in what *Wisden* aptly described as a 'bruising, bar-room brawl of a Test'. The umpiring was again very poor, with the local official B. C. Cooray having a game to forget. Some of the decisions were scarcely credible: Jayasuriya was given out caught at slip when he edged a full toss into the ground; and Graeme Hick hit a catch back to the bowler and got away with it. It was just that sort of match, and it inevitably led to some frayed tempers, swinging our friend Mr Singh into action. Jayasuriya was fined for dissent at that decision, and Sangakkara and Atherton were reprimanded for a verbal spat. I also felt that the Sri Lankans were indulging in another sharp practice. In our second innings, with spin the only option, they substituted Nuwan Zoysa, the gangling left-arm seamer and very immobile fielder who had bowled two expensive overs, with a more able, close to the bat, catcher. It was said that Zoysa was injured. I saw no sign of that, and this seemed to be only confirming a ploy of which I had been warned by the South Africans, who had hosted the Sri Lankans prior to our tour.

It was also the game when Nasser Hussain finally refound his form with the bat, scoring a gutsy hundred to turn things around for him. It had been obvious that this had been affecting him, but throughout his lean period, which lasted almost a year, he had still captained the side exceptionally well. I have always believed that the captain/batsman is an all-rounder and Hussain was still doing one part of his job very well. His problem was that because he cared so passionately about the game, he was getting too emotionally involved. He needed to relax and remember how good a player he was.

As vital as his century was, the innings I recall most vividly in that game is the 46 Graham Thorpe scored in the second innings, which far eclipsed the 59 he made in the first. Chasing an awkward 161 to win, he assessed the situation perfectly and played an uncharacteristically aggressive innings. He realized that his usual, nurdling style was no use here on a difficult pitch, and instead took the challenge to Muralitharan, hitting him back over his head on a couple of occasions. He may have fallen with a few runs still required but he had got us over a critical period in our run chase, which we achieved for the loss of seven wickets. If he had gone early I am not sure that we would have won that Test match.

It was here that we realized it was the end of the Test road for Graeme Hick. In that second innings he had every chance to win the game for us and show everyone how good he was, but he dithered around and got out to an appalling shot off Jayasuriya, who was bowling his left-arm spin over the wicket, giving Hick room to hit over extra cover and getting bowled middle and leg. He did not have to do that in the situation. I had always had faith in him and wanted him to do well, but even I now had to come to terms with the fact that he did not have a Test future. Technically he was fine – and I never agreed with those who said that fast bowling was his downfall – but mentally he was not there. He never played another Test for England.

It was also at Kandy that I gave the team an almighty bollocking. Apologies for the industrial language, but it is the most appropriate expression, mainly because it was such an unusual thing for me to do, especially during a match. In fact, I can only remember handing out one other bollocking of similar vehemence – and this after a match – when we had lost a NatWest series game to Zimbabwe at the Oval in 2000. That was an appalling performance, which prompted me to let fly afterwards, but even then I tried to end my rebuke with some humour – despite the fact that Dean Conway (and most of the press corps for that matter) always insists that I haven't got any – saying: 'But it wasn't a train smash, just that the steam engine came off the railway line.'

There was no such levity in Kandy. But more than that it also emphasized how the relationship between me and Hussain was developing; how we were beginning to appreciate each other's contributions. It came at teatime on the first day, with Sri Lanka looking well set at 216–4. It was another steaming hot day and the players were beginning to look tired. Another bad session and the Test series might be over for us. Hussain came to me: 'Duncan, I can't get anything more out of these guys,' he said. 'You've got to speak to them. Give them a bollocking.' Usually I wanted the captain to speak in these situations, but I recognized this as being slightly different. I waited until they were just about to leave the dressing room. 'Right, you lot, listen up,' I said very firmly, causing them all to look at me, startled and surprised. 'This is bloody pathetic. We're one down and if we carry on like this, we'll be two down and that will be that. We've got a chance here if we pull our fingers out. You look like raggy-arsed rangers, now tidy it up.'

They responded. Darren Gough poked his chest out and ran in with the venom which was later to earn him the man of the series award, and with good support from Andrew Caddick by the close we were batting, Sri Lanka having been dismissed for 297. The tide had turned. We went to Colombo for the third Test full of confidence, and it showed, especially in the batting of Thorpe, who hit an unbeaten first innings hundred and then came good again when we needed him in another tricky chase; this time finishing unbeaten on 32 as we made the 76 required with only four wickets remaining.

Curiously though, that Test reminds me of one thing above all else: an incident I had with Mike Atherton. It occurred during that second innings run chase. Hussain had injured his hip flexor while fielding earlier in the match, and so could only bat at number seven. He was clearly struggling and therefore called for a runner. There was much discussion about this in the dressing room, because it might have been the better option for Hussain to come off. That was certainly what Atherton thought. But I decided to send out the runner. Atherton then said in front of everyone: 'That could be a costly decision you've just made.' It was crazy that he was saying such a thing when we were under so much pressure, and publicly too. I was annoyed but did not bite back; reasoning that, as with Caddick at Lord's the previous year, silence is often the best policy in such heated matters, and so left it. For then anyway. But I made sure that I went to his room later that night. I explained that he should never have spoken like that in front of the other players. To his credit he apologized immediately. 'Just please remember that in future,' I said and walked out. I think I gained a lot of respect from Michael Atherton that evening, although I didn't realize that until it was brought to my attention that he had written so in his subsequent autobiography.

We had won four Test series on the trot, which was some achievement. The players were deservedly rewarded with their win bonuses, but it always bemused me that none of the back-room staff benefited in a similar way following such an outstanding achievement. Of course, they should not receive the same as the players, who, after all, are the ones who perform out on the field, but they play a vital role, and their sole objective is to win too. They do everything they can off the field to ensure that the players can win on it. One night during the subsequent one-day series (over which it is best to gloss, because we got hammered 3–0) I had dinner with Lord MacLaurin. 'I think it might be a nice idea to reward the management team with a bonus as well,' I suggested. He agreed wholeheartedly.

When we returned there was an ITMG (International Teams Management Group) meeting at Lord's at which MacLaurin handed me a letter about those bonuses. I did not open it until afterwards, but you know what? Inside, it said that every single member of the management team would receive a bonus, apart from ... yes, you guessed it, me! Not that I complained, but when Dean Conway and the others on the management team discovered that I did not receive anything, they threatened to return their money to the ECB in protest. 'Just leave it,' I said.

But at least while I was at Lord's for that meeting I received a bonus of a very different kind. There was some confusion as to the exact whereabouts of the meeting (bizarrely it ended up being on the steps of one of the Middlesex CCC hospitality suites because lunch was being laid up inside), which resulted in some hanging around. Thankfully though, Middlesex were playing a Championship match, which I sat watching quietly. Batting for them was a left hander, whom I had not seen before. He looked good to me, well organized and compact, so I later made some enquiries as to his identity. His name? Andrew Strauss.

7

Down to Earth

The three words used as the title of this chapter accurately sum up what happened to England in the summer of 2001, when Pakistan and Australia were the visitors. 'With a thud' might also be added, as the euphoric afterglow of the four series wins dissipated amid five Test losses out of seven.

The season actually started quite well, with a win over Pakistan at Lord's in the first of two Tests against them, but, boy, did it go down hill from there. But I was especially glad of that first win because it vindicated my decision to rest certain players who were on central contracts. At the time it was not something which had been seen before and naturally caused a rumpus in the press as well as in the counties, but we went into that first Test very fresh and were rewarded with a victory by an innings and 9 runs. In fact, it was probably one of our most clinical Test wins during my time with England. Even in that game, though, we had lost the toss and I sensed that we had a defeat coming if we kept doing that (we had lost five consecutive tosses in Pakistan and Sri Lanka). And so it came at Old Trafford in the second Test; batting last on a wearing pitch eventually became too much for us as the reverse swing of Waqar Younis and Wasim Akram, allied to the wily spin of Saqlain

Mushtaq, transformed an opening partnership of 146 between Mike Atherton and Marcus Trescothick into 261 all out.

The bad omens for the summer were probably there when Nasser Hussain broke his thumb in the first Test against Pakistan, beginning an unfathomable succession of injuries which were to blight the season, and leading to dilemmas over the captaincy and unfavourable comparisons with the Australians' seemingly more hardy approach to injury: skipper Steve Waugh scoring a century in the final Test at the Oval virtually on one leg after straining a calf in the third Test at Trent Bridge.

Craig White had already missed the two Pakistan Tests with a back injury, but during the Ashes series Hussain missed two Tests, Graham Thorpe four, Michael Vaughan all five, and Ashley Giles four. Having said that, though, the Aussies were just too good for us. You cannot escape from that fact whichever way you turn. However, I would have liked to have seen what would have happened if we had had our full complement throughout. Unsurprisingly the Australians, that Steve Waugh incident aside, did not have any injuries.

As ever there had been so much hype about the Ashes but we were hammered 4–1; the one victory coming at Headingley where Mark Butcher played an extraordinary innings of 173 not out after stand-in skipper Adam Gilchrist had tempted us with a declaration. It has been said that it was generous but I disagree with that, because history tells us that any chase of over 250 in the last innings of a Test is difficult. So to reach 311 in 90 overs, especially when one considers how variable the bounce was early on, was a notable effort. And we won by six wickets – that is a real thrashing in anyone's book.

Butcher might never have even been playing in that game, for we had seriously considered dropping him on disciplinary grounds after it had emerged that he had been out late drinking during the previous Trent Bridge Test. We had even talked about who his replacement might be – David Fulton of Kent – but as I always tried to do in these situations, I decided it best to seek the views of some of the more senior players as to the severity of Butcher's indiscretion. They all assured me that it was not too bad. I also knew that Butcher always had problems with sleeping, so it was often better for him to go out rather than fret in his room. It might interest you to know that I never imposed curfews but always said that individuals should accept the consequences if they were caught by either me or the press. However, this was still worthy of a fine and a stern talking-to for Butcher. At least he was not dropped though. I felt that would have been a case of cutting off one's nose to spite one's face. But just imagine how different his career might have been if he had not played in that match.

Otherwise much of that summer was filled with speculation about the winter tour of India. It was hinted midway through that Alec Stewart and Darren Gough might be going to make themselves unavailable for that part of the winter, both apparently wanting a rest. But the problem was that both then wanted to go to New Zealand in the second half of the winter. I never believed in players picking and choosing games or tours, so I knew this was brewing up into a confrontation with two of England's more senior and high-profile cricketers. But as soon as these whispers began I was of the opinion that such matters should not be sorted until the end of the summer. We had the Ashes to worry about, and I thought that was all we should be concerned with because we were not doing particularly well anyway.

David Graveney had spoken to me about the availability problem at Headingley and I sensed he wanted me to speak to Stewart especially, but for those reasons mentioned I did not want to, and anyway I always maintained that in matters of selection it should be the man in charge of that area who speaks to the player. In other words, Graveney, the chairman of selectors, should have been communicating with him. I did tell Graveney my thoughts on the matter, though, saying that I felt no one should pick and choose their tours, but as I did so, I sensed that he had already been speaking to Stewart about it.

Whatever, I did not want to be fussing over it then. I wanted to sort it out after the Test series, even if that meant delaying the announcement of the winter tour parties, which was due to take place the day after the conclusion of the final Oval Test. But none of this seemed possible, and what frustrated me most was that there was no ECB policy on this. However, when I did state my policy, everyone else within the ECB and the selection committee then seemed to be in agreement and was willing to back me on it. Maybe they were glad somebody had stuck their neck out and were then all too happy to follow on behind.

This matter was bound to come to a head during that Oval Test, and so it did. I went into the ground on the last day of that Test, and could immediately hear a heated debate between Stewart and Hussain. There is a room to the side of the main dressing room, specially reserved for the coaches, but still I could hear what was going on next door. Stewart was clearly voicing his opinions about the situation, saying that he needed a break and had the right to pull out of the tour, so I decided to walk in and get a coffee. I just said good morning to them – Mike Atherton was there, too, but was only sporadically entering the debate – got my coffee, stirred it and walked out on to the balcony to contemplate the day ahead. I just wanted to let them know I was there but also that I was ignoring their debate. Stewart continued to make a noise, but I knew that it was not the time to become embroiled in an argument. But I also just wanted to see if I would be confronted about it. In truth I did not want it discussed until the end of the match. We were 3–1 down in the series and all I was interested in was trying to drag the score back to 3–2. That would not have looked too bad, would it?

But I was a bit down as I stood on the balcony looking out over the Oval, until Atherton appeared and said: 'Stick to your principles, Fletch, you are doing the right thing. You're doing a good job.' That was very thoughtful of him, especially as there were clearly other matters weighing on his mind, it being his farewell match. Equally thoughtful was this note he sent me after the match:

Conrad Hotel
Sunday evening

Dear Fletch,

This is a short note to thank you for your work over the last couple of years. I think you have done an excellent job and I will always remember the four series wins on the trot that we had with enormous fondness. I hope that you and Nasser continue to combine well over the next 18 months or so. This Ashes series should be taken in context: we need to learn from them and improve, but we have also had injuries and can compete and beat all other nations.

Two things have struck me over the last year if we are to move on: the sooner the players are under the sole control of the board the better. We can't have a situation whereby the players have two employers. Secondly, and I know that you don't agree with me on this, but I think, under central contracts, we need to have a more hands on approach with our players during the home season and in between Test matches. This can only come if the board has a national facility to use.

I will no doubt see you around next summer. I may be on the other side of the fence by then, but I'll try to remember how difficult the game can be! If you ever need any help/advice or thoughts on a player you just have to ask.

Best wishes
Athers

When we got to India that winter one of the first things I said to Hussain was: 'I'm really going to miss Ath.' And I did. I enjoyed him both as a person and a cricketer; his attitude was always spot on, despite the terrible pain he was in with his back – something he never complained about. There is no better recommendation of the guy's character than the fact that he agreed to captain the side for two Tests during that summer's calamitous Ashes series. Hussain was injured for a second time (Jason Gillespie breaking his little finger), Graham Thorpe was also incapacitated and Stewart was reluctant to do it after having led the side to defeat at Old Trafford in the second Test against Pakistan. Added to this Mark Butcher had ruled himself out after his torturous flirtation with captaincy in 1999 – a stance with which I could not disagree, having seen his dejection first hand. So Atherton knew we were in a hole, even though he had always vowed never to captain England again after stepping down in 1998. He agreed straight away – albeit with a wistful chuckle – when I phoned him to ask. That summed him up.

At least we got to say a proper farewell to him at the end of that Test at the Oval with the special dinner we had arranged for him afterwards. However, before I could go and enjoy myself at that, there was the question of an important meeting arranged by David Graveney to finalize the touring parties and to ensure that every-one was agreed on my principle about Stewart and Gough. It was to be in my room, with Hussain to be present too.

I did not realize that Stewart was going to be there, but sud-denly he came knocking on the door. It appeared that Graveney had asked him to come without warning Hussain or me. I was surprised, but it did give me the opportunity to speak to Stewart and state my case emphatically. Graveney opened the conversa-tion, but he rather too quickly abandoned his responsibility as chairman of selectors and handed it to me to explain the issue. 'Thanks, Grav,' I said rather cynically. I began by telling Stewart that I was disappointed at the way he had behaved in the dressing room. I raised my voice and Stewart was a little bewildered. 'I really respect you, Duncan, but there is no need for you to raise your voice at me,' he said.

'Listen, Stewie, you raised your voice about me in the dressing room, now it's my time to raise my voice in this meeting.' Graveney then asked us to settle down. To which I replied: 'Grav, you handed this meeting to me and I'll run it now, thanks.'

I told Stewart that there was no way that anyone, whoever they were, could pick and choose their tours. Allowing him to do that would set a dangerous precedent. I told him that if he wanted to choose one form of the game over the other, then that was fine, but to say that he wanted to go to New Zealand, but not India, was unacceptable. Later I could see why he might have wanted a rest in such a crowded schedule but then I definitely had to stand by my no picking-and-choosing-of-tours policy. Gough had accepted that and was just going to play in the one-dayers that winter. It was the only time in my long association with Stewart that I was disappointed with him, because he was a top professional. He might not have been happy, but at least we shook hands and he left the room.

I will freely admit that now I was the one who was in a state of shock. When Graveney and Hussain left too, I stood in there in my room, thinking, 'Where is this going to end up?' My feelings were very similar to those after the racial incident in Sri Lanka. I had put my job on the line with my stance, because I had taken on two current superstars of English cricket in doing so. I was a little unsure of how much support I had, whether among the players or within the ECB. 'Have I overstepped my authority?' I asked myself. But thankfully my stance was seen as honest and fair, and was accepted by everyone.

That might have been the end of Stewart's Test career, which on reflection would have saddened me, because he is a good man whose always wholehearted performances for England deserved a more fitting finale than that. We decided to go with Essex's young wicketkeeper, James Foster, for India and I liked what I saw. Yes, he was raw and had some technical deficiencies in both his batting and keeping, but I felt that he was someone we could work with for the future. He really wanted to play for England and his mental toughness was up there with the best I had encountered. Despite the fact that he received a lot of criticism that winter, we felt he should be given a home series and he would definitely have played against Sri Lanka the following summer but for an untimely injury; he broke his arm while practising in the nets at Chelmsford.

It was desperately disappointing for him but deep down I was chuffed for Stewart. I was never one to see age as a barrier and as long as the individual was performing to his usual high standards then I was happy to pick him. In fact, I will say openly that I always felt that I was looking for any opportunity to reselect Stewart. We were never looking at anyone else if something happened to Foster and there was certainly no grudge against Stewart for missing the winter tours. Stewart had begun that season well for Surrey and desperately wanted to play again for England, so it was with some degree of satisfaction – and a little anxiety as to what his reaction towards me might be – that I went down to the Oval for Surrey's match against Lancashire to tell him he was back in. We shook hands again and both said that whatever had happened between us before was now forgotten. And it was. That one incident aside I would like to think I got on with Stewart as well as I did with any England cricketer. When I went to a testimonial dinner of his in 2003 I was astounded when he took up a large part of his speech with praise for me. He did not need to do that, but I think it emphasized what great mutual respect there was between the two of us.

*

When we did get to India, the early net sessions and practice matches were most disconcerting – and not because of the standard of facilities, which we will come to later in this chapter – but because of the very obvious lack of firepower in our bowling attack. As well as missing Gough, Andrew Caddick had, along with Robert Croft, pulled out of the trip for security reasons in the aftermath of the terrible events of 11 September. My stance on that was that if the tour was on, I felt that everyone should go. Not that I felt that such a decision would be held against them in the future. They were told that at the time and I believe we adhered to that afterwards.

I remember being on the golf course at home in Cape Town with H. O. de Villiers on that fateful day in September, before returning home and switching on the TV. If I am not watching sport, I generally watch the news channels and I sat there in stunned silence as the shocking events were replayed time and time again. I doubt if I was the only one whose immediate thought at its first sighting was that I was watching a movie. I was soon thinking: 'What is going to happen now?' – not only about world peace, but also our tour of India.

Obviously our small cricket tour meant nothing in the greater scheme of things but its viability was clearly going to be an issue. I was soon on my way back to London to attend a meeting about security, and there was naturally a lot of uncertainty among the players. But eventually the tour was declared on, with us having a squad vastly different from the one which had triumphed in the subcontinent the previous winter. There was no Atherton, Stewart, Gough, Croft or Caddick, and Graham Thorpe was only to play one Test in a highly distracted state of mind before returning home in a vain attempt to save his marriage. Our bowling attack now centred around Matthew Hoggard, Richard Johnson and Jimmy Ormond, none of whom was the type of 'hit the pitch' bowler I thought we required in India, especially as I had noticed during their tour to South Africa how the Indian batsmen had been discomforted by the short, rising ball.

Andrew Flintoff was that sort of bowler, but the selectors, in their infinite wisdom, had decided to leave him behind, and of his own accord he had asked if he could go to the National Academy in Australia. It took me one net session in Mumbai to realize that we needed to do something about this. I spoke to Hussain and said: 'I don't think we've got enough firepower to cope here.'

'I'll leave it to you,' said Hussain. I immediately got in touch with the ECB to summon Flintoff from the academy in Australia, despite the fact that we were getting negative vibes from there about his fitness. But I had a lot of faith in Flintoff, and he responded superbly when asked to open the bowling with Hoggard in the second and third Tests, playing with great accuracy and stamina.

It was during the first Test at Mohali that ECB chief executive Tim Lamb arrived, and one of his statements during a casual conversation over breakfast stunned me. Even with Flintoff there, I was still bemoaning the situation with the bowlers and I said that we could still do with Caddick being there. Lamb then suddenly turned to me and said: 'We could still get him out here.'

'How?' I enquired, rather bemused.

'Listen, what we could do is to get the press to put some spin on him,' he said in all seriousness about the possibility of using the press to influence Caddick into reversing his original decision. As he said that he turned behind to speak to Hussain about it, and with that I glanced at Phil Neale who gave me a startled look. The comment had scared me, because I could not believe what I was hearing. I wondered in what other circumstances the ECB might also manipulate the press. It became a running theme throughout my tenure, right until the very end when I know that, just before my resignation, a high-ranking ECB official approached three or four members of the press to ask whether they thought I should still hold the job and what their reaction might be if I did.

As you may have gathered, my relationship with the ECB often bordered on the suspicious, no more so than once in Pakistan when Tim Lamb was negotiating a new contract with me. We met in a hotel and he threw the contract on the table for me to sign. As I have mentioned, I could be overly blasé about things like that and usually would have signed immediately. But for some reason I decided not to. 'Just let me read through it please,' I said. It was lucky I did. I discovered that the contract had changed dramatically. Suddenly now a notice period, previously not there, had been slipped in. I do not know whether that was accidental or not, but a three-month notice period had definitely appeared. I would not sign it.

That was nothing, though, compared to the pathetic politicking which dogged the whole Indian tour. It had begun before the first Test at Mohali with a row which did not even initially involve us; the Test – and maybe even the tour – was in danger of being cancelled because of the consequences of decisions made against six Indian players by ICC match referee, Mike Denness, on their tour of South Africa. Most severely punished was Virender Sehwag, whom Denness had banned for one Test. That should have been the final one of that trip, but when India refused to accept Denness as match referee for that game the ICC declared it an unofficial Test match.

So when Sehwag was included in India's squad for Mohali then the ICC were threatening to deem this unofficial too. In all of this the Indian board president, Jagmohan Dalmiya, was throwing his weight around and leaning on all and sundry. Eventually the Mohali Test did go ahead with Sehwag serving his suspension – and us taking a hammering by ten wickets – but in the background Dalmiya was beginning to turn his attention to us rather than the ICC, his target hitherto.

Family portrait. Standing (left to right): Allan, Gordon, Colin and myself; sitting (left to right): my late father (Desmond), Ann, my mother (Mary), and John.

Setting out to collect cattle for dipping.

Winning the School Under-15s Cross Country.

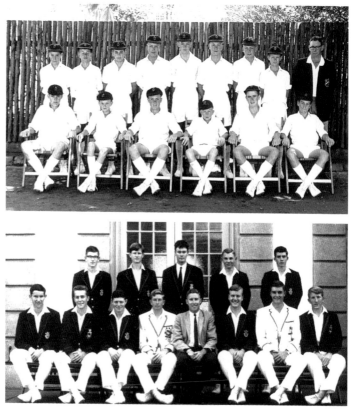

Top: Rhodesia Under-15s: I'm sitting third from the right. Leading at an early age. Man-management skills were already needed when handling lads a lot bigger than me.

Middle: Captain of the Prince Edward First XI in 1966. Nick Erskine, who is mentioned in these pages, is the Master in Charge.

Right: Lucky me on an important occasion: Marina and I on our wedding day.

Somewhere in the Zambezi valley on escort duty. We have landed in the bush to investigate something suspicious.

Packing for my only international tour as a cricketer, the 1983 World Cup.

Playing against Bermuda in the 1982 ICC Tournament, which we needed to win to qualify for the 1983 World Cup.

Playing against Australia at Trent Bridge in our first game in a World Cup, on the way to a famous victory. Dennis Lillee the bowler, Rod Marsh the keeper.

Two of the old brigade, Nasser Hussain and Mike Atherton, who people warned me to be wary of. As on numerous occasions these doubters were far from the mark and I enjoyed them both on our tours together.

The great all-rounder Alec Stewart and I share some fun in June 2000.

Victory in Pakistan, December 2000. Nasser Hussain and I with the trophy after an emotional series win.

A very good management team in Pakistan at an unusual but memorable restaurant in Lahore. Nigel Stockill, Matt Maynard, Dean Conway, Mark Saxby, Colin Gibson, myself, Phil Neale, Tim Boon and James Avery.

Celebrating our series victory over Sri Lanka in 2001 after a niggly tour. Andrew Caddick catches me unawares with a bucket of ice-cold water.

The management team with the trophy after the series win in Sri Lanka, 2001. The size of this team sure did grow as tours went by. Bob Cottam, Dean Conway, myself, Phil Neale and Nigel Stockill.

Nasser Hussain with a brave and skilled 106 in the 1st Test at Christchurch, March 2002, which set us up for victory and a 1–0 lead.

Adelaide, 2002, and one of Michael Vaughan's great centuries in Australia. It was always a pleasure to watch him bat.

The team celebrates a Steve Harmison wicket during the ICC Champions Trophy of 2004.

What a year 2004 was. Michael Vaughan, Andrew Strauss and Mark Butcher celebrate our 3–0 drubbing of New Zealand.

Deep in thought with Michael Vaughan during the West Indies series of 2004. I was fortunate to work with two very good captains in Vaughan and Nasser Hussain. Different, but both outstanding.

Celebrating another series win over the West Indies in August 2004, bringing an end to a great English summer.

A cup of tea and quiet chat with a trusted and very good friend, Dean Conway. We started and finished together. There was always laughter with him around.

One of the many pleasures of touring. Marina and I at the Taj Mahal.

Marcus Trescothick with one of his favourite shots during the tour of South Africa in 2004. He played some very valuable innings during that winter tour, especially at the Wanderers in Johannesburg.

KP (Kevin Pietersen) was always willing to listen to advice.

Simon Jones has just taken Michael Clarke's wicket during the 3rd Ashes Test at Old Trafford in 2005. It was a great feeling to back someone and then see them play a vital role in such an important series as the Ashes.

Matthew Hoggard getting the valuable wicket of Adam Gilchrist in the 4th Ashes Test at Trent Bridge. He was a good workhorse for many series and was always willing to bowl.

The crucial partnership. Geraint Jones with a very important 85 in the 4th Ashes Test of 2005 at Trent Bridge. His partnership with Andrew Flintoff gave us the momentum we desperately needed at a vital time.

We've done it. Ashley Giles and Matthew Hoggard leaving the field of play after a very nervous partnership between the pair saw us home to victory in the 4th Test.

Another gutsy performance by Andrew Strauss as he celebrates a century to draw the 5th Test at the Oval and ensure that we have won the Ashes.

Celebrating at the Oval: Kirk Russell, Troy Cooley, myself, Nigel Stockill, Tim Boon, Phil Neale. Kneeling are Peter Gregory, Matt Maynard and Mark Saxby.

Marina with the players' wives, girlfriends and other relatives after the final day's play at the Oval.

Above: What a great honour. A very proud day. I am sure this photo does not need any explaining.

Right: After the 2005 Ashes victory my family decorated the house to celebrate Marina's and my return.

My son Michael receiving an award for me from Princess Anne.

Great day. Receiving my OBE at Buckingham Palace with Marina and daughter Nicola.

Andrew Flintoff and I after a tough tour and an important win in the 3rd Test in Mumbai, March 2006, ensures we draw the series with India against most people's expectations.

He was prepared to take the Australians on, as you should, if you want to be successful against them. Paul Collingwood played some great innings during the tour of Australia in 2006/07, and none more so than his double hundred at Adelaide.

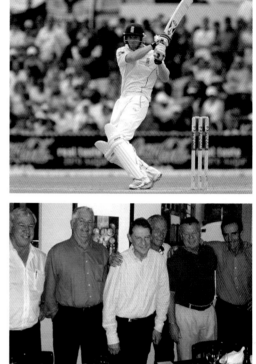

Right: Dinner in Sydney, January 2007. Five Rhodesian captains with my mentor Alwyn Pichanick. Jack Heron, myself, Alwyn, Brian Davison, Mike Procter and John Traicos.

Below: Victory at last. Celebrating after winning the Commonwealth Bank ODI series in Sydney after a very tough winter.

His vehicle of vexation was an intended sixth one-day international. His predecessor at the Indian board had agreed a five match series when we returned to India in January (having returned home for Christmas after the third Test in Bangalore), but Dalmiya wanted a sixth match and began using that summer's tour to England and England's tour to India in 2005/6 as pawns. The 2002 summer clash was scheduled to be a four Test series but Dalmiya now threatened not to play the fourth Test at the Oval, if we did not accept the extra one-day match, because we were only playing three Tests in India. This was a saga which dragged on interminably during that pre-Christmas Test tour.

I saw no reason to play it and was dead against agreeing to it, because I knew that it would give us even less preparation time for an already crowded programme, with us straight off to New Zealand afterwards for five more one-day internationals and a three-Test series. That was a programme which had been carefully planned, not just so that the team could go home for Christmas after the Test series, but also to enable me to have more time to work properly with the one-day squad. Before that one-day series were normally rushed into the schedule straight after the Test matches, sometimes lasting no more than nine days. That was no time in which to work with the players on their one-day games.

So I asked the ECB if the one-day series in India could be immediately followed by the one-day series in New Zealand, making it one long tour of one-dayers before the Test series began against the Kiwis. We even had time for warm-up matches in both countries. This can obviously only happen when there are split tours, and not always then, but was repeated when we toured Bangladesh and Sri Lanka in 2003. But adding another one-dayer would, in my eyes, eliminate crucial practice days and almost defeat the initial object.

As always with this sort of thing, meeting followed meeting. But the one thing that concerned me most was that I was led to believe that, even though Tim Lamb came out to India early for the first Test at Mohali as an ECB representative, not once did he go and meet Dalmiya to settle this issue. Lamb then went home and John Read, the ECB's director of communications, replaced him for the second Test in Ahmedabad, and it was left to him to attempt to solve the problem. There was enough going on by then, what with my worrying about the inexperience of the team and also the Thorpe situation, so I did not need to be involved in these negotiations. What is more I thought it ridiculous that it should have been Read who was charged with trying to sort this out. So when he called a meeting about it, I had had enough. I said to him: 'Look, you've just come here as Tim Lamb's messenger boy. It's not my job to sort this out. So go back to Lamb as my messenger boy and tell him that. That's all I've got to say.' Read was shocked. I know that because he met Phil Neale along the corridor after he had left me. 'Jeez, Duncan can be really abrupt, can't he?' was all he could say.

It rumbled on and on, so much so that during the third Test in Bangalore I remember sitting in the dressing room with Lord MacLaurin, who was also out on a visit, and Terry Blake, the ECB's commercial director, who had replaced Read as ECB representative, still discussing the matter. I eventually just said: 'Leave me out of this. I've got to concentrate on the Test.'

At least we enjoyed raising Indian hackles by playing in the Test series with a spirit and cussedness which surprised and, often, angered them. We did, of course, lose the series 1–0 but we competed manfully in the last two drawn Tests – Craig White scoring a fine century in the second – and who knows what might have happened if rain had not intervened in Bangalore in the third? What caused most antagonism was the bowling of left-arm spinner Ashley Giles. I explained earlier how I liked him to bowl over the wicket, pitching the ball on the stumps. But here Hussain, being the deep-thinking captain that he is, came up with a plan, which I wholeheartedly supported, of bowling just outside leg stump in a bid to frustrate the Indian batsmen on what we knew were going to be very flat pitches. It went back to my misgivings about our attack and I was proud of Hussain because he did not want the team to 'just pitch and play'. He wanted them to make the Indians scrap for every run, and there was no better vindication of our tactics than at Bangalore where Sachin Tendulkar was stumped for the first time in eighty-nine Tests.

As well as Andrew Flintoff did in the Test series in India, it was in the ensuing one-day series that he really made a name for himself; the image of him ripping his shirt off in celebration in the last of the six games – when he secured a tie by bowling Javagal Srinath – being an enduring one. Some did not like that expression of delight but I did not mind it at all. He had every right to be ecstatic (having also hit a vital 40 earlier) and it showed he had some character. As long as that sort of thing is not happening all the time, then I do not have a problem with it. To draw that one-day series 3–3 was a special effort by the players (strengthened by the return of Caddick, Thorpe and Gough, who had made himself available for the winter's one-day series only). Marcus Trescothick was thoroughly outstanding with the bat, especially in the first match, which we lost by just 22 runs, where he scored a magnificent hundred (England's fastest ever at the time) despite a stomach bug, only then to be seen off by an outrageous LBW decision when victory looked likely. Every side, including Australia, has struggled at times in India, so for us to perform so well really pleased me.

That blasted sixth one-day international was not confirmed until 27 December, even though the ECB quite rightly rejected proposals for the 2005/6 tour to be a full five Test series. The one-day series was rejigged to include Cuttack as the extra venue, with Calcutta now to host the first match instead of Mumbai. We suspected that Dalmiya might have had something to do with this as Calcutta was his territory and it meant we now had to warm up for the tour there, where he could call the shots. There was no point practising, as originally planned, in Mumbai (where the facilities at the Wankhede Stadium were good) and then flying across the country to Calcutta to play, so it was organized for us to prepare in Calcutta – an ample opportunity for further shenanigans in an attempt to disrupt us. The most obvious and sensible thing would have been for us to practise at Eden Gardens where we were to play and where we were pretty certain we would be provided with facilities of the standard required by an international team, but instead we were told that we had to practise at the Calcutta Cricket and Football Club (CCFC), at least for the first four days of our time there.

That surprised us as did the fact that our first two practice sessions were to take place in the afternoon, the morning obviously being preferable because there would be no restriction on time because of the light. However, we were assured that floodlights would be available so that our practices could extend beyond 5 p.m. if we so desired. As always we stated our requirements for these practices, which were no different from that which any international team expects anywhere in the world: 2 nets, 1 throwdown net and 8 net bowlers (4 seamers and 4 spinners). These arrangements had been confirmed in a fax sent to John Carr at the ECB by Mr Niranjan Shah, the honorary secretary of the BCCI (Board of Control for Cricket in India), nine days before our arrival.

We got there and it was a shambles. Nothing more, nothing less. The two pitches provided were soft and damp. There was no way that you could practise for a one-day game under those conditions. The best a batsman could hope to do was survive. The netting had so many holes in it that there were a number of near misses for players as balls flew through into the next net. There was no throw-down net and the four net bowlers who were there had been cobbled together by our local liaison officer. Oh, and when they turned the lights on, it was like being in a badly lit alley. Practice was duly abandoned with tempers fraying all around. It felt like a deliberate ploy to unsettle us. As I said, this was Dalmiya's territory. He must have been really enjoying this.

I sent Phil Neale to Eden Gardens to check out things there. Surprise, surprise the nets were in good order and there seemed no valid reason why we could not practise there. We discovered later that evening when Neale spoke to Dalmiya that the reasons they were giving were security issues relating to some repair work being undertaken at the stadium at that time. This was apparently going to be completed so that we could practise at Eden Gardens on our fourth day (as previously scheduled). By chance, though, Neale had earlier bumped into the deputy commissioner of Special Branch, a Mr Gaurav Chandra Dutt, who was in charge of security. He said that if the Cricket Association of Bengal (CAB) were prepared to allow it, he could provide security for us at Eden Gardens. In fact, he said it would be easier that way. And anyway the security we had at CCFC was so negligible that to use it as an excuse was nonsensical.

Dalmiya knew about this and could have changed our second and third day practices to Eden Gardens, but, of course, he did not want to. There was a real furore because some quotes falsely attributed to Neale appeared in the local media, expressing our dissatisfaction with the net facilities. We were not happy, true, but wanted to go through the correct channels first, and we were upset that it seemed like we were berating the CCFC – they did what they could and were very hospitable, it was just that their facilities were of a club rather than international standard.

Letters were fired back and forth between Neale and the CAB before we were granted permission to move our fifth day practice from CCFC to Eden Gardens. On top of this the opposition provided by the Bengal XI for the subsequent warm-up match was

8

Tragedy

Even as I consider what to write about this incident in 2002 I am becoming quite emotional, so you can imagine what it must have been like at the time. I am, of course, referring to the tragic death of Ben Hollioake, who died in a car accident in Perth, Australia, while England were involved in the second Test of the tour to New Zealand. I know that I will struggle to put into words fully the emotions involved and the effect it had on the team, but I hope by telling the story that I can convey some of the grief and terrible emptiness which affected us all during that traumatic time.

It was 10.30 a.m. on the third morning of the match in Wellington when Andrew Walpole, our media relations manager, tapped me on the shoulder and asked to speak to me in confidence. He often did that during play, and as ever, I gave him a jocular, mock-dismissive reply: 'Oh, come on Wally, don't irritate me while I'm watching,' I said. I could never have known how inappropriate that comment was.

'No, no, Duncan, it's very serious,' he replied, his tone and demeanour immediately alerting me to the gravity of his message. We went to the back of the viewing area and he told me what had happened. It had not yet been 100 per cent confirmed, but it was thought that Hollioake had died when his car spun off the road after a night out with his family.

I did not have a clue what to do or say. I told Walpole not to tell anyone else while I collected my thoughts. I returned to my seat, with a mass of thoughts rushing through my head. 'Do I tell the players? Is cricket really that important that I keep this from them?' were a couple of the questions I was asking myself. As I was contemplating all this, I realized that in front of me Michael Vaughan had received the news via a text message on his phone – a silent one, of course, because mobile phones were not allowed to be on during hours of play. It soon became clear that some of the other players downstairs in the dressing room knew too, so I had little choice but to go around the rest and tell them quietly.

Mark Butcher and Graham Thorpe, as Hollioake's Surrey team mates, obviously took it especially badly, both in tears in a dressing room which was consumed with sadness and disbelief at the news. Still a key question remained for me, though: what about the two batsmen in the middle? Nasser Hussain and Mark Ramprakash were together after Butcher and Thorpe had been out that morning, but there was still some time until lunch. There was nothing we could do until then. They battled on oblivious to the tragedy which had overtaken us. All I could do was make sure that I was first to them when the break did come.

It was terrible. Hussain was devastated. His initial reaction was: 'Fletch, we can't play on.' Initially I did not disagree. I was as shocked and stunned as everyone else. I was not sure that these guys were mentally right to go out and continue playing cricket. They were all in pieces. How can anyone really comprehend what we were all going through at that time? How many people have been through something like that in their sporting careers? Obviously Pakistan at the 2007 World Cup, but not that many, I'm sure.

Hollioake had been with us just a month before. He had been with us through the whole of the winter's one-day programme. I had played golf in a four-ball with him at the end of the one-day series in New Zealand before he had left for Australia. That was the last time I saw him. It is a nice memory because he was his usual self; friendly, pleasant and humorous.

He really was a quality individual. I had first been impressed by him when Glamorgan played Surrey in a National League match at Pontypridd in 1999. It happened to be Jacques Kallis' debut for the Welshmen and he smashed 155 not out to announce himself in the Principality, giving Surrey a good thrashing. They were not happy and most of their players could barely bring themselves to shake the Glamorgan players' hands at the end. But Hollioake alone came into the Glamorgan dressing room and went around warmly congratulating every Glamorgan player. And he was sincere about it. It might only sound like a minor thing, but it was the sort of thing I often looked out for as a coach. I had heard much about him but this immediately announced him to me as someone with some real character.

I had such high hopes for him as a cricketer. I thought we were shaping up into a very useful team with both Hollioake and Andrew Flintoff coming through as all-rounders. I think Hollioake would probably have turned out to be as effective as Flintoff; he certainly had the talent and was strong-minded too. But most importantly I think he had the intelligence to be a very good cricketer.

I think that he would have wanted us to carry on in Wellington. 'That would definitely have been his wish,' I said to Hussain and he agreed, so he and Ramprakash went back out to bat with black armbands on. And full credit to them, and the rest of the team, they performed remarkably well in the remainder of the Test.

There was obviously a minute's silence on the fourth morning, which was extremely emotional with many players in tears again. But we came out battling and the only thing which prevented us from winning that Test, and in doing so honour Hollioake's memory in a fitting manner, was the rain which had blighted the first two days. And the fact that Lou Vincent somehow managed to score two of the worst Test fifties I have ever had the misfortune to witness; their shocking technical quality added to by a number of ridiculously obvious reprieves from the umpires. We were also severely criticized for not declaring sooner here, but that was ridiculous. As we shall see, we had had a scare in the first Test which we were already carrying as baggage and then there was this Hollioake scenario. It would have been very understandable if we had thought 'let's just get this match over with'.

The next problem was Hollioake's funeral. Obviously everyone wanted to go, but there was a problem with the flights and also the fact that there were only five days before the final Test in Auckland. Some were closer to Hollioake and desperately wanted to attend, but if only a few were to go, how could you prioritize in such a situation? Eventually it was decided that Hussain, as captain, should be the team's representative and take Hollioake's England blazer (which Hollioake had left for our video analyst, Malcolm Ashton, to take home for him), and that at the same time as Hollioake's memorial service in Perth we should hold our own private service in Auckland.

All I can say is that was a sad, sad day. We all dressed in our number ones and went to a memorial at Bastion Point near Auckland Harbour, where Phil Neale read a service and prayer, and then Mark Butcher brilliantly sang a song to the accompaniment of his guitar. It was both beautiful and emotional, and I will never forget the eerie silence as we all walked back to the bus.

When I got back to the hotel, I thought to myself, 'How am I going to get these guys up for a Test match?' I had no chance really and unsurprisingly we lost the last Test. We did not play well but, without wishing to make too many excuses, umpiring decisions went against us in a low-scoring match, Chris Harris scoring a crucial 71 after being clearly caught at short leg early on (the players barely appealed because it was so obvious) and Andrew Flintoff being adjudged caught behind when there was clear daylight between his bat and the ball.

This loss led to what I thought was some callous reporting – some journalists blithely slating us for throwing away a 1–0 lead when not considering what we had been through. I know that it affected me considerably, so goodness knows what it did to the players.

New Zealand is normally a very pleasant place to tour, but this turned out to be a most difficult trip, both on and off the field. I suppose that I should have realized that it was going to be tough after we lost our opening warm-up one-day game in Hamilton. We had arrived from India in buoyant mood after clawing that one-day series back to 3–3, but immediately looked lacklustre in a game which we should have won after scoring 288. Northern Districts were not the sort of side we should have been losing to.

I also caused something of a furore with some comments I made in a press conference before that match. They were unusual in that this was the first time I had ever publicly criticized a top player, but on this occasion I felt that I needed to say something. The person in question was the former Indian batsman Sunil Gavaskar, who had been making some particularly derogatory comments about the England team's performances in the recently finished series in India. He had described our approach as only being 'good for people suffering from insomnia', also saying: 'Thank God it was a three-Test series and not a five-Test one, for Indian cricket would have lost a great number of spectators seeing the fare dished out. Why our cricket board are keen on having a five-Test series when England visit India next is beyond comprehension for, without the slightest doubt, they are the most unattractive and boring side to have played cricket in India.' Phew, strong stuff, and it was especially rich when you consider his well-earnt reputation for slow scoring.

So when I was asked for a comment in Hamilton about these remarks, I said just two things: 'First it's very important to realize that he's on the International Cricket Council [ICC] panel and should have an unbiased opinion and secondly it's very sad when a good wine goes sour.' I was very disappointed with Gavaskar. He was a cricketer for whom I had always had the utmost respect when I was playing. Often I would be asked who was the greatest player I had played against, and while I never thought I could answer that, I always said that Gavaskar was the one for whom I had the greatest amount of respect. As well as in India, he had scored hundreds away from home, and especially in the West Indies, where a lot of players who have been termed 'great' have not done so. He also scored all his runs without a seam attack to back him up, and that is important in my view, because it is all very well doing it when you have some quick men to bully the opposition. But after these comments, which I think might have been made because he had a problem with the English press rather than the cricket team, I lost respect. He had not recognized how well we had played in India, especially as we were missing many key players.

Ted Dexter, then the president of the MCC, also later put in his halfpennyworth about the Indian trip by saying that he thought Hussain had been 'pushing the laws of the game to their limit to gain advantage', in announcing that the ICC had asked the MCC to look into closing the apparent loophole in the laws which allowed such negative tactics. There is nothing like a bit of support from a former captain, and has he ever complained when Muttiah Muralitharan bowls over the wicket to left handers or when Shane Warne goes round the wicket to right handers?

All sorts of things seemed to be going on at this stage. There was even a row brewing between the players and the ECB concerning the issue of the amount of time wives and girlfriends were paid for to join the team. The criterion at the time was that your partner was permitted two weeks' paid holiday if you were away on tour for sixty days. But there was a very valid argument that because we would be abroad for 148 days out of 180 (with only a brief time at home for Christmas) four weeks should be paid for. However, the ECB would not budge, despite being very receptive to our thoughts and requirements after that.

It was also about this time that Graeme Hick conducted a newspaper interview back home in which he had an unnecessary pop at me, saying something along the lines of 'there have never been any coaches for England' when asked which of them had helped him most during his times with England. So I probably did not need us to lose the first two one-day internationals; the second when we were embarrassingly skittled out for 89 in Wellington. It was now that Christopher Martin-Jenkins suggested in *The Times* that England might be better served by having separate coaches for Test and one-day cricket, therefore implying, to my mind anyway, that I was not good enough to do the job. To be fair to him though, as he did in Sri Lanka earlier, he did follow it up with a positive piece after I had spoken to him. However, that came about over a dinner at which he had never mentioned that anything that I was going to say was going to be on the record. That sort of thing always made me wary of the press because often you can divulge something which might be used at a later point.

Ian Botham also commented that we were picking too many bits-and-pieces cricketers. I think he must have been referring to Paul Collingwood, but I tackled him on the subject: 'What about Chris Harris?' I said. 'He's a bits-and-pieces cricketer.'

'Yes, but he's played over two hundred games,' replied Botham.

'What about his first twenty though?' I asked, my point being that too often in England players are judged too quickly, with criticism thrown blatantly around before the player has had a chance. Ian Harvey is another example of someone who might have looked like a bits-and-pieces cricketer when he started but progressed into something much more in one-day cricket. Andrew Symonds, too.

Picking too many bits-and-pieces cricketers was a constant criticism during my time with England. When I was conducting a tour of the counties prior to the 2005 season it was a topic Worcestershire's coach Tom Moody raised. 'Name me one,' I said.

'Anthony McGrath,' he replied. I tried to explain that McGrath had never been chosen for the England one-day squad as a bowler. He had been chosen as a 'finisher' with the bat – something England had been lacking for a long time. I had been mightily impressed by his efforts in the C&G Trophy in 2002, which Yorkshire went on to win. First in the quarter-final at Chelmsford it was his 72 not out which defeated Essex and then in the final, even though Matthew Elliott's hundred attracted greater acclaim, it was his 46 not out which finished proceedings. Anybody who knows cricket understands that the real pressure is on the guy who comes in at number six and has to be there at the end. That was why we picked McGrath. It did not necessarily work out, and because other bowlers were not performing, we ended up using him as a medium pace bowler as well.

Botham made me laugh later in that New Zealand one-day series when I asked him who he would pick – it had come down to a straight choice between Owais Shah and Ben Hollioake. 'Hollioake,' he replied. Why? 'Because he does a bit of everything'! I've said it before but that's what you have to put up with in English cricket – people running with the foxes and hunting with the hounds.

At that stage that first week in New Zealand was the hardest I had endured as England coach, so I was especially pleased that we managed to claw the series back to 2–2 (Collingwood taking 4–38 in the third match). It came to a decider in Dunedin and I believe we deserved to win that game. I cannot put it any other way than to say that I thought that we were robbed by two plumb lbw decisions which were not given. We had not batted particularly well, but had posted a competitive total, which New Zealand were struggling to chase down. One of those decisions went in favour of Craig McMillan whose 44 was vital. Sadly, the standard of officiating during this tour was some of the worst I ever experienced.

Matters off the field were also clearly out of the ordinary. I cannot recall one Test series during my tenure with England when there was not an issue which might have had a negative effect on the side. So here it was the so-called 'fattie debate'.

Six players had joined us for the first class leg of the tour, but when they arrived it was obvious that some of them were not fit. The most glaring example was James Ormond. I did not name him specifically at the time, but when a photograph was taken showing his paunch in a less than flattering light it was fairly obvious who I had been referring to when I had said at Lincoln University in Christchurch before our three-day game against Canterbury: 'Some players could have looked after their fitness better. They were caught out a little bit when they pitched up here and weren't able to get into match fitness as soon as they would have liked.' I had spoken to Ormond and Richard Johnson in India and told them that I did not think they were fit enough for international cricket. Both of those two were typical county cricketers who thought that what they did at county level was enough for international cricket. It was not. It was a shame because I thought Ormond was a good bowler – very skilful – but it seemed as though he was just unfit and lazy.

It was, therefore, no surprise that he did not figure in any of the three Tests. I must make mention of the first one in Christchurch because it was such an incredible game of cricket for many reasons. It was the first time we had seen or used a drop-in pitch, and it intrigued us no end. When we arrived at the ground I can honestly say that I have never seen a greener pitch. New Zealand duly won the toss and inserted us, whereupon Hussain played one of his finest innings. It was typical of his character that he should chisel out 106 in a team total of just 228, as the ball darted all over the place. Due to what happened later in the match I am not sure that people fully understood how good an innings it was, and it is easily forgotten amid the subsequent big hitting. Because, after we had bowled them out for 147 – with Matthew Hoggard taking 7–63 – the transformation in the pitch was remarkable. Suddenly now it was flatter than anywhere – probably only bar Antigua – in the world.

Graham Thorpe helped himself to a rapid double century and Flintoff smashed his first Test century, leaving New Zealand a mammoth 550 to win. But what came next nearly drove me to distraction. There was no way that they should have even come close to winning that match, but, yes, that is what happened. Nathan Astle played extraordinarily well to record the fastest Test double century of all time, but I could not believe what I was seeing from the England bowlers. They just did not have a clue what to do; they were unable to think on their feet. Eventually there was a break and I said: 'Look guys, it's a one-day situation. You have to vary your pace.' Thank goodness Hoggard was listening and soon after he snared Astle with a slower ball. It was wide but it had deceived Astle and he was caught behind. However, once the dust had settled on the victory – which was by 98 runs after all – I realized it was one of our top wins, because New Zealand had been to Australia beforehand and gained considerable credit in drawing all three Tests.

If only the rest of the series could have been like that, but circumstances conspired against us, as they did against Mark Ramprakash, for whom this tour was destined to be his last appearance on the international scene. I was disappointed for him, but on that trip I saw it in his eyes that, mentally, he was shot at this level. I realized that we were wasting time investing in him at international level. It was all so reminiscent of the Graeme Hick scenario in Sri Lanka. They were both quality players, whom I would have loved to have worked with in the England set-up when they were younger. I just would never have dropped them. You cannot just pick on form alone because quality will come right for you eventually. How long did Australia persevere with Mark Taylor when he was struggling? That is what should have happened with these two, but because they felt they had to score runs straight away they put too much pressure on themselves.

I remember first working with Ramprakash when he came out as a replacement on my first tour with England – to South Africa in 1999/2000. I gave him some throw-downs in the nets and was stunned by his technical proficiency. I walked out and said to Hussain: 'How did we ever leave this guy out of the tour?' Hussain laughed and replied: 'The problem is that he gets so locked up in himself that it affects his batting.' He was right. It was difficult for Hussain because he was close to Ramprakash but even he agreed that the time had now come to move on. We had tried hard to keep him in the side, even opening with him at one stage, but as much as Ramprakash tried to relax, he just could not do so in the international arena. I will never forget an incident on that tour of New Zealand when it was decided to use a nightwatchman at the end of a day's play to protect Ramprakash. I went up to him to tell him, and I swear that I have never seen a more relieved cricketer in my life. His appointment with hell had been postponed.

Ramprakash's technique was comparable to that of Jacques Kallis, Daryl Cullinan and Ricky Ponting – the best practitioners in the world – but sometime before that tour I had said to Hussain: 'We really need another technically strong youngster to emerge. Where is he?' Remarkably he appeared, quite by chance, in New Zealand. Before the final two Tests we had needed cover for the injured Mark Butcher, so we summoned the best batsman at the National Academy in Australia – a nineteen-year-old by the name of Ian Bell. It took just one indoor net in Wellington for him to become the talk of the squad. During practice both Michael Vaughan and Marcus Trescothick came up to me and said: 'This guy can really play – there's something top quality about him.' I found that interesting, not least because Bell might be challenging those two for their places. So as he practised I began to study him out of the corner of my eye – I never liked to make a show of watching a player because that would put undue pressure on him – and I, too, was mightily impressed. He was composed and I liked the way he was putting things together. 'We might have to play him against Sri Lanka,' I mentioned to Hussain, in reference to the first series of the 2002 home summer.

By the time we were back in England I had still not altered my opinion. I thought that it would be a good opportunity to blood Bell, but I could understand why there was so much debate about it and also why Hussain wanted John Crawley, who had a good history of playing Muttiah Muralitharan. Selection overall was not easy because of the ticklish issue of those players who had made themselves unavailable for the winter tours, such as Alec Stewart, whose position we have already considered in the previous chapter. But we had a meeting and it looked as if we were going to go with Bell. Soon after I was sitting in the office of Hugh Morris (ECB performance director), along with Rod Marsh, who had taken up his appointment as director of the ECB National Academy the previous October. I asked Marsh about Bell, because he had spent the winter with him. 'He's not ready,' he replied. 'He needs to go back to county cricket and get some scores.' That was fair enough, and it was a view also shared by Bell's Warwickshire coach, Bob Woolmer, who phoned me to say: 'Just be a bit wary. He's a bit young.' So I phoned the selectors immediately to tell them that I thought that we should omit Bell. But then a few days later I was astounded to see Marsh being quoted in the press, criticizing the selectors for not picking youth (Marsh was not then a selector, not becoming one until the following year). He could only have been referring to Bell, because he was the only youngster up for selection. I thought that very odd, considering Marsh's earlier comments to me. It was not to be the last time I was left scratching my head over Marsh.

Indeed, we were to be at loggerheads again that summer, this time over Simon Jones. The previous summer I had been handed a list of players whom the selectors and academy hierarchy were considering for the first academy intake. There were two glaring omissions. Neither Jones nor Steve Harmison was on it. I was already panicking a little in case either Darren Gough or Andrew Caddick broke down, so I needed some fast bowlers to start coming through. From what I had seen, these two fitted the bill. I said to the selectors: 'I don't care who you take, but those two must go.' They replied that they did not think Harmison would go because there were already signs at that stage that he suffered badly from homesickness. My reply was that I thought he would because Andrew Flintoff, his great buddy, was going as well.

As for Jones, the selectors were concerned that he had not played a great deal for Glamorgan. My reply to that was that I thought he had potential and that is what academies should be about. I think fast bowlers can progress almost overnight. Batsmen take time and spinners take even longer, but the quickies can suddenly discover that they can intimidate the batsmen and they are away.

Anyway, it was at the start of the 2002 season that I happened to be down at Sophia Gardens watching Glamorgan play; in fact it was against the Sri Lankans in a match after the first Test, which had been drawn at Lord's. I was keen to see Jones bowl, because there had been some good talk about how he had performed at the academy, and there was even a thought that we might consider him for the second Test at Edgbaston. So I was somewhat taken aback to see how short his run-up was. I agreed that when I had been at Glamorgan in 1999 it had been far too long, but this was ridiculous. I reckoned that it needed to be about another five metres longer, and as chance had it, there was a pile of sawdust positioned right on the spot where I thought he should begin his run-up. As I was envisaging this, I was joined by Steve Watkin, by then Glamorgan's academy director and a bowling coach whom I rated highly. I asked him what he thought. He agreed entirely.

Not long afterwards we played Sri Lanka at Old Trafford where Jones was used as a twelfth man to acquaint him with life at a Test match. I spoke to him about his bowling, and he admitted that he was lacking rhythm. 'I think you need to lengthen your run-up,' I told him. 'Are you sure?' he questioned, but he agreed to go back to Cardiff and speak to Watkin about it. Again, by chance, I was down at Cardiff after that match and I saw Jones, who was talking with Lynn 'The Leap' Davies, the former Olympic long jump gold medallist, whom Jones had used a lot earlier in his career, especially to cure his no-ball problems. Davies also agreed that the run-up needed to be lengthened, and he should know – it is the same principle after all, of achieving sufficient momentum and rhythm before taking off behind a given line.

So Jones lengthened his run-up (even though it was not as long as before) and bowled really well for Glamorgan. So well, in fact, that he was selected for the first Test of the second series of the summer – against India at Lord's. However, during his debut he suffered a side injury, and another dispute arose because Marsh said on TV that it was wrong for him to have lengthened his run-up (blaming me for it) and that was the sole reason why he was injured. What annoyed me was that I had only acted on a consultative basis and that, as I later discovered, Jones had actually had the same injury while bowling off that very short run at the academy.

My most vivid memory of the Sri Lanka series is of the final Test at Old Trafford, where we managed to winkle them out on the final afternoon to leave us requiring 50 to win off just 6 overs. Hussain came hurtling off the field in a state of hyper-excitement – more so than I'd ever seen him before – and said to me: 'You handle the batting order. I'm too excited.' He was basically handing the captaincy over to me because he wanted to concentrate on his own batting. I think it showed that there was a lot of respect flowing both ways in our captain/coach relationship. It was a tricky situation for me though, because there were so many different permutations we had to think about, even in such a short chase. Did we promote Alec Stewart if the seamers were on? Or Graham Thorpe if the spinners were on? It seemed like we had the whole team padded up ready, but thankfully no one else was required, bar the openers Michael Vaughan and Marcus Trescothick, who played superbly to see us home with an over left.

The Sri Lankans made the mistake of thinking that if they could stop the boundaries by spreading the field straight away, then they would be OK. As it was, Vaughan and Trescothick were not only able to pick up a run-a-ball at will, but also pierce the boundary fielders with their power. It was scintillating stuff, and the win really pleased me because, having won the second Test at Edgbaston, there was a lot of talk that we were good at obtaining a lead, but not so good at retaining it. So it was good to get that monkey off our backs.

The resultant one-day triangular series with India was certainly unforgettable but for the wrong reasons. In the final India managed to chase 326 for victory, having been 146–5 at one stage. It was going to be Hussain's day, having made his only one-day international hundred – complete with gestures to the media – but Mohammad Kaif and Yuvraj Singh were our destroyers-in-chief as they rescued their side from the mire. Hussain probably went a little overboard in making his point to the press that he thought he should be batting at number three. I think that was always his best spot, but I also think that his problem in one-day cricket was that he never fully realized that he did not have to hit the ball as hard as he thought he had to. He was a great timer of the ball, but too often, especially when trying to hit over the top, he would unnecessarily give it the kitchen sink, as they say.

We also decided to use Stewart in a different role in this series, often batting him as low as number seven or eight. He had never done that before, but the true professional he was, he was willing to try to learn new tricks. He was not like some, who might have been arrogant and all-knowing in such circumstances, and thus threw himself into it with the enthusiasm of a debutant. So I worked hard with him in deciding how to deal with yorkers at the end of an innings; showing him how to alter his grip on the bat slightly, and then transfer his weight backwards while opening the face of the bat to dig them out. I also talked to him about another change of grip, turning the blade in his hands before the bowler released the ball, so that when he attempted a hit over the top with a straight swing of the bat, the opened face would skew the ball over the off side. I remember him doing that at Headingley against Sri Lanka in a match reduced by rain to 32 overs per side, where he scored a wonderfully inventive 38 not out from number eight. And after he he had played the shot, he turned to me on the balcony and signalled his satisfaction. Little moments like that make you warm inside as a coach.

I also spoke to Stewart about his wicketkeeping and about catching the ball with his hands up so that his wrists absorbed the pace of the ball rather than his shoulders, as you see in the conventional method. He took that on board too. If only the bowlers had been as receptive during the India Test series. We drew it 1–1 but really should have won it. I have already mentioned two crucial parts of it – the Trent Bridge Test where Rudi Koertzen gave Rahul Dravid not out and he went on to make a match-saving hundred in the second innings and the Headingley Test where we bowled abysmally – but in general we were not able to execute our plan against Sachin Tendulkar. This was different from the one employed in India – where we used Ashley Giles to bowl outside leg stump – because of the obvious variation in the pace of the pitches in the two countries. We had noticed that Tendulkar seemed uncomfortable against fast, short-pitched bowling, so we decided to test him out with that, but then suddenly changing to bowling wide outside his off stump, frustrating him by not bowling straight to his strength. However, as his 193 at Leeds indicates, it did not always work!

India then hammered us by eight wickets to send us tumbling out of the ICC Champions Trophy, which took place in Sri Lanka in September, but I recall that trip for only one thing: a phone call I received from Graham Thorpe during the opening dinner. He had not been with us since the first India Test at home in order to attempt to sort out his marital problems, but at the end of the summer he had declared himself available for the winter's Ashes tour. That had been good news, because we needed his experience out there. This was not good news, though. He had had a rethink. He did not feel able to commit himself now. It seemed like a huge blow but it was only the start of our travails before yet another Ashes debacle.

This 2002/3 tour will be remembered for many things, probably most notably Hussain's decision to bowl first at Brisbane, but its build-up will always be recalled for the fitness – or lack of it – of a number of key individuals. They were Andrew Flintoff, Simon

Jones and Darren Gough. Flintoff had had a hernia operation, Jones still had his rib problem and Gough was still struggling with the knee problem which had first presented itself in the last one-day match at Dunedin in New Zealand. We were roundly criticized for selecting those three, but what people did not appreciate was that we did have a backup plan and I thought we were justified in giving those three as long as possible to recover. If we had not, we would have just been going with a second-rate bowling attack. We took specialist medical advice, and it told us that Flintoff and Jones would definitely make it, as long as they did the necessary rehabilitation work. They had to complete their programmes to the maximum; they did not. Gough was a risk but we were prepared to take that because he was, after all, the only bowler in the original party to have previously taken a Test wicket in Australia. So while physio Dean Conway took an awful lot of stick for this situation, it was out of his control, and most annoyingly in the cases of two players, their fault. The only good to come out of this was that the ECB eventually appointed a medical officer – Peter Gregory. Poor old Conway had been crying out for this appointment for two years.

We initially sent Flintoff to the academy for further rehabilitation but that proved fruitless too, so eventually it was decided to send him home in mid-December. We were in Sydney at the time playing two warm-up matches for the VB series, and I had to stand in front of the press and protect Flintoff. I did not blame him publicly but inside I was seething. He knew that, and came to me afterwards and said: 'Thanks very much, Duncan.' That was totally unlike him to do that. He knew what I thought of his actions – or lack of them – because we had had a heated meeting in my room earlier in the tour, where he was emotionally upset.

We had our backup plan, though, because Alex Tudor and James Anderson were at the academy in Adelaide. I had insisted on these two being part of the intake, especially Anderson, whom the selectors and Marsh did not initially want to go, and also Tudor because I felt that he needed to dramatically improve his aerobic fitness – he seemed too keen on doing upper body weights instead of strengthening his lower body which is so important for fast bowlers. Both were called up, of course, although Anderson came despite reports from the academy that he was not ready. I found that strange because all the batsmen I seemed to speak to, including some of our one-day squad who spent time at the academy before joining us, were saying: 'He can really bowl, can this lad.' And he proved that when he played in the VB series, bowling so well that he stayed with us as cover for the two final Tests which separated the two stages of the one-day series.

I was still a little unsure about Marsh at this stage, but another small happening in Tasmania made me think further. I had been invited to do a breakfast question and answer session in Tasmania by an old friend of mine, Brian Davison, with whom I had played in Zimbabwe and who was now living Down Under. There were about 200 people there and it was an enjoyable event. But long after I'd left one question was still whirling around in my head. It had been in two parts; the first: 'How is Rod Marsh doing at the academy?'

'Fine,' I replied. Part two, though: 'Do you find that he undermines you at all?'

'No, not all,' was my response, but 'What about those incidents involving Bell and Jones?' I was asking myself long afterwards.

So to that decision in the first Test. Generally, I am a 'bat first' man, but there were mitigating circumstances here, and I can say in all honesty that I agreed that we should bowl first. Indeed in the post-match press conference, I unequivocally said that. 'Did you support the captain?' I was asked. 'Yes, I did,' I replied emphatically. I did not skirt around the issue, as some coaches might have. I remember Scyld Berry coming up afterwards and praising me for that. He said a lot of previous coaches would have sat on the fence on that question. He also seemed to be implying that quite a few of the other pressmen had been impressed by that too.

Many of the other senior players agreed with the decision and I think it is opportune that I should allow you to read these words: 'Brisbane – if there is to be any lateral movement off the seam it will be on day one. However, the pitch is generally slow on the first day and the bounce tennis ball-like. The best days for batting are two, three and four. It has turned towards the end of the match in recent years but is by no means a raging turner.' Rod Marsh wrote those words. We had asked him to give us an appraisal of every pitch and what we might expect. Now, I might have some doubts about him elsewhere in this book, but what I am not doing is totally blaming him for this decision. But it is undeniable that his comments were a small contributory factor. When we had first seen the pitch it was green, so we already had mixed feelings then, especially with the inexperienced bowling attack which we had. Of course, with the benefit of that wonderful thing – hindsight – we were wrong, but everything seemed to be telling us that if there was going to be an occasion to bowl first, then this was it. It was some consolation that when we met up with Matthew Elliott later in the tour, when he appeared for Australia A against us, he said: 'That pitch at Brisbane always confuses us. Whenever Victoria play there, we never know whether to bat or bowl first.'

Simon Jones suffered a horrible knee injury on that first day at Brisbane. That is readily recalled. But is it also recalled that that left Hussain a bowler down after inserting the opposition? Probably not. As if all the furore about fitness pre-tour had not been enough, Jones' misfortune set an alarming trend for the rest of the tour. We lost a key bowler in the first innings of the first three Tests.

In all the injury list was scarcely credible. John Crawley bruised a hip and missed the second and third Tests; Alec Stewart bruised a hand which ruled him out of the fourth; Andrew Caddick had a sore back which ruled him out of the third; Ashley Giles had his wrist broken by Steve Harmison in the nets prior to the second and Harmison himself had sore shins which ruled him out of the first. And that was just those originally selected. Those injuries which afflicted the replacements make even harder reading. Chris Silverwood, called up to replace Jones, bowled just four overs before his ankle gave way; Craig White, called up a week into the tour, strained a side and missed the final Test; Alex Tudor, who replaced Gough, was hit on the head by Brett Lee, and the final straw came when Jeremy Snape, who had arrived with the one-day party, had his thumb broken (also by Lee) from the first delivery he faced on tour.

Australia racked up 492 at Brisbane, but funnily enough all but one of our plans for their batsmen worked. Before each Test one of my strategies was to go through the opposition order and identify possible ways of dismissing each of them.

For example, we had talked about bowling bouncers at Matthew Hayden, because we considered him a compulsive hooker. Not just any old bouncers though, carefully directed ones which were leg side of him, tucking him up and offering him no room to free his arms, only allowing him to hit in the deep fine leg area. We did that early on and he top-edged it just over Jones' head at fine leg for six. But we did not try it again for some time. The bowlers were intimidated by him. He set out to bully us on that first day and he succeeded. By the time he did succumb in that fashion he had scored 197. The only one who did not fall to our plan was Ricky Ponting, who was bowled, somewhat bizarrely, around his legs via his thigh pad off Ashley Giles. But the rest did. 'But how come they scored so many?' I hear you ask. Because we did not get enough balls in the right place, that is why – just as we had not with Tendulkar at Headingley the previous summer. Plans to dismiss a batsman do not work unless you can bowl five or six balls an over in that area. That is what the Australian bowlers did to our batsmen. We were only managing one or two an over where we wanted.

Michael Vaughan might not have scored too many in that first Test, but in the second at Adelaide he announced himself to the Australians as a batsman who was going to cause them serious problems for the rest of the series. Three hundreds and 633 runs at an average of 63.30 certainly proved that he was that, but he might never have begun that impressive sequence after he injured his knee during the warm-up in Adelaide. It led to a rather odd, and almost embarrassing, situation. Vaughan immediately went off for treatment but by the time it came for Hussain to toss up, there had still been no definite decision on his fitness. I felt sorry for physio Kirk Russell, who was on his first full trip after Dean Conway had decided to limit himself just to the one-day trips.

But Vaughan had gone off with Russell to the nets to try it out. There was much stalling and wavering as Hussain stood looking out of the window with his blazer on, ready to toss up. But eventually he just said: 'Right, he's going to play.' It was a big gamble, and there were some worried faces around after we had won the toss and decided to bat. Every run he made was watched with anxiety and concern. And there were a few of those by the end of the day. One hundred and seventy-seven, in fact, before he was dismissed just before the close. It showed the character of the man; very gutsy, stubborn and resilient. I had first noticed how brave he was in Sri Lanka in 2001, when we had been given a ropey net in which to practise in Matara. It had a nasty ridge on it, which made deliveries rear up dangerously. A couple of more experienced batsmen tried it and immediately walked out, shaking their heads. 'Somebody could get killed in there,' they were saying. Not Vaughan though. He went in and had a full net. That really impressed me.

On another occasion in 2001 we were playing Australia in a one-dayer at Bristol when he broke a finger in practice. He still wanted to play, and I had to speak to him firmly to tell him that there was no way he should play. In the innings at Adelaide he actually fractured a bone in his shoulder when hit by Jason Gillespie, but carried on. When he did not field during the Australian innings there were calls from the Aussies that he was shielding his knee, but in fact it was his shoulder. He copped a lot of sledging in that game, especially from Justin Langer who felt he had caught Vaughan at cover when he only had 19, but they soon realized that they were wasting their time with such chat.

The Ashes were lost when we were hammered again at Perth, and no respite came from three warm-up matches we played before the VB series, losing all three against New South Wales, Australia A and a Prime Minister's XI. As much as those losses upset me, there was a small incident which disappointed me even more. It came after the loss against the Prime Minister's team in Canberra, when John Howard came into our dressing room to thank us for the game. Not one of the team got off his seat to shake Howard's hand, and some sat with their caps still on. In my opinion that showed a total lack of respect. I know that they were disappointed after losing, and most of the time I was willing to stand up for them, but not here. It goes back to my Prince Edward days where I learnt the value of respect. This was the Prime Minister after all; they should have had the common decency to afford him more respect. I walked away from the ground that night, thinking: 'That was terrible.'

And our one-day form was so terrible that Ian Botham suggested that the academy side should be representing England rather than the team who actually were, only increasing the pressure on us for the final two Tests. All the talk was of a whitewash and I was determined that that would not happen, but I also knew that I had a mighty task on my hands to lift a demoralized squad. But in fairness they never gave up. We battled hard at Melbourne, roared on by the Barmy Army, who were just brilliant. We always felt that they were the only people in English cricket who supported us at all times and we really appreciated that. That is why we always made a point of thanking them after a match. They might just have had something to celebrate because there were some worried Australian faces around when they were chasing 107 to win. They had a history of struggling in small run-chases and it showed. Who knows what might have happened if captain Steve Waugh had gone early? He should have done, because he edged Steve Harmison behind but no one appealed, and then hit a catch to Hussain who had cleverly come in close on the off side, only for it to be revealed as a no-ball. But they eventually scrambled home by five wickets. We were 4–0 down. I now knew that I had to do something different if we were to avoid that dreaded whitewash.

There is a big dressing room at Melbourne, used by the Aussie Rules teams, in which I decided to call the whole squad around. I got them into a huddle, with arms linked, and gave it my best motivational stuff. I am not normally one for Churchillian rousing speeches, but I felt that this moment called for something different. Hussain did not usually like them either, but even he conceded afterwards that it had had an effect. It may or may not have been the reason for us winning the final Test in Sydney but at least I felt that I had tried my damnedest to make sure we did not go home with the wrong sort of history-making exploit accompanying us. There had not been an Ashes whitewash for eighty-three years. We often spoke about making history during my time as coach, but that was not the sort we ever wanted to make. It is to my eternal regret that we did so four years later.

It annoys me to some degree that that Sydney Test is remembered for Waugh's hundred, despite all its drama in coming off the final ball of the second day. We played some solid cricket and thoroughly deserved to win in front of the second-biggest Sydney crowd in history. It was said that we had only won because Australia were without Shane Warne and Glenn McGrath (the first time the two of them had both been missing from a Test together for over ten years), but what about all the injuries we had suffered throughout the tour? It was time for Lady Luck to cast a little glance our way for a change and we thrashed them by 225 runs.

9

The Zimbabwe Crisis

I know that it annoyed many people, and from the outside could have been considered incongruous, but at the time in 2003 I made no public comment about my thoughts regarding whether England should go to Zimbabwe to play their first game of the World Cup. Here I was, a Zimbabwean, most definitely better placed than anyone else to pass judgement, keeping my counsel. But there was very good reason for it. In fact, two very good reasons, neither of which has ever been mentioned or considered by those criticizing, of which there were many, but most of whom I considered ignorant of the real situation in Zimbabwe.

The first was that I was still travelling on a Zimbabwean passport then. As soon as I had set foot in Zimbabwe the authorities could have done whatever they wished with me. Great Britain would have had no right to me then. Just look what happened to those two English *Sunday Telegraph* journalists who were arrested for not having state accreditation during the 2005 elections in Zimbabwe – you should not be thrown into jail for that.

It was all a game to the Zimbabwean authorities and the same could easily have happened to me. Because if I had made public comments with which the Zimbabweans had not been happy (say, suggesting that on moral grounds the tour should be cancelled), and the tour had been declared on by the ECB, then they could easily have put me in jail. It would not have been a case of whether it was right or wrong, but just some fun to them in order to humiliate the British. People must be careful of making judgements on what happens in some African countries by blithely comparing them with what happens in Britain. It is just not the same.

Secondly, many of my wife Marina's family were in Zimbabwe. And it is a small country where everyone knows everyone else. Again, any comment which was perceived as adverse might have had repercussions for them. For me these were pretty compelling reasons not to pass comment, but I also felt no urgent need to do so, because I knew that I was doing all I could behind the scenes to help the squad.

The issue had begun to raise its ugly head during the Ashes tour beforehand. One evening skipper Nasser Hussain came to my room, as he did on occasion during tours to mull over things and have a chat. He came straight to the point. 'I've got a problem,' he said, 'and I don't know how to handle it.'

'What is it?' I asked worriedly.

'It's Zimbabwe,' he said. 'I don't want to go there and be seen to be like Mike Gatting when he led his rebel tour to South Africa. I don't want my name attached to a tour we should never have gone on. On moral grounds I'm not sure whether to go and I don't want to use security as the reason not to go.'

I told him that I thought it did boil down to a moral issue, because I felt that security was not a problem. The worries I outlined above were different; an international sporting team would never be in danger as a group and in that respect I think Zimbabwe is a good deal safer than most other countries. But I said: 'Nasser, on the moral issue, you have to be very careful where you draw the line. There are many countries in the world where, perhaps, others should not play sport on moral grounds. What is also important is that you speak to other people, as I feel that I could unduly influence you because of my moral obligations to Zimbabwe.'

Naturally, there was a chance I could be biased. Without being arrogant, I had helped put Zimbabwe cricket on the world map. I captained them to victory over Australia in the 1983 World Cup and played a major part in the country adjusting to international status after it became independent in 1980. If England did not go to Zimbabwe, I could be helping to destroy everything that Zimbabwe's cricket administrators had worked so hard to create.

But, of course, this was not just about me. I had spoken to many people within the Zimbabwean cricketing fraternity and they thought the tour should go ahead, because it would do untold harm to the game there if it did not. But I suggested to Hussain that there was a vehicle that could help him and the team make their decision. 'What is that?' he asked.

'The Professional Cricketers' Association [PCA] and in particular Richard Bevan [their group chief executive],' I said. 'Ask him to canvass some older players, who have experience either of Zimbabwe or of rebel tours, because I think they will help you make your decision.'

I did not know then how great a lead Bevan would take in the decision-making process, but from that point on I fell out of the equation. I made other enquiries among non-cricketing Zimbabweans I knew but there was no general feeling one way or the other. Some wanted the game to go ahead, others did not. These were people living in the country and they did not know what to do: how were a group of English cricketers supposed to make that decision? While we were in Australia I met a couple from Zimbabwe who had had their farm seized by the so-called war veterans and had been forced to emigrate, but even they were not sure whether it was wrong for England to play in Harare.

There was also another consideration, which might seem trivial and unconnected, but which I think was very important in creating a certain mood among the England players. Before the Australia tour we had been promised that if we did not make the final of the VB one-day series then we could return home for a few days before travelling to South Africa for the World Cup. Of course, we did make that final, pipping Sri Lanka into second place, but there was still time enough to get home for a short break, the best of three final against Australia having been decided in two (lost) matches. The side was jaded, having been away from home for over three months, and I thought the break would do them good.

But the ECB was having none of it, even though we had already sent Steve Harmison back to be with his wife who had just given birth. I was summoned to a meeting with David Morgan, whom I knew well from my time at Glamorgan and who had just taken over as chairman of the ECB at a most difficult time, where he told me in no uncertain terms: 'They cannot go home. It is your responsibility to tell them.'

I was annoyed because I knew that my head was on the block with the players. But I would like to think that they did not make a fuss about the issue for my sake. However, I do also believe that this irritation could have contributed to some of the steadfastness shown later in the Zimbabwe issue.

This air of having been harshly treated lingered as we arrived in South Africa. I look back now and think how disgraceful it was that this group of players was expected to play cricket – in the World Cup no less – in such an environment as that in which they now suddenly found themselves. Morgan, Bevan and Tim Lamb, the ECB chief executive, were all there in Cape Town negotiating, placating and sometimes pontificating. Predictably there was little thought of cricket. Zimbabwe, Zimbabwe dominated every waking hour. And for me there were plenty of those, as I could barely sleep. At the famous Cullinan Hotel, situated at the entrance to Cape Town's waterfront, there were meetings after meetings, often ending late at night, and then we were expected to be up at 7.30 a.m. for practices starting at 10 a.m., which ended up being a joke, with minds elsewhere, and everyone mentally and physically shattered.

One night I had just dozed off to sleep when at about 3.30 a.m. the phone rang. It was Lamb. 'Can I come and talk?' he said. 'What are we going to do?' he asked. He was emotional and seemed to be struggling under the pressure of the situation. He wanted the team to go to Zimbabwe. And I agreed. I told him so then.

It annoyed me that people like Bob Bennett, the former Lancashire chairman who managed England on several overseas tours, later said in the press that this situation could have been much better handled if there had been an old-style manager (like him, presumably) present. That is just laughable. I might have been keeping quiet in public but behind the scenes, as I have said, I was working as hard as I could for Hussain and the team. As you have seen, we had a very different arrangement from the old days, when, it should be remembered, the players could easily be dictated to. They did not have a voice like the PCA to fight their corner then.

I was in charge of the tour, as the old-style manager would have been, with everyone reporting to me, but I also had Phil Neale as my operations manager. We had all bases covered. We already had Lamb and Morgan out there, so what would someone like Bennett have been doing anyway? On plenty of previous tours there had been problems with discipline despite these old-style managers.

It was decided to ask the ICC if the game could be switched to South Africa, which, in my opinion, was what should have happened long before this. As you know, my feelings for the ICC are not wholly warm, and here I think they lacked common sense in not realizing much earlier that there was a potential problem with staging games in Zimbabwe, and Kenya too – because it is easily forgotten that New Zealand pulled out of a match there. They should have just told the South African authorities that all games should be held there in South Africa. How much simpler things would have been then.

As it was, Malcolm Speed, the ICC's chief executive, came to speak to the players. His manner was perfunctory and it upset Hussain especially, who felt that Speed was not prepared to listen to what he and the players had to say. It was interesting to observe the various stances, not just of individuals but of the cricketing governing bodies, too, during this time. The situation turned political, nothing at all to do with cricket. The ICC seemed interested in little other than money, while the United Cricket Board of South Africa could only see as far as the smooth running of their tournament. That is all they were bothered about. Nothing else.

I thought David Morgan did a good job overall in the circumstances, his negotiating skills especially to the fore throughout. I shudder to think what it might have been like if someone plucked from the counties and much less diplomatic had been there.

Then came the famous letter from the Sons and Daughters of Zimbabwe, threatening the players: 'Come to Zimbabwe and you will go back to Britain in wooden coffins!' That certainly scared many of the players. But from the moment I heard about it I considered it a hoax. End of story. I was brought up in war-torn Rhodesia, so was used to an environment of fear, but the players were not, so I could understand their apprehension. But I was amazed that some players thought that, if they went to Zimbabwe, their families might be at risk back home from rebel Zimbabweans. That letter just did not concern me in the slightest. You will have read before of my early life in Rhodesia, and some of my experiences during the battle for Independence. Such incidents mean you have a very different outlook on what life security is.

Before a final decision was to be made we welcomed two incredibly brave visitors, who came to speak to me and Hussain. They were the Zimbabwean players Andy Flower and Henry Olonga, smuggled in by a member of Zimbabwe's opposition party, the MDC (Movement for Democratic Change), who had spoken to the whole team before taking me and Hussain into an adjacent room, where we met Flower and Olonga. Those two were rightly to become heroes for their stance against what they perceived as the death of democracy in their country. They told us then of their plan to wear black armbands during their games in the tournament in order to mourn that. They even suggested that we might consider wearing black armbands if we did decide to play in Harare.

Hussain and I took this back to the players but I sensed that they were not for turning, and it came to a final meeting, called by Richard Bevan and the PCA lawyer, Gerrard Tyrell, where a decision was to be made. I wanted to speak first, so I asked Hussain if I could do this – he knew I would not take long – before I left. That was always going to be the best course of action, because I knew that it was going to be a long debate and that this was a players' meeting. So I stood up and said: 'Guys, if you ask my opinion I think that we should go to Zimbabwe. But I understand your concerns and it is now up to you to make that decision.' I then left the room. And they decided unanimously not to go.

I was disappointed, but only from the World Cup point of view in that I knew that we were going to lose four points for conceding the match to Zimbabwe, making our task of qualifying from Pool A all the more difficult. I was not disappointed with the players because I believe that everyone is entitled to their opinion, so long as it is clearly thought through, and I was happy that they were making a unified decision rather than individuals breaking ranks and making their own decisions, which could easily disrupt the team ethic. If there was one slight element of frustration in my mind it was that I doubted whether the players really knew what the situation was like in Zimbabwe.

I now faced one of my more difficult times as England coach. How was I going to motivate these players to play good cricket, when anything but cricket had been occupying their minds for what seemed like an eternity, but was actually only a couple of weeks since we had arrived in South Africa? I immediately called Steve Bull, the team's part-time psychologist, to ask him to come out to Cape Town. We used Bull a fair bit and he did some good work with the team during my time, so I had no hesitation in using him now – the team needed some psychological help in order to get their minds back on the job in hand. We booked the Newlands ground in Cape Town and had an enormously benefi-cial session with Bull. From there we went straight to the nearby Techs Mutual club ground and had one of the most enjoyable workouts for a long time. All the tension of the Zimbabwe issue was being released.

We easily disposed of Holland in our first game but then I was immediately confronted with a tricky call for the next game against Namibia in Port Elizabeth. Hussain was struggling with a stiff neck and looked unlikely to make it, so we had a quick deci-sion to make about who was to be skipper. I never had an official vice-captain in my set-up, because I felt any member of my man-agement team could step into the role.

In this instance it was widely assumed that Marcus Trescothick would take over the captaincy. I disagreed. We were not sure how long Hussain was going to be out for and I felt we needed a more experienced captain, especially if he also had to skipper the next match against Pakistan. So we went for Alec Stewart, who had pre-vious World Cup captaincy experience. It caused a furore because

Trescothick had captained a few games previously but I also thought it best for us if he concentrated on his own game. Trescothick did that reasonably well enough against Namibia, scoring 58 but we almost came an enormous cropper as their opener Jan-Berrie Burger smashed a run-a-ball 85 to give us some serious jitters as they chased 273.

Hussain was back for the Pakistan game, though, and we won in thrilling fashion; a game best remembered for the devastating swing bowling of James Anderson, who wrecked the Pakistan innings with 4–29. Most pleasing for me was that he bowled Yousuf Youhana first ball with an out-swinging yorker, after I had mentioned beforehand to him about Youhana being susceptible to such a delivery. That had been a good toss to win in Cape Town but in Durban against India we fell foul of losing a crucial toss. Their score of 250 seemed only respectable but as soon as we went out to bat the drizzle began to fall and the ball skidded and squatted alarmingly; a seamer's paradise exploited by Ashish Nehra who took 6–23.

We still had a chance in the tournament though, but Australia in Port Elizabeth stood in our way. It was certainly a game not easily forgotten. In fact, there are few one-day games in my life which I look back on with real regret and, sadly, this is one of them.

I am certain that nine times out of ten we would have won that game from that position. Chasing 205 to win, they were 135–8, surely game over. But, of course, Andy Bichel was in the middle of a golden spell, having already taken seven wickets and he guided them to victory. I am sure that Hussain rues bowling Anderson rather than Andrew Caddick for the penultimate over (in fact, he came to me and apologized afterwards), but I would never chastise my captain for that. He acted on a hunch at the time and you have to back that. It was brave of him to admit his error. But it should not even have come down to that: the game should have been over by then. What annoyed me was the way the bowlers in general did not stick to basic principles towards the end of the match when tensions were running high.

Similar failings accounted for the other games I regret. The first was the previously mentioned final of the NatWest series at Lord's in 2002 where India managed to chase 326 for victory, having been 146–5 at one stage. I just remember thinking: 'Come on, guys, we just shouldn't be losing games like this.' But we did.

Next was a game just before the World Cup in Tasmania where we contrived to lose to Australia by 7 runs, with Shane Watson and Brad Hogg stymieing us at the death – well, that is what the record books say, but rather it was silly batting on our part, players looking to hit boundaries when all they needed to do was take singles. We might have been better prepared mentally to win the World Cup match if we had won that.

And the final game which galls me is the ICC Champions Trophy final of 2004. There has already been mention of an lbw decision which went against us in that game but we should have walked that game in any case. It was an important lesson to our bowlers not to get too smart and think that the game is over before it actually is. In fact, the mindset associated with that probably goes back to the problem of playing too much cricket at domestic level. In county cricket because there is so much cricket, players do not often play every game to the end. By that I mean that if the situation looks bleak, they often take their foot off the pedal, because they know that they have another match starting the next day, or if not then, then some day very soon. The desire – and also the knowledge of how – to fight right until the very end is missing. That is not necessarily the fault of the players, but rather the system in which they are forced to operate. It creates the wrong mindset.

There were a couple of postscripts to the World Cup campaign. First was a sign of things to come with a hefty fine for Andrew

Flintoff. Not from the ICC for on-field behaviour, but sadly, from me, for some overly drunken revelry.

Before we headed for home there was a day off where Flintoff was required to attend a function with some other players in the evening. It transpired that he and Steve Harmison had gone out at lunchtime and had a few drinks too many. When they returned, Flintoff, in particular, was in a bit of a state, loudly making a fool of himself with Castle lager bottle stickers on his forehead. He was still keen to get on the bus with the other players but Phil Neale dealt with it well and made sure he did not.

I was not there but when I came to hear about it soon afterwards, as usual I did some investigations as to what had exactly happened. What swung it for me was that three or four of the players told me that Flintoff had been an absolute disgrace – an embarrassment to English cricket, as they said. He was still pissed when I called him to my room. I saw no other option but to fine him a huge amount of money. Sadly it was not the only time I had to do that.

And second was Hussain's decision to step down as skipper of the one-day side. It was the right decision. Throughout that winter of one-day cricket the pennies had been beginning to drop: we needed to make some dramatic alterations to our one-day policy. It was too late to change things then, but I vowed that after the World Cup we needed to focus on youth, and develop a side for the next one. We so lacked agility in the field that it was almost embarrassing. But it was also clear that we needed some proper preparation time before the next World Cup – we had not had that in 2003 because of the crammed nature of the schedule in Australia. So when the authorities came to me to suggest that we play a series against Bangladesh just before the 2007 World Cup in the West Indies, I refused in no uncertain terms. As it was we arrived there knackered again, but we will come to that.

We were actually knocked out of the 2003 World Cup when a

game between Pakistan and Zimbabwe was rained off in Bulawayo. The news filtered through while most of the players were on the golf course, but Hussain knew he was going to have to do a press conference, so he headed straight for my room when he returned from the golf. He wanted to know my thoughts on the future as regards one-day cricket. 'I'm going to go with youth,' I replied, a move I had been contemplating ever since the second Test of the Ashes tour that winter when I had heard one of the older players lament 'here we go again' as we collapsed.

'Fine,' he responded. He was not one to bear grudges, and just walked downstairs to announce his resignation as England one-day captain.

I spoke to Alec Stewart soon afterwards and told him that I did not want him to announce his retirement immediately, because I did not want them all doing so at the same time. I spoke to Andrew Caddick about that too, explaining to them both that I wanted to go with youth but that it would not affect Test selection. They subsequently staggered the announcement of their retirements. It was always my policy that I would go and speak to players I considered to have been great servants for England, and tell them to retire, rather than unceremoniously dropping them. Too many coaches take delight in that, in being able to say that they dropped a 'legend' of the game. That is wrong in my opinion, and such players should always be allowed to go out on their own terms. The only one during my time who acted of his own accord without first speaking to me was Darren Gough, who retired abruptly from Test cricket after the second Test against South Africa at Lord's in 2003.

Before that game, though, there was still much to happen. First there were the grillings I received from the ECB concerning the Zimbabwe issue. These particularly infuriated me because there were a lot of misconceptions about it. But I was fortunate that David Morgan was so supportive and I was able to continue in my desired role of being in total charge of the team while abroad, rather than that 'old-style manager' of which we have already heard too much.

After we had easily disposed of a very poor Zimbabwe side in two one-sided Tests, it was time for the one-dayers and a new look side, as well, of course, as a new skipper. Michael Vaughan was always going to be the next captain in my eyes because, as I have said, I thought Marcus Trescothick a good deputy but not the main man.

Vaughan had a bit of a mean streak in him which I liked, and the ability to put players in their place if they stepped out of line – an essential quality for any leader. We began with three one-dayers against Pakistan, and we took a huge risk with some of the selections, with the likes of Anthony McGrath, Rikki Clarke and Jim Troughton making their debuts. I wonder to this day what the media would have said if we had lost. But it paid off with three handsome victories, and Vaughan really impressed with his captaincy. That then continued in the following NatWest series against Zimbabwe and South Africa, which we won by hammering South Africa by seven wickets in the final, having dismissed them for just 107. It was no contest. What a turnaround in our one-day fortunes. To beat two of the top one-day international teams in Pakistan and South Africa with a remodelled, inexperienced side was a very good start after the World Cup.

Having two international captains is never an easy situation, and I can imagine how difficult this all must have been for Hussain. I could just imagine him sitting at home watching the one-day games and seeing all the enthusiasm among this group of young players, and thinking, 'What's going on here?' He would not have spoken to anyone about it, because he could be very introspective in situations like this, but I knew that it must have been playing on his mind.

It was also difficult for me. When we turned up for the first Test at Edgbaston I noticed that every time I spoke to Hussain, Vaughan's name seemed to crop up. Hussain and I had really clicked as a combination but now Vaughan was in the mix as well, because I had spent so much time talking to him during the one-day series. It got so bad that after the second day of practice I decided not to be seen speaking to Vaughan at any practices, to try to steer clear of him as often as I could. It was the only way I could find of dealing with this situation. Otherwise I felt that a close relationship with the one-day captain would have played on Hussain's mind.

The last thing we needed was for South Africa to win the toss and amass a huge total. But that is what they did, scoring 594–5, with skipper Graeme Smith making 277. This drove Hussain to the edge. He felt that he had lost the team in the field, and so came to speak to me on the third day. He told me he was thinking about packing it in. My response was that I thought he should carry on, at least until the end of the series. But unbeknown to me he later spoke to Vaughan about taking over, and also called David Graveney up to the game.

So it came to the last day and again Hussain called me in for a meeting, with Graveney there too. I looked into Hussain's eyes and knew it was over. I had changed my mind completely. Graveney said that he thought that Hussain should carry on. But in my mind I knew that he should not. The timing might have been bad, and Vaughan would probably have preferred to have consolidated his position in the team that summer, and then take it on in the winter, but it had to happen then. I said to Hussain that his time was up. And so it was, with Hussain emotionally resigning the Test captaincy.

The trouble was that we only had two days in which to prepare for the second Test at Lord's, a ludicrously short period for everyone to digest what had happened and focus on another important Test match. That we were thumped by an innings and 92 runs was no surprise. But something happened after the match which was to have huge ramifications for the rest of the summer. Not just because we had lost but because it was Vaughan's first Test in charge, there was a huge media scrum afterwards for quotes and reaction. But the ECB had not had the vision to realize that this was going to be the case.

Andrew Walpole was on leave, and instead of ensuring that someone suitably experienced was there to manage this difficult scenario, the authorities plunged Mark Hodgson in at the deep end. He was way out of his depth, and it showed. Usually it would be either the captain or coach who would go and speak to the media after the match, but not both, unless we had spoken to each other in the meantime. So Vaughan was taken off to speak to them, and then I received a message that they wanted to speak to me. I tried to stall them because I wanted to speak to Vaughan first but it was chaos, and the TV people, especially, were becoming very fidgety. I did not want them to wait any longer because I knew that if you made them wait then it would only lead to the questions becoming more personal, so I went and did my interviews.

I learnt an important lesson that day because for the one and only time I used the words 'I don't know' in response to a media question. I was being totally honest because, in truth, I did not know. Vaughan had said to them beforehand that he thought South Africa might have been 'more hungry' than us in the Test. So when I was asked why he had said that, I said I did not know. I had not spoken to him, that was the problem, but before I could explain myself I was lambasted: 'What, you as England coach, do not know?' they were saying, and, of course, it was plastered across all the papers the next day.

This was the just the beginning of a summer of antagonism in the media. Anyone would have thought that we lost the series 5–0 but in fact we drew it 2–2. Yes, we let things slip at Headingley in the fourth Test but we responded with some character to win the final Test at the Oval, especially Marcus Trescothick who hit a superb double hundred, to give Alec Stewart a fitting send-off in his last game before retirement. Stewart might not have had the best of summers, but his enthusiasm was unquestionable right until the end – you would never have guessed that his career was winding down by the way he went about things.

At times I took advice from Mike Atherton on these matters, and his thinking was: 'The best way to deal with the critics is to win on the field – that is the only way to shut them up.' He was right, but there were a lot of them to shut up that summer. First to put his oar in had been Geoffrey Boycott, as already mentioned, and then it was Henry Blofeld's turn in the *Independent*:

Duncan Fletcher, who came to the England job with an impressive reputation, has not delivered the goods. His influence appears to have kept Phil Tufnell, a far better left-arm spinner than Ashley Giles, out of the England dressing-room. It is highly probable that his is the controlling hand in the refusal to bring back Graham Thorpe, who must surely now be brought to the rescue. Fletcher has outlived his usefulness and may even be hindering the advance of England's cricket. His time has come. What has happened at Edgbaston and Lord's is ample testimony to that.

As luck would have it I came across Blofeld soon after. During the fourth Test at Headingley, Marina and I were invited for a meal by David Morgan and his wife, Ann. As we entered the restaurant I noticed that Blofeld was there. I said to Morgan: 'He's written a nasty piece about me. I just want to discuss the matter with him.'

'It might be a good idea,' said Morgan in total support. So I did. I walked across to him, even though I had never spoken to him before, and said: 'Mr Blofeld, is it possible to have word with you about the recent article you wrote about me?' He did not even greet me, but instead just bellowed: 'F**k off! I don't want to speak to you.' It was embarrassing because there were other people in the restaurant, but I refused to go, saying that I could not believe what he was saying.

Standing up, he then told me to 'f**k off' again. I was not going anywhere, so I just sat down opposite him. Realizing I was not leaving, he sat down too.

'You blanked me,' he said.

I had no idea initially of what he was talking about, but he explained that I had not spoken to him at the Lord's Test against Australia in 2001, when the Queen had come to meet both teams. When he mentioned it, I recalled the incident. I had half-recognized him while a whole group of people were lining up on the stairs in the Lord's pavilion, but was not totally sure who he was. It showed the arrogance of the man that he thought that everyone in world cricket should know him. Unbelievably he said to me: 'You don't know how important I am in English cricket. I could have helped your coaching career.' As if I needed someone like him to help me. But he had calmed a little by the time I got up and had even suggested that we have dinner at a later date. On returning to my table I mentioned the discussion and Morgan, in his usual diplomatic manner, went over later to have another chat with Blofeld to smooth things over. I hoped that might be the end of the matter, but I had not banked on this individual being quite as relentless as he proved.

The next morning as I arrived at the ground I was met by Peter Baxter, Blofeld's boss as producer of BBC Radio's *Test Match Special,* who was full of apologies. He had already heard about Blofeld's outburst, because Blofeld had apparently got to the ground earlier. I had the impression Baxter had been down this road before with him. It amazed me that a man who tries to come across as so cultured and educated in the media could behave in this manner.

There was more scorn to come from the journalists. Later in the summer came criticism from Michael Parkinson in the *Daily Telegraph*: 'Ah, the coach! Take your partners for the Duncan Fletcher Two Step, a simple dance. Two steps forward and one step back. Two steps sideways, one step back and repeat ad nauseam,' he wrote among other things.

As with Boycott and Blofeld I wanted to have my say, so I asked Andrew Walpole (by now back in situ) to attempt to contact Parkinson. Unfortunately he could not, but quite by chance during the Oval Test, Walpole came to the dressing room and said: 'I see your friend Mr Parkinson is here.'

'Just see if he will have a word with me, please,' I asked.

'Are you sure?' replied Walpole, maybe a little worried about how the meeting might pan out. But it was arranged and we met in the players' dining area behind the dressing rooms; not the best place to meet a man of his stature (and I have always had enormous respect for him). Here I explained to him my philosophies, strategies about coaching and areas of concern in English cricket. He actually apologized to me and said: 'I'd rather have my job than yours,' before saying that he would like to play golf with me at the next mutually convenient opportunity. We never did play that round of golf, but the following winter when we were doing so well in the West Indies, he wrote another piece, quite different in its tone, in which he said: 'Duncan Fletcher has produced a mettlesome team and those, including your correspondent, who doubted he had either the resources or the strategy for the job, must eat humble pie.' It is amazing how attitudes can change when a journalist is in possession of the full facts and a proper perception of the difficulties of the job.

10

Record Breakers

Please forgive me for digressing, but I hope that the significance will soon become apparent. It was in the summer of 2003 that Michael Vaughan attended the British Grand Prix at Silverstone as a guest of Vodafone, who at the time sponsored the Ferrari F1 motor racing team as well as the England cricket team.

By all accounts he enjoyed the day. But it was not just the social side of the event which took his fancy. Because when we joined up as a squad soon afterwards, I have scarcely seen him so animated. 'Fletch, you should have seen how smart the Ferrari team looked – all in the same uniform, so clean as well, even in the pits! This is something we've really got to work on,' he purred.

Ah, they were sweet words to me. 'You're preaching to the converted with me,' I replied. He was, because I have always believed in a strict team dress code. I believe that if you want to be a top side, then there is a certain set of disciplines which needs to be in place. You know the old adage: 'Look the part, play the part.' I believe in that. It brings pride to what you are doing.

That is not to say that in the past the England squad did not have a dress code. They did. But there had been a certain reluctance attached to it, which meant that a good deal of scruffiness crept in. Especially amongst some of the older players.

So, beginning with our tour of Bangladesh in the winter of 2003, we made a conscious decision to smarten our act up. On the surface it might seem a minor thing but I genuinely believe that it was a big factor in the unprecedented success which England enjoyed in 2004, culminating in a record-breaking eight Test match wins on the trot. Because, hand in hand with it, went an increased work ethic and a greater emphasis on physical fitness, which meant that in Bangladesh the team worked harder than any other side with which I have been involved. This was right up Nigel Stockill's alley. In the past his job as physiologist had been made very difficult when the captain and senior players had been reluctant to train hard. In contrast Vaughan was adamant about the need for fitness.

So in conjunction with Stockill we decided to introduce a buddy system for the fitness training, making sure that each pair comprised one conscientious player and one less than enthusiastic trainee. Thus we paired Andrew Strauss, on his first tour, with Andrew Flintoff. Immediately we saw some special qualities in the new boy Strauss, who showed no deference to Flintoff's greater international experience when Flintoff maybe wanted to ease up. It got to the stage when we moved on to Sri Lanka for the second stage of the winter that Flintoff pleaded with us for a new buddy. But everyone bought into the idea, even the old sweats Nasser Hussain and Graham Thorpe, who were paired together. Those who know those two might consider that a bad pairing – two fitness fiends – but Thorpe had just become involved with a new lady friend, who was a fitness instructor, so he was the enthusiastic one who was egging his old mate on. All credit to Hussain though; he might not have liked it, but he just got on with it without any excuses.

Maybe he was just happy to be on the trip. After the summer

series against South Africa there had been a lot of press talk regarding his England future. It had not been easy for Vaughan having an ex-skipper in the dressing room, but I was strongly in favour of Hussain going on tour that winter, especially when considering the third part (after Bangladesh and Sri Lanka) in the West Indies. I knew that we would definitely need his experience there. I also knew that he was dying to go, and this led to a rather unsettling episode at the team's end of season dinner.

We had selected the squad that evening but it was not to be announced until the next day, and as we sat having dinner Hussain kept staring at me. He barely took his eyes off me all night, so much so that Phil Neale, who was sitting next to me, felt moved to mention the fact.

But it was always my policy not to speak to players after selection meetings – the only time I did was with Alec Stewart when he was recalled after that rumpus over his pulling out of the India tour, but that was an isolated exception, because I needed to smooth things over early on. The situation became so awkward with Hussain that evening that at one stage I did mention to Neale that maybe I should go and speak to Hussain just to reassure him. But I stuck to my guns and even though I am certain that he did not enjoy his food, at least he received his good news the following morning.

In Bangladesh the fitness sessions in the gym were compulsory for everyone. And that meant everyone, including myself, all the medical staff (which included a doctor, Mark Ridgewell, on his first trip), Andrew Walpole and even analyst Malcolm Ashton. It created a wonderful atmosphere and really bonded the whole squad. Everyone had to wear the same kit, which resulted in me being fined when I wore the wrong top. Mind you, it had been decided that everyone had to wear one of those ghastly training vests, in which I would not be seen dead. I was not at the age where I wanted to be showing off my 'guns' (biceps) like that!

It is probably instructive if I give you an idea of the relentless training schedule we followed in the run-up to the first Test. We played two three-day warm-up matches but that did not mean any let-up in the work. For the second of those in Savar, we would be up every morning at 6.15 a.m. in order to catch the bus at 7 a.m. to go to the ground, which rather ridiculously was a journey of at least an hour and twenty minutes. The distance was not great but the roads in Bangladesh are chaotic; there are just too many people crammed in to that small country.

So by 9.30 a.m. play would be underway in temperatures of 40°C and 80 per cent humidity. By 5 p.m. when play ended we would go straight out on to the outfield for forty-five minutes of fielding and fitness. We would split up into three groups and go through our favourite fielding routines, like the crossover and ten catches, which would test everyone's lungs as well as their hands. We would be on the bus by 6 p.m. and as soon as we returned to the hotel we would all pile into the gym for another forty-five minutes to an hour of fitness on either the treadmill or the exercise bikes. We would just have time for supper before crashing into bed and starting the same schedule again the next day.

It really was incredible how hard everyone was working, and it made them proud to see how their body shapes were changing. It was a bit of a gamble in a way because we still had to make sure that we achieved the results on the field, and even if we did, it would be difficult to judge how much effect this hard work was having. But it was a united decision that this was what we wanted to do.

We also decided to be more up front with the press, but this almost immediately backfired, as we felt that we were terribly let down by them. At the press conference to sum up the two Tests, which we won easily against Bangladesh, I was asked about our bowling during the series. In the first Test I thought Steve Harmison and Matthew Hoggard should have bowled Bangladesh out for 150 at most – maybe even 100 – on the first day, where the ball swung and seamed beautifully, but the hosts ended up scoring 203. I thought that the press had misinterpreted how those two especially had bowled that day, and I singled out Hoggard as one who needed to think more about the line he had to bowl when the ball was swinging. He actually won the man of the series award for his nine wickets (but he came bottom of the averages out of the five bowlers used) and in the press conference I was questioned by Angus Fraser, who is a big fan of Hoggard because the Yorkshire-man often seeks his advice. Fraser asked: 'Do you think that England should now revolve their attack around Matthew Hoggard?'

I made the mistake of using the word 'no' in my reply, but what I was trying to stress was that we could not think about that at that stage, because Harmison had returned home injured after the first Test and both Andrew Flintoff and James Anderson were missing through injury. The next day I was lambasted in the press. 'Hoggard the hero slated by Fletcher' was the type of headline used, and it was not just the headlines which were critical, because that was the usual excuse of a writer when I tackled him – 'I don't write the headlines,' he normally said. I know that, but the head-lines are taken from the text and here that was critical too. What I had said had been taken totally out of context and sensational-ized. I phoned Hoggard straight away to explain what I had actually said, because he was not involved in the subsequent one-day series in Bangladesh and Sri Lanka, and had returned home. I did not want him to think that I was criticizing him from afar without speaking to him first. My words had been twisted. So much for being more open with the press.

Flintoff did return from his groin injury in time for the one-day series in Bangladesh, and he was magnificent. He won the man of the match award in all three games, and deservedly so. We lost the toss in all three, which meant batting second in difficult conditions with the heavy dew making the ball move around quite fierily. Just consider his three scores: 55 not out (off 52 balls), 70 not out (off 47 balls) and 52 not out (off 39 balls). Forget the opposition, that is quality finishing; he bowled pretty handily too.

So to Sri Lanka. My first memory is of Dean Conway buying me a red T-shirt with the words '10% valley boy' emblazoned across it. The boy from Mountain Ash had '100% valley boy' on his. It was Rugby World Cup time and this was Conway's idea of drumming up some additional Welsh support for the England vs Wales group game, which England just about won after a serious scare. I am not really sure who I was supporting in that game.

But I was definitely supporting England in the final against Australia on that famous day of 22 November 2003, a day off for us in between two abandoned one-day internationals in Colombo – the story of our one-day series there after losing the first match in Dambulla, where we were bowled out for just 88 on a shocking pitch; so poor (it was a new ground) that even some of the locals were saying we should not have played on it. We batted poorly though, again not recognizing quickly enough what a good score was, and so paying the price.

However, despite my support for Clive Woodward's men, I was very nearly stitched up by some of the more conniving members of the press corps on that day of the final. As I have said already, I love rugby. I love watching it, but what I do not enjoy is watching it with a large group of people. I dislike all the supposed know-alls who continually shout at the referee and try to impart their deluded knowledge to everyone else. I would much rather watch it on my own so that I can view it in some depth and detail, not just seeing the game being played, but observing what is going on off the ball as well. I had watched half of that England v Wales match with the others in the team room, but soon got fed up with the running commentary and went to my room at half-time to watch the remainder of the match.

The tournament had begun while we were in Bangladesh, and even when Conway asked me to go to his room to watch some matches, I refused. I would just rather be on my own – or with Marina, of course, because she knows when to keep quiet! And while we were in Bangladesh I had resolved to get myself fitter – if I was badgering the team to do so then I felt I needed to lead from the front – and I had set myself the goal of running on a treadmill for an hour. I had never done that before, and twice I managed to do it. So then I set myself the further goal of running for the length of a rugby match, and while watching Ireland on the gym TV I managed to do that.

Therefore when it came to the final I decided to watch the match in my room, while everyone else watched it in the bar of the Taj Samudra hotel in Colombo. But when I saw that England were all over Australia in the first half, I decided to go to the gym and run for the second period. To do so I had to walk past the bar, where the pressmen were gathered with the players. Some of them saw me and thought I was being disrespectful to England by not watching their rugby team in the World Cup final. So they tried to summon some photographers to capture the moment for a sensational piece they wanted to write. If only they had known what I was doing.

At first the fitness instructor at the gym could not find the remote control for the TV, so I was going to run back to my room so as not to miss anything, but he eventually found it. Then, of course, the match went to extra time and I had done enough running for that day, so I rushed back to my room to watch the thrilling climax. Well done to England, but it was a day which was soured a little for me when I discovered the motives of those pressmen.

I thought we did pretty well ourselves in the first two Tests against Sri Lanka, showing a lot of character. To lose the toss at Galle and manage a draw was some effort. When we turned up at the ground three days before the Test we were amazed to find that the pitch was so green. It had been rolled but there was so much grass on it that there seemed no way that they would be able to remove it all before the start. I asked the groundsman about this and he just laughed. Sure enough, when we arrived for the start of the match there was not a blade of grass to be seen on the pitch, just dried mud. Next to it were huge piles of grass. I still do not know how they do it, but they have a method which even strips the roots – and, boy, does it aid Muttiah Muralitharan.

Hussain missed that Test with flu, so Paul Collingwood made his Test debut – what a place to make it! But he acquitted himself well. He is a very quick learner, who wanted to utilize the forward press, and did so to good effect in the second innings where he probably looked our most accomplished batsman in a fine rearguard action. We were still clinging on with nine wickets down when rain intervened with four overs left.

We lost the toss again at Kandy, but still somehow survived again. That we did so was mainly down to a brilliant defensive hundred from Michael Vaughan, again displaying his deep well of courage. It was such a different innings from those which he had played in Australia, when he first introduced himself as a world-class player. But it was every bit as important. And Gareth Batty and Chris Read also demonstrated good character, sticking it out on the final afternoon with seven wickets down.

We had not been sure about Hussain's fitness before the match, but I was keen for him to play. He had scored a hundred here on the last trip in 2001 and one for England U19s some time before, and I have always believed that players doing well on certain grounds is a reliable indicator. After Collingwood's impressive debut we decided he should play, too, so we left out a seam bowler to accommodate them both. Hussain might later have wished that we had not made the effort, for he ended up being at the centre of a ridiculously overblown row with Muralitharan.

It concerned alleged comments made by Hussain to the controversial off-spinner as he arrived at the crease in the first innings. I, like all the England team, was very disappointed that Muralitharan should squeal to the umpires about it in the first place. As Graham Thorpe described it at the time, it was like 'telling tales out of school'. But, of course, it resulted in a disciplinary hearing with match referee, Clive Lloyd. I went on the offensive from the outset in that. Before Lloyd could begin, I said: 'Clive, can I start please? I think it is very wrong that the game is coming to this: that as soon as someone says something on the field it comes to a meeting like this.'

I think that put him on the back foot immediately. Throughout the meeting I fixed my eyes upon Muralitharan but he refused to look at me. Hussain was very honest about what he had said – that he had sworn and referred to Muralitharan as a cheat and a chucker, but only to his team-mates, and not directly at Muralitharan. The video evidence was inconclusive and there was to be no penalty for Hussain, which was only right.

What irked us most about this was that the behaviour of some of the Sri Lankans during the series was far worse; especially wicketkeeper Kumar Sangakkara, whose language throughout was terrible. But did any of our players go running to the umpires? Of course, they did not.

We now had a selection dilemma on our hands for the final Test in Colombo. We realized that we could not play so many batsmen again, so it boiled down to a straight choice between Collingwood and Hussain. And it was a close run thing. Personally I thought that we had to go with Hussain, because of his greater experience. Yes, Collingwood had done well in difficult circumstances (he had scored 28 and 24 at Kandy), but it was obvious that those sort of scores were not going to win us a Test match. Hussain had played many match-winning innings before, and might do so again. However, the selectors back home, who then still had a say in team selection for overseas Tests, wanted Hussain out. I always felt that in such situations the selectors could be unduly influenced by the press. They were not there on the ground to assess the nitty-gritty of the conundrum, but Vaughan and I were, and we stood by Hussain. OK, we eventually lost the Test heavily, but that was not Hussain's fault.

We fielded poorly in that Test, ironically with our two most usually safe fielders, Marcus Trescothick and Ashley Giles, dropping vital catches. That match emphasized how an away team's innings in Sri Lanka can be composed of two distinctly different parts. They could be termed PM (pre-Muralitharan) and AM (after Muralitharan), with the turning point usually the twenty-fifth over when the off-spinner is introduced to the attack. PM is mainly against the seamers, who during that tour were not that special. So, that can often be an opportunity for a flyer for the upper order batsmen. But AM is a completely different game.

What is most interesting is that if another spinner is bowled PM, he is usually dealt with comfortably. But if he operates AM he is a different proposition. Muralitharan has this incredible effect on batsmen. He creates a great deal of doubt, turning the ball to such an extent that you do not know how much the other bowlers are going to turn the ball. And that is all you need for a batsman to struggle. Once the doubt creeps in, the bowler is laughing. Also the batsmen AM go into a shell not wanting to expose new batsmen to Muralitharan's wiles.

Mind you, we did not play Muralitharan as well as we had in 2001. It will probably not surprise you to learn that, given my theories on spin, I do not think that we played the sweep and sweep/slog shots enough. What I think happened was that the players became affected by what was being said and written in the press. I was telling them to do one thing (i.e. sweep) and then if they got out doing it, they were being lambasted in the press. So they were confused as to when and when not to use the shot, which requires a lot of confidence to play.

It was a pity that we lost that last Test, because we had put in so much hard work. My worry was what the opinions would be about the effects of the increased fitness work. Had it been worth it? Had it worked? I thought that it had built character, and my view always goes back to what the sports psychologists say: that if you put in the hard work, you will not throw the towel in. It is easy to quit if you have not done the work. So the reason that sportspeople who work hard are successful is that they do not want to waste all the effort that they have put in. Simple, really.

Not that I thought things would be so simple when we went to the West Indies in the final segment of the winter. But I was feeling surprisingly confident before it began. At the pre-tour press conference I was asked by Mike Walters of the *Daily Mirror*, a man who always seemed to come up with one pertinent question: 'Duncan, you've been on plenty of overseas tours now – isn't it time that you won away from home?' We had triumphed in Pakistan and Sri Lanka in 2000/1, but I knew what he meant, because that now seemed a long time ago. 'Yes, it is,' I replied with confidence and certainty. There was none of the usual talking around the answer. That was it: I had laid my cards on the table, but I did it because I thought that the work ethic which had begun in Bangladesh was paying dividends. It had tapered off slightly in Sri Lanka because you cannot continue such high levels of exertion for too long – and anyway Sri Lanka is rather hotter – but even there the training was more intense than on any previous tour. And we continued with it in the Caribbean, with the buddy system still in place.

Not that any of this prevented there being some negativity in the build-up to the Test series; there always is some of that, as I have already pointed out. This time it again surrounded the number of players used in a warm-up match – the one we played against Jamaica in Kingston. We requested that it could be a twelve-a-side match, with only eleven batting and fielding, but that only prompted outrage in certain sections of the press, because it meant the match not being accorded first-class status. Who cares about that? The carping was so old-fashioned and out-of-date. We wanted some practice for as many players as possible. The criticism then became even more vehement when Mark Butcher twisted his ankle and we drafted in Paul Collingwood to play as well as a thirteenth player.

No matter, whatever we did beforehand was spectacularly vin-dicated, as we won 3–0 (with a draw in the fourth on the feather bed of a pitch in Antigua) to claim a first Test series win in the Caribbean since 1967/8. That last Test aside, the pitches were the liveliest I had encountered in my time with England, and the West Indians clearly thought that they could ruffle us with pace, picking the excitable pair of Tino Best and Fidel Edwards. Thus, I was very glad to have the experience of Nasser Hussain, Mark Butcher and Graham Thorpe in the middle order. They all made valuable contributions, with Hussain's supposedly contentious selection being proved absolutely correct. But the star of the show was undoubtedly Steve Harmison, who won the man of the series award for his 23 wickets at 14.86, including an incredible 7–12 in the second innings when the West Indians were humbled for 47 in the first Test at Kingston.

It was some turnaround for him because he had returned home after that first Test in Bangladesh under something of a cloud. That was the first time that the question of his homesickness had arisen. While Bangladesh is not the easiest place to tour he had passed some dangerous comments which suggested he might be happier back home. I think, too, that the press had also got wind of the fact that some of the other players were not overly enam-oured of the situation either.

But ironically, with the benefit of hindsight, it might have been one of the better things to happen to him. We were firm with him (as we had been when we did not give him a central contract that winter) and told him that he had to go home and sort himself out. We put a programme in place which did not make things particularly comfortable for him, involving a lot of travelling to Loughborough for treatment. But in fairness he did knuckle down, and, of course, it is now well known that he trained hard with his beloved Newcastle United FC during this time, so that when he rejoined us for the West Indies trip he was in excellent shape.

People ask me if I was surprised by his emergence in the West Indies, and I reply that I was not. It should have happened earlier really. He had shown in the final Test of the South African home series of 2003 at the Oval that he had something, so he just needed to kick on from there. The key for Harmison is that he bowls the correct length. If he can understand that quickly in any certain match (because it obviously varies on differing pitches), then he is OK. At the Oval I had sat him down and explained that I wanted him to visualize hitting a spot about six inches above the stumps. That way I thought that if he erred on the side of full – which he does sometimes – he would then hit the stumps. What I did not want to happen was that he was driven. He is the type of bowler who needs a very simple, clear direction and I was quick to remind him of this in the Caribbean. His mind was on the task here though – unlike South Africa in the winter of 2004/5 – and it was much easier for him. That his mind is uncluttered is crucial for him. Mind you, that is true of all top sportspeople. But the great ones have this uncanny ability to focus their minds wholly on their task, whatever the distractions. Harmison does not seem able to do that always.

But both mind and accuracy were again in unison in the second Test in Trinidad with a six wicket haul in the first innings, as we triumphed comfortably by seven wickets. A touch of gloss was taken off the win for me by the fine meted out to Simon Jones, who bowled really well for his five wickets in the second innings, after the most minor of confrontations with Ramnaresh Sarwan. All Jones did was clench his fist and shout 'Come on' after he had dismissed Sarwan leg before.

This match again highlighted some problems which I outlined earlier. Yes, the old scenario of the match referee not being in total control of the happenings of a Test match. Here I was incensed with umpire Billy Bowden. There was some rain and bad light in this game, and the first time we had come off for this, Bowden had put his light meter up in the air and then decided to offer the light. It looked as if he had used his meter. So the next day when it might have been to our advantage to stay on, he suddenly offered the light without using his meter. I spoke to match referee Mike Procter, but he said I had to speak to Bowden. Typical palaver. I went to Bowden and he said meters were not being used. 'You're misleading the public,' I told him.

That led me to speak to Bowden and his colleague Daryl Harper about an idea to resolve this. Basically the umpire should use his naked eye to determine whether it is too dark to play. And then when he has made that decision for the first time in a game he should take a light meter reading, record it and that should the benchmark for the rest of the game. Even if the batsmen do not accept that first offer the umpire must still take the reading, otherwise the opposition could be at a disadvantage later in the game. Since the umpires thought this a good idea I suggested they took this to their hierarchy at the ICC.

None of this was a particularly controversial issue, though. There was a big one of those brewing elsewhere on this tour. I am, of course, talking about the great Chris Read/Geraint Jones debate. Who should be England's wicketkeeper/batsman?

For me it had begun in Bangladesh. Marcus Trescothick usually has the safest of hands at first slip but suddenly he was dropping the odd catch, and in Sri Lanka and the West Indies too. But he was only dropping ones to his right when a left hander was facing, and to his left when a right hander was on strike. In other words they were Read's catches. I think that Read knew that he had a problem too, because during a game in the West Indies I happened to see him go to the laptop computer, on which all the match footage is stored, and he muttered under his breath: 'That was mine' in reference to a catch which Trescothick had dropped. That was beginning to bother me, and was reinforcing doubts I had had when Read came to South Africa on my first tour in 1999/2000. Alec Stewart was the number one keeper there, and he was a pleasure to work with.

I have always liked my keeper to stand in when I do the regulation slip catching practice. Stewart did this and enjoyed it, but Read just would not do it. He complained that it was not realistic – the only keeper I know to have said that. I think, like everyone else, that he has lovely hands, but in my opinion he operates within a very narrow channel. In other words he does not drop too many, because he does not go for a lot of catches which he should be attempting. Maybe if he was prepared to do that practice he might be able to widen that channel.

Read's batting worried me too. I thought that he really struggled facing the spinners in Sri Lanka. Yes, he did well to help us scrape that draw in Kandy, but quite how he survived is almost a mystery; he could have been out at any time. He still struggles to play spin to this day. It is something that I have spoken to him about, and rather ironically it was his playing of a particular spinner which initiated the chain of events which eventually led to his being dropped from the Test team. It came between the second and third Tests during a three-day match we had against the Carib Beer XI at the Three Ws Oval in Bridgetown, Barbados. We played Read as a batsman but decided that it was time to hand

Jones a game behind the stumps. He had been impressing in the nets and I soon realized that I was not the only one who had doubts about Read. Michael Vaughan mentioned the situation to me, and I said that I did not think that we had the complete package in Read. We were not getting enough from him in the field. He is a very quiet lad after all. The wicketkeeper needs to be the motivator and Read was not being that.

So in that match at Bridgetown we bowled the opposition out for 129 but were 121–3 at the close of the first day, on a pitch which was turning sharply. Read was 0 not out overnight and I said to Vaughan (who was having a game off and did not have to be at the ground) that he should come there the next morning. They had Dave Mohammed in their side, a one-time West Indian left-arm wrist spinner, and he was soon causing problems, most notably for Read, whom he dismissed for just nine. Jones came in, and although he had one lucky escape – a missed stumping – he was soon tucking into Mohammed with relish. The night before when Read and others, including Graham Thorpe, were batting, Mohammed had looked like one of the best spinners in the world, now with Jones smashing him about, he looked pretty ordinary. Jones looked so confident, hitting three sixes, that soon Vaughan and I were saying: 'We might have to make a change here.'

It is at this point that I would like to clear up probably the biggest misconception of my time as England coach. I have been castigated for dropping Read for Jones without the knowledge of the selectors and without any selector being in the West Indies. That is not true. David Graveney was in Barbados for the third Test. He knew all about our deliberations about Read and Jones. In fact, Read was very nearly left out of the Barbados Test. Play was delayed on the first day there, and still no firm decision had been made about who was going to play. As they had in Sri Lanka, the selectors still had a say about the team for overseas matches.

But Graveney had said to me and Vaughan: 'You two guys know more than we do. We will be influenced by your decision.' However, despite my misgivings about Read, I was a bit worried about making a change. We were 2–0 up and the West Indians could still level the series. Before the warm-up Vaughan, Graveney and I discussed the issue. I stated I wanted Read. Vaughan seemed keen on Jones taking over. Graveney was not sure what to do, probably preferring Read for political reasons.

At this stage I went to take fielding practice on one side of the field, leaving Vaughan and Graveney talking, still deliberating about the keeper. Vaughan then interrupted that practice by calling me over again. 'What are we going to do?' he asked. I walked over and bluntly said: 'We are going with Read,' and promptly walked away again. I had further practice to attend to. 'No, come on, let's discuss it,' said Graveney. I ignored the request.

Read had his last chance in Barbados and did nothing again. So for the last Test in Antigua we dropped Read and selected Jones to give him a Test in preparation for the following summer. Graveney, who flew home after the Barbados Test, knew that we were going to do that. So if the other selectors did not know about it, then it was Graveney's fault.

When the decision was announced, the MCC were playing the champion county, Sussex, at Lord's in the English season's pipe-opener. Rod Marsh was in the dressing room with all the MCC players, most of whom had been his winter academicians, when he discovered what had happened. I have it on good authority that he went ballistic. That was disgraceful in my view. Even if he was upset at the decision and did not know anything about it, he, as a selector, should not have behaved as he did in front of this group of impressionable youngsters.

Naturally when we returned from the West Indies, there was a meeting at Lord's to discuss this. It was frosty, I can tell you, and I am not talking about the weather. As well as the Jones/Read scenario the selectors were unhappy with Mark Butcher and Michael Vaughan; Butcher for some comments he made about them which they deemed unacceptable, and Vaughan for his comment that Jones would now be given a fair run in the side. As I walked into the meeting I saw photocopied press cuttings of these comments on the table, cynically placed as proof and then used in the discussion.

Vaughan was just trying to give Jones some confidence. But Marsh was particularly vehement in his assertion that both Vaughan and Butcher should be disciplined. I was bullish in their defence. Originally the selectors wanted both fined with letters of reprimand, but after much debate only Butcher received a letter.

But we still had the Read/Jones issue to talk about. There was a really aggressive atmosphere in the room. Marsh came on strong, wanting to know what right I had to be dropping Read. Marsh clearly did not know what had happened. I found it astounding that Graveney had not informed him of what had actually taken place. So I told Marsh exactly what had happened. To which there was a stunned silence. Marsh then turned to Graveney and asked him why he had not been told that. Graveney stuttered, paused and eventually apologized.

To his credit Marsh also eventually apologized to me. But it is a subject which has run and run in the media, without their having true knowledge of the facts. They will know now.

Of course, the squad for the subsequent one-day series had already been selected, so there was no way that Jones could play in that. This allowed Read another chance in that form of the game, and in the first match at Georgetown he won the man of the match award for his 27 off 15, as we chased 157 to win in a 30-over contest. He did show me there that he could bat well in certain situations, and might have a limited role to play.

Rain blighted the whole series, which ended 2–2 with three

matches totally abandoned, but some succour came first in the shape of the magnificent facilities we encountered in St Lucia, where we played two games. I have seen few better grounds in the world, and was delighted that we were told at the time that this was to be our base for the 2007 World Cup. And further comfort came from an unexpected source. The day after the final one-dayer we played golf, and Brian Lara asked if he could play too. So, as we were heading back to the hotel on a bus afterwards, Lara and Vaughan sat next to each other discussing the series, with Lara admitting that he found Andrew Flintoff a difficult bowler to face. I was seated in front and it was fascinating to hear Lara say: 'I think you guys have got the makings of a young, exciting side. The only area of concern is the wicketkeeper. That wicketkeeper, he is not the one.' It was interesting to receive a similar opinion to ours from an outsider looking in, a great of the game too.

New Zealand were our first opponents in the summer of 2004, and this produced an interesting match-up between the coaches, as I came up against John Bracewell, formerly in charge of Gloucestershire. I had first come across him as an excitable off-spinner, who had toured Zimbabwe with Young New Zealand in late 1984, and a misinterpreted incident then had led to an edgy relationship between us thereafter. I was captain of Zimbabwe during that series and in one of the matches one of the New Zealand opening batsmen had edged a ball behind. When he was given not out by the umpire, there was naturally something of a reaction from our players. One of them uttered the words: 'You effin' cheat.' It was not me who said it, but I will give you a clue and tell you that until very recently he was coaching Derbyshire! I was at first slip and was laughing when the batsman turned around to see who had said those words. The batsman thought it had come from me and from there on I was a marked man during the series.

Back to that game and I already knew that I was worrying Bracewell because I was sweeping the living daylights out of his off-spin; so much so that he refused to bowl straight at me, pitching the ball so wide of my off stump that I could scarcely reach it. It got so bad that at the end of one over I picked up my off stump and jokingly placed it back in the ground outside the return crease. So when he eventually dismissed me in one game he gave me the almightiest of send-offs, swearing at me. In those days that was not the done thing. There was plenty of chat while a batsman was in, but as soon as he was dismissed, that was it. To give him a send-off was like kicking him when he was down. I still think that is wrong, even today. So I reacted angrily to Bracewell's words, even brandishing my bat in his direction; so much so that the umpires had to intervene.

Because of that, there was a general uneasiness between us when we met on the county circuit, although the ridiculous rumour that that was the reason why I was not interested in selecting his Gloucestershire players when I became England coach was totally wide of the mark.

What I would say is that Bracewell had tremendous success at Bristol in one-day cricket but it should be remembered that Gloucestershire were never out of the championship second division during his tenure. It was interesting that on a visit around the counties in 2000 to ask county coaches for players whom they thought of as potential England Test candidates outside of the current squad, Bracewell gave me at least six of his own players. Whereas as Bob Woolmer at Warwickshire gave me only one – Ashley Giles. Bracewell also did himself no favours with the England players when he wrote some disparaging player profiles in the programme for an international we played at Bristol during his time there. That really upset many of them and no doubt fired them up to make sure they did well against his side in 2004. Of course, they also had the 2–1 defeat of 1999 to motivate them.

Things could not have gone better, despite the fact that there was some pressure on us after the winter wins in the West Indies. A 3–0 win was really satisfying; an indication that the team was making progress and a winning mentality was taking root. There was little doubt that the major story of the series was the emergence of Andrew Strauss, after Michael Vaughan injured himself in the nets prior to the first Test at Lord's. We had seen that mental strength of his in Bangladesh and I had little doubt that he would succeed. In fact my initial thought was that one day he would captain England. Of course he did so, but even before then I was slowly changing my mind a little because I saw how dozy he could be – forever leaving things behind at training and in hotels (and that is important in terms of captaincy, because you need to be sharp all the time) – but there was definitely something special about him. So special in fact that he forced Nasser Hussain into premature retirement. I say premature, but I always thought that Hussain was going to retire at some stage in that summer, but maybe not as early as at the end of that first Test.

Strauss had scored a brilliant debut hundred, which set Hussain thinking about the potential make-up of the side for the second Test if Vaughan returned. Hussain called me to his room in the Landmark Hotel, Marylebone Road, on the Sunday evening to ask me for my thoughts about his retirement. There was no way that I was going to tell him flatly to retire, but what I did say to him was that it is always good to retire at the top of your game; also to go out on one's own terms and not leave the game grumpy because you have stayed too long. I told him how nice it might be to score some runs the next day and if we could beat New Zealand, it would erase all the painful memories he had of being booed at the Oval in 1999. I knew how much that had hurt him. The rest is history, as the cliché goes: a hundred to win the game at Lord's. Farewells do not come much better than that.

If only the script had been so easy to write and enact for the one-day NatWest series in 2004. With a series of thoroughly disappointing performances we did not even qualify for our own final, but it does have to be said that in those group stages every side which won the toss then went on to win the game. We won the toss just once, at Headingley against the West Indies, and hammered them by seven wickets. But otherwise the pitches seamed around early on and we just could not defend the totals we posted when the pitches went flat. We were hampered by the fact that Andrew Flintoff could not bowl throughout the competition, and he missed our first three matches (one of which was rained off) before playing as a batsman and scoring two very good hundreds. It was suggested that we had rushed Flintoff back from a foot injury in desperation at our stuttering form. It was nothing of the sort. We had word that he was fit and that he was going to play for Lancashire, so we said that if that was the case, then he should play for us. He had not been out for that long, so would not struggle with his general fitness because these were only one-day games and not Test matches.

I was extremely frustrated because I felt that not enough thought was going into how we selected our one-day sides. It seemed that anyone in form was being picked and then a strategy was being developed around those players. For instance, Robert Key was included for this series on the back of a glut of first class runs, but we could not really find a suitable position for him in the order. So after the series was over I suggested a meeting be arranged with the selectors at the Belfry, where I put forward my strategy for one-day cricket.

Firstly, I said that we needed a top three who could use the first fifteen overs (with their attendant fielding restrictions) effectively. That did not mean that we had to be 100–0 at the end of that period in every match, but those players had to 'think on their feet' to see what any particular pitch was worth. But they did have to have the ability to score 80–100 in the first fifteen overs on appropriate pitches. That is why it is crucial those players have long spells in those positions to gain as much experience as possible. That was an area in which we were to be particularly hard hit by injuries and illness, with the loss of Marcus Trescothick and Michael Vaughan. Technique is also important for these players in that they must be able to cut and pull effectively.

At number four in the order I wanted a player who was mentally strong; one who was able to see the innings through. It is a difficult job, especially if the top order fails. Then at five and six I wanted batsmen who could turn a game in the space of a few overs. In other words the likes of Flintoff, Kevin Pietersen and even Somerset's Ian Blackwell. At seven there should be a batsman who can finish an innings, a player who can manipulate the bowling around cleverly – for example, Paul Collingwood. Preferably at number eight would be a bowler who could bat usefully, like Ashley Giles, and ideally someone similar at number nine, because you need to bat as deep as possible if you are to win the tight games. And at numbers ten and eleven you would have your specialist bowlers.

If you have a flying start to your innings you can rejig the order and, say, drop number four down to allow the bigger hitters at five and six to capitalize. Of course, this is the Utopia. And only really during the home summer of 2005 did we come near to it. It is very difficult to find suitable players to fit all those roles, but I said to the selectors that was the goal I was aiming for. And they all agreed, apart from Rod Marsh, who expressed some hesitation about it, but had no alternative strategy.

But we used that strategy of mine to select the team for the NatWest Challenge against India and the ICC Champions Trophy, and I would like to think that it worked. We beat India 2–1 (winning the first two) and reached the final of the ICC tournament, a match I have already looked back upon with real regret. Suddenly we looked a good one-day unit. However, the problem in England is that if something does not work for a couple of games, then it is assumed that the plan is all wrong and change is demanded. So when Andrew Strauss failed a couple of times at number four in 2005, everybody forgot how well he had played against India and against Australia (in the ICC Champions Trophy at Edgbaston) in that position. We played poorly in the one-day series against South Africa at the end of the 2004/5 tour but it did not mean that the overall plan was wrong. The problem there was that the top three were just not getting any runs – just two fifties between them in seven matches. No wonder we were losing.

Not that we did any of that in the second Test series of the 2004 summer. Losing that is. Four matches against the West Indies and every single one of them was won. Seven on the trot; in fact ten out of eleven, only that draw in Antigua –where the pitch is so flat that I do not think anyone can win these days – preventing a full house of wins in 2004 up to that point.

I was especially pleased that Ashley Giles had such a productive series, snaring twenty-two wickets. Flintoff might have been a deserved man of the series for both his 387 runs at 64 and his fourteen cheap wickets, but Giles turned his whole career around to put himself on the international map. I had always believed in him, as had his teammates, but it obviously took the public, and the press in particular, a lot longer to do so. I think his dismissal of Brian Lara in the second innings of the first Test at Lord's might have been the moment when Giles at last realized that he belonged at the highest level. He bowled the great man with a magnificent delivery, which turned sharply out of the bowlers' footmarks, to claim his 100th Test victim. It was a defining moment for the most professional cricketer anyone could wish to have in their side. And his increased confidence was reflected in the team's comfort with being favourites and constantly winning. A lot of baggage was shed that summer.

One would have thought that the selection process for the winter tour of South Africa would be simple. But it was not. At the meeting, the selectors had seemingly determined upon their final composition and were trying to move swiftly on to picking the winter's academy squad when I said: 'Look, guys, we need to look deeper into this.' The problem that had been overlooked was that, while we had cover for every other position in the team, we did not have anyone in reserve should Andrew Flintoff pull up lame. And there was a good chance of that. Unquestionably he was the most important member of our side and I was asking: 'What happens if he pulls out on the morning of a Test? How do we balance our side then?' My suggestion that we take Paul Collingwood to cover this eventuality was greeted with the response: 'But he is not in the same class as an all-rounder.' I agreed with that, but he was the next best thing we had. It had been blithely assumed that we would take a bowler to fill that extra place, and then when it was announced that Collingwood was going, there was a lot of talk that Ian Bell, who had done so well on his debut in the final Test at the Oval, should have been preferred. However, I had done a fair bit of homework on that and I was told that Bell's little seamers were not in the same class as Collingwood's.

Before the tour of South Africa we had a one-day tour of Zimbabwe. Ah, Zimbabwe again. It had been said that the events of that 2003 World Cup should never be allowed to happen again. So what happened now in November 2004? Virtually the same thing, that is what. This time the ECB decided to try to take early control, commissioning Des Wilson, chairman of their corporate affairs and marketing advisory committee, to undertake a report on the viability of the tour, especially on moral grounds. His paper concluded that the tour should not go ahead. But it was never properly discussed by the ECB and was rubbished by the ICC, inevitably leading to Wilson's resignation.

At the start of the 2004 season we met Wilson at a 'do' designed for the players to get to know the ECB officials better. He told us: 'You will have nothing to do with this affair. The ECB will deal with it entirely. If you are asked about it, just say – "The ECB are dealing with it."' After the events of the World Cup that was what everyone wanted to hear.

Better news followed for the players when they were told that they could take it as read that they would not be going to Zimbabwe. If only it had all been that simple. As the summer progressed the debate raged and still there was no definite decision. The situation was further clouded by the row over the rebel white cricketers, which resulted in Zimbabwe being temporarily suspended from Test cricket during mid-summer. It is worth mentioning the fact that we were scheduled to play two Test matches in Zimbabwe during the 2004 tour. That fact was quickly forgotten when people were criticizing the schedule for the subsequent South Africa tour. 'Undercooked' was the word being bandied around with great abandon, but those two Tests, allied to a warm-up match against South Africa A, would have easily been sufficient preparation.

Having been told categorically that we were not going, then all of a sudden the tour was back on when the ICC started to throw their weight around, threatening England with hefty fines if we did not fulfil the obligation to tour. As a result the ECB released a statement saying that if individual players objected to the Zimbabwe tour on moral grounds, then they would not be forced to go, and their decision would not be held against them in the future. It was wrong of the ECB to do that in my opinion, not least because I was not consulted on the matter, but also because it was in complete contrast to the previously mentioned situation where Alec Stewart and Darren Gough wanted to miss the India tour of 2001/2.

I felt strongly then they should not be able to pick and choose tours, and ensured that they were not able to do so, but this was effectively what was happening here. Where did that leave me as coach? In a position with very little control, that is where. What happened if the whole of the selected squad refused to go? And then the next group of players in line after that? As I have said, my view has always been that if any tour is on then the whole group of players should go. OK, we live in a democratic society where individuals are allowed to make their own decisions, but my take on that goes back to a common theme I have already stated regarding Zimbabwe: do the individuals concerned really know the full facts? Do they really know enough to make an informed decision?

During the final Test of the summer, against the West Indies at the Oval, the whole squad had had a meeting at our hotel, the Grange City near the Tower of London, where it was decided that whatever happened regarding the Zimbabwe issue, we would stick together as a team. It was becoming clear that we would have to go because of the financial penalty if we did not. If only for that reason I thought we should go, even if, on other grounds, I was less sure than I had been in 2003. The situation in the country had definitely worsened since then, but still the people I spoke to were unsure whether we should tour. From a personal point of view I was slightly more relaxed because I knew that I would be receiving a South African passport in September (on account of my mother's birthplace – Kimberley), on which I could travel.

So I said to the players: 'Look, I know that you have a moral issue about this tour. But there is another moral issue to consider – if we do not go, then how is that going to affect your mates at your county?' I had been told by the ECB that the counties would definitely be financially affected if we did not tour. Corners would have to be cut somewhere as a result of a fine, and they were likely to be centred around the annual handout given to the counties.

However, during the ICC Champions Trophy tournament which followed, I began to hear whispers that certain players were considering not going to Zimbabwe. Ironically our first game was against Zimbabwe and our easy win by 152 runs at Edgbaston convinced me that we would be unnecessarily flogging our best players by taking them. I thought it would be an ideal opportunity to look at some younger players. So I spoke to Michael Vaughan and we agreed that it would be wise to rest the senior players from the tour. And subsequently that would have eased the decision for the ECB, as well as hopefully not upsetting the team ethos too much.

Our next game was at the Rose Bowl in Southampton against Sri Lanka, where the captain and I organized a meeting with chairman of selectors David Graveney, ECB director of cricket John Carr and Rod Bransgrove, the chairman of Hampshire and at the time helping the ECB with communications and policy issues, in order to inform them of our intentions. They all agreed it was a good idea but they had to clear it with David Morgan first. Lo and behold, as Vaughan and I returned to the dressing room, we were told that Steve Harmison wanted to have a chat. There was nowhere suitably private, so we had to speak quietly while standing in the corner of the dressing room, where Harmison told us that he was pulling out of the tour. 'Hang on, Harmy,' I said, 'we're going to rest you and other senior players anyway.'

'No, no, I'm going to the press to tell them,' he replied.

What we later discovered was that Harmison had already told his tale to the paper for which he contributed a ghosted column. That was how much he was interested in the team. This was turning into a muddle because, after we had spoken to Harmison, he, annoyingly and against our wishes, then told all the other senior players that they were going to be pulled out. That was not what we wanted, because we still had to speak to David Morgan. So when Morgan heard about this scenario, he was insistent that everyone must go, including the skipper. He was not happy: I was not happy, and for the one and only time during our relationship, which had begun when he was chairman of Glamorgan when I joined them in 1997, we ended up at loggerheads. This was a far cry from the occasions when we used to share a glass of red wine – or two – at his Newport home.

He summoned me to an 8 a.m. meeting the following day at Lord's, at which Graveney and Carr were also present. It was not a pleasant meeting. Morgan said that Graveney and I had made a mess of the situation. I thought he was accusing me of misman-agement, which upset me. I challenged him about this, and told him that we had tried to stop Harmison going to the press. We had even got Richard Bevan of the PCA to phone his agent (John Morris, the former England cricketer) in order to try to solve the problem, but time was against us because this was all happening on a Saturday night, with publication of Harmison's column due the next morning in the *News of the World*. I thought I was being castigated for just trying to sort out a predicament which was not of my own making or instigation.

But Morgan was unwavering in his view that Vaughan had to tour. He told Graveney to ask Vaughan to phone him. This is where I seized an opportunity. I realized that I had to phone Vaughan quickly and did so, telling him that it might be for the best if he said he would go to Zimbabwe. There was no quibbling or arguing from him. He just said he would. No question.

So the problem was solved, with Andrew Flintoff and Marcus Trescothick being rested, although Flintoff annoyed me a little by later stating that he would not have gone anyway on moral grounds. He did not need to say that. Ashley Giles behaved mag-nificently. We told him that he could miss the trip but he said: 'If my captain is going, then so am I.'

In order to warm up for Zimbabwe we went to Namibia to play two one-day matches, vowing all along that we would go to

Zimbabwe so long as the goal posts remained the same and there was no attempt to use us as political pawns. However, just as we were leaving Namibia, we heard that a number of British journalists were not being granted accreditation to cover the tour in Zimbabwe. It looked as if those goal posts were already being shifted, and that immediately concerned the players. Their initial reaction was: 'We're not going then.' And I agreed with them. I was hauled before the press in the corner of a departure lounge at Windhoek airport, but all I could tell them was that we were going to meet Richard Bevan, who had some information for us in Johannesburg, where we were due to catch a connecting flight to Harare anyway. 'Here we go again,' I thought. The memories of the Cullinan Hotel in Cape Town began to flood back.

Michael Vaughan and I met Bevan in a café at Johannesburg airport. Money was still a major talking point, namely the fine the ICC might impose if we decided not to go. We needed to speak to the players but that was easier said than done in such a public environment (we were all in transit just like other travellers), especially with the press milling around too. Some were more subtle than others, and even though I did not show it at the time, it made me chuckle inside when we walked into the business class lounge to find Scyld Berry, the wily old fox of cricket journalism, sitting there quietly. He knew something was boiling.

Rather rudely we had to eject some people from a small glass-panelled lounge, used as a smoking area, which was the only place available to have some kind of reasonably private meeting. During the course of this we became aware that Ehsan Mani, the ICC president, had expressed the view that there would be some sympathy towards England if they called off the tour because of their journalists not being allowed in. That one comment swayed the players. They were definitely not going now.

Michael Vaughan spoke to David Morgan, who was in Harare

with his deputy Mike Soper and John Carr, and Morgan said: 'Stay in Johannesburg until you hear from me.' Unfortunately all of our bags were already on the plane being readied to go to Harare. This was where Phil Neale came into his own, doing a superb job to get all the bags off and booking us into the nearby Caesar's Palace Hotel. At this point I refer you back again to that criticism clamouring for the need for an old-style manager. I bet he would not have done half the job that Neale did here.

So here we were again, cooped up in a South African hotel debating about whether to go to Zimbabwe. It seemed hardly credible. The players' stance was hardening by the minute. That was why David Morgan felt compelled to send John Carr from Harare. Even after he gave the news that the media ban had been lifted, he was required to allay fears, which he did well. The tour was on. But, of course, that was not the end of the story. Our delay meant that the first match, on Friday, 26 November, had to be cancelled, because we only arrived in Harare at 2 p.m. that afternoon. To me that just meant that the tour would now comprise four matches rather than the scheduled five. It had been Zimbabwe's fault – by not accrediting the journalists – that we had arrived late.

But David Morgan phoned me just before we left Johannesburg to say that the Zimbabwean authorities wanted us to play back-to-back matches on Saturday and Sunday. 'No way,' I said, but Morgan was keen for us to do it. One part of me might have wanted the extra game so that we could have a look at some of the youngsters, of which there were many in the party. But the other part was adamant that there was a principle at stake and that under no circumstances was I budging.

Thankfully, once I had explained my reasons, Morgan understood, and made sure that we only played four matches. But still there was more controversy; this time about our hotel accommodation. Beforehand I had told John Carr that if the players were having to go to Zimbabwe under sufferance, then they should be lodged in the best hotels. In Harare that meant staying in the Meikles Hotel, which is the best of a bad bunch. But that caused a problem with Zimbabwe Cricket, who had a deal with the Zimbabwe Sun group, which owns the Monomotapa Hotel in Harare, where all international touring teams stay. We were begrudgingly allowed to stay at Meikles, but while we were playing one of the two one-day matches in Harare David Morgan came to me. 'We have another problem,' he said. 'They [Zimbabwe Cricket] are saying that we cannot stay in the best hotel in Bulawayo [the Holiday Inn] but instead must stay at the Rainbow.' I knew the Rainbow Hotel well. Let us just say that I did not think it was up to the standard required by any team, let alone an international touring team. I was really beginning to feel sorry for Morgan at this stage, because he had been put through so much on this whole issue – and dealt with it very well in my opinion – but I just said: 'Tell them no way. If we have to stay there, we are leaving.' Morgan agreed and was extremely supportive. This was similar to the pact we had made that if Robert Mugabe came near any of the grounds at which we were playing, we would leave immediately. This final episode was the Zimbabwean authorities' last attempt at one-upmanship. They denied this, saying that the Holiday Inn was full, but Morgan, through his multitude of contacts, discovered that it was not. So, mysteriously, rooms were suddenly found for the whole of the England party after we had threatened to leave. Funny, that.

So on to South Africa. This was an extremely difficult trip for me personally; much more so than my first one with England in 1999/2000. Then there had been no pressure because England had slumped to new depths in the previous summer against New Zealand. So I was able to go about my business without too much scrutiny. But now there was a high level of expectation. From the outset eyes were trained upon me. Cape Town is my home after all, so I suppose that it was natural that there should be a different level of interest in someone returning 'home' with a burgeoning England team. I was in Cape Town for much of the build-up, watching and listening to what was being said about the England team. It was not complimentary, with some commentators like Mike Haysman even ridiculing us. That made me angry because I had already been upset by the way he and Pat Symcox had treated Eric Simons when he was coach of South Africa, almost precipitating Simons' departure with their negative comments.

So all this talk made me retreat into a defensive bubble. Maybe unnecessarily so. For I will admit that if I had my time again, I would treat this tour differently. The problem was that I so desperately wanted to win. There had been a general feeling in South Africa that I had made a big mistake in taking the England job. So I wanted to prove people wrong. Interestingly, when I had first taken the England post, there were not too many people interested in it. But once I resigned, there were a lot more wanting it. So I reckon I must have done something right.

Where I think that I erred in South Africa was that I went overboard in my desire not to be seen talking to any South Africans. That was always a problem for me because I knew many of them so well. Even when they toured England in 2003 with Simons as coach, I had to be careful about speaking to them too much. Otherwise I could have imagined the comments: 'Is he with us or them?' the cynics would have been asking. That tour was particularly strange because Simons is such a good friend, but I think those that I know well understood the situation. Anyway, there is not always that much opportunity to catch up. Teams rarely stay in the same hotels, so a quick word at the ground is usually as much as you can manage.

The situation was complicated by the fact that there was some talk of my applying for the post of South African coach, which was going to come up at the end of the series, with Ray Jennings only having been given a short contract. That was rubbish. I was never going to apply for that. But I was approached about doing so. In a somewhat ludicrous manner, though. One of the South African security personnel protecting the England squad had been told by a member of the United Cricket Board of South Africa to ask me if I was interested. Naturally I just told him it had to be done in a more official manner than that.

I probably should have communicated more with people I knew, but I must stress that I was never rude to anyone. Sometimes when I was, say, walking over to the nets at a ground, with my mind firmly in concentration mode and maybe head down, I might have not seen certain people. But if I did see anyone I knew, I would always greet them, but rarely stop to hold a conversation.

No matter what else happened, we won the Test series 2–1; all I ever wanted, as I have said. Proudly for me it was the second occasion on which we had prevailed in four series on the trot during my time as England coach. Beating South Africa was a fine achievement because it is not an easy place to win; only Australia (twice) had done so in Test series since South Africa's readmission to international cricket in 1991/2. It was certainly tense stuff and I do not think that I have ever been as nervous as I was on the final afternoon in the fifth Test at Centurion, where we held on grimly for a draw after slipping to 20–3. Again the skipper, Michael Vaughan showed his tenacity and grit with a battling 26 not out in over two hours to save the game in concert with Andrew Flintoff, who also played very well in rearguard action.

We should really have been 2–0 up after the second Test in Durban, where we were a little unlucky with the weather on the final day, but we did not play at all well in Cape Town and allowed them back into the series. Then came the decisive match at the Wanderers in Johannesburg, which we won because of the astonishing bowling of Matthew Hoggard, who achieved the remarkable match figures of 12–205, including a second innings 7–61 on the final day to bring victory almost single-handedly, as the rest of our attack struggled. He used the pitch and the overhead conditions superbly, but I am convinced that if Shaun Pollock had not stuck to his usual defensive ways, then we might not have won that Test. Pollock plugged away outside off stump, when if he had bowled straighter, we might never have scored 300 in either innings.

The tour lost some lustre with the 4–1 defeat in the one-day series, but that might have been very different. We won the first game and tied the second, but for all the excitement of that match at Bloemfontein it should never have come to that; no side should be able to chase 270 under lights at that ground. Nor in Port Elizabeth, which is exactly what happened in the third game. We should have been 3–0 up, but the worrying trend of the bowlers being unable to defend targets manifested itself in the most untimely manner. Yes, we missed Andrew Flintoff, who had returned home to have an ankle operation, but we knew that we could not keep using that as an excuse. Nor the fact that the players were tired. They probably were, but not as much as they thought.

One who might have had cause for complaint in that department was Geraint Jones. We did not realize until afterwards that he was the only player who had played in every single match of the winter. That was probably why it was a mistake to ask him to open. We had first moved him up the order, at my instigation, when we faced Wales in a warm-up match during the summer of 2004, but I thought I was the only one who truly believed in him performing such a role. That is until we had a management meeting in South Africa about the issue. All of the senior players were arguing forcefully for his inclusion as an opener. If anything I was a little bit reluctant then because of the timing. Because, after experimenting with him at number three in a couple of NatWest series matches in 2004, he had done well at number seven thereafter in Namibia and Zimbabwe.

But uppermost in everybody's minds was the worry that Vikram Solanki, who was our other option as opener, would always struggle against the highest quality bowling. I have never seen a higher back lift – his hands reach head-high – or so much general movement in a batting technique. I was keen on Andrew Strauss at four because I felt that he could not hit the ball hard down the ground in the first fifteen overs. So we went with Jones, and he did not have a good time there. What I would say, though, was that at least he was reaching 30 quite often. It was not as if he was continually getting out cheaply – like many of the other top-order players were. It could only be the mental breakthrough which was required for him to succeed in that role. He certainly has the shots for it. We continued with him at the top of the order in the summer of 2005 but were eventually forced to drop him down when it was felt that it might be adversely affecting his confidence.

There was one huge positive to come out of that winter's one-day cricket. His name is Kevin Pietersen. He was not originally selected for the South African leg, but he had played just two games in Zimbabwe when I said to Michael Vaughan: 'We've got to get this guy to South Africa.' It was glaringly obvious that he had to be a part of the one-day side we were attempting to build. It was wrongly thought that Pietersen replaced Flintoff in South Africa. He did not. He was coming anyway. And he made some impression. Three hundreds under the most intense pressure and abuse from his fellow countrymen is not a bad riposte. I think he probably handled his homecoming a little better than I did that winter.

11

Ashes Regained

Where to start with the summer of 2005? In case you did not know, we won the Ashes that summer. The Australians might have gained more than ample revenge in 2006/7 but that is no reason not to recall our 2005 achievement with pride and delight. It was so damn spectacular and gripping that, as I have mentioned, I wrote a book about it (*Ashes Regained*). That apparently was so revealing that Australian coach, John Buchanan, ordered all his coaching staff to read it before the rematch.

Come on, John, as if I would let slip anything I did not want to. As I said privately at the time, I was hoping that the Aussies would have been worrying more about the stuff I had left out than anything I had put in that book. Injuries and many other factors – which, of course, we will come to – scuppered that, but there was definitely detail I could not reveal then. Of the Australian batsmen I knew would be a threat in 2006/7 I did not even touch their techniques in that book.

There were other things I could not say. I will tell you one for a start. During the one-day series which preceded the Test matches there was a furore about the guards of honour lined up to greet the teams as they entered the field of play. This reached its apex at

Edgbaston where Australia's Matthew Hayden was accused of swearing at the children who formed this guard. There had been a similar problem in the previous game at Durham.

I will come clean and admit that I wanted this to be a problem for the Australians. I had spotted in the Twenty20 international at Southampton that most of their players had intentionally managed to avoid going through the tunnel as there was a gap between the boundary boards and the boundary rope where the tunnel started. So I persuaded Dave Clarke (the ECB's events audit officer) to ensure that the tunnel always began at the boundary boards so that there was no way that the Australians could peel off and avoid going through the flags of St George. They had shown a sign of weakness and I was keen to exploit it. It seemed to work.

There were other examples. Take the saga of the substitutes. Ricky Ponting's famous blast at me during the fourth Test at Trent Bridge after being run out by substitute Gary Pratt was one of my more-chronicled moments in this series. I can say now, though, that I saw a Ponting outburst coming, if not necessarily in that manner. Having played the NatWest one-day series we had a pre-Test series meeting with Sri Lankan referee Ranjan Madugalle. Those meetings are de rigueur, involving both captains and both coaches. At this one Buchanan brought up the issue of substitutes and basically accused us of taking our bowlers off for massages after their spells in the one-day series. How can you have a massage in one over? Because that was the period our players were off the field for. I was not happy with that and said to Madugalle: 'He's making a big assumption.' Buchanan butted in: 'I'm not assuming.' As he was saying that, I said: 'Well, then, you are accusing us of—'

I could not finish my sentence. Madugalle stepped in then and told us to settle down, but, as he did so, I happened to look at Ponting. Those little eyes of his were staring darkly at me. He was fuming.

Not fuming quite as much as he was at Trent Bridge, though. It was the Saturday afternoon and Australia had followed on for the first time in seventeen years. Ponting's partner Damien Martyn had called him for a suicidal single to cover and Pratt had run him out with a direct hit. I was not even watching. Not live anyway. I was making toast in the dressing room. I heard the roar and looked up at the TV. Ponting was clearly out – maybe the most crucial wicket of the whole series (the team certainly thought so when they later invited Pratt to join the open-top bus celebrations).

It was soon clear that Ponting was not happy. I left my toast and went out on to the balcony. Ponting was by now nearing the boundary's edge. He looked like he was swearing. He looked up at me and said something. I do not think he was complimenting me on my excellent choice of substitute (if I had been meaning to have a really good fielder I would have asked Warwickshire's Trevor Penney, who happened to be with us and was then still the finest fielder in county cricket). That was when I smiled – yes, remarkably, I smiled. I do do that sometimes. And, boy, did Ponting lose his temper. It turned out that I had burnt my toast, but in an instant I knew that England would win the Ashes. A day later we went 2–1 up and that was how the series ended.

It was so obviously the wrong time for Ponting to complain about substitutes anyway. Pratt was on the field for Simon Jones, who was in hospital having an X-ray on an injured ankle. He was certainly not having a massage in readiness for another bowl. He did not play again that summer, not until the next year when he broke down with a knee injury in India.

Look, I will admit that once we knew that the Australians were becoming incensed by the substitute saga that we did play on it a bit. Why shouldn't we? It was like the guard of honour thing. Anything to gain that small advantage. But most of the time players were off the field to have a pee. There is such a strong emphasis on rehydration these days that some cannot go a whole session without needing to relieve themselves.

Players did have to see the physio on two or three occasions. Those like Michael Vaughan (knee) and Andrew Flintoff (ankle) had had operations and when there was even the slightest pain in those areas they naturally wanted it checked out.

When Ponting was fined 75 per cent of his match fee for his behaviour I thought that was the end of the matter. Although I did believe that he should have also, along with Simon Katich who was seen swearing after being out, received at least a one-match ban. Lesser players than Ponting would have been punished in that manner. Katich was probably lucky that he swore in the same match as Ponting misbehaved, otherwise he would have been severely punished.

I even shook Ponting's hand outside the dining room the day after. But it was not the end of the matter. Ponting did a radio interview in which he dragged the affair up again, accusing us of not playing within the spirit of the game. That really riled me. As if the Australians were whiter than white all series. Even their use of substitutes could be questioned – Brad Hodge deputized for Michael Clarke in the third Test at Old Trafford (and took two superb catches) but then Clarke miraculously recovered from his back problem and appeared without a runner when it was time for Australia to bat.

The Australians kept saying that we were not playing in the spirit of the game, but all that showed to me was a total misunderstanding of what the spirit of the game actually is. For me the spirit of the game means that you can do something within the letter of the law but it must be something that you are happy for any young player, especially a schoolkid, to copy. For example, running off the field to go to the toilet is something you would not mind a youngster doing. But when you question an umpire's decision, which you are allowed to do within the laws, would you really like youngsters to do that? The answer is no. It is not in the spirit of the game.

Therefore, I thought Ponting set a poor example during the series with the manner in which he often challenged the umpires' decisions, sometimes backed up by a couple of colleagues, as in football. There were also another couple of occasions when his players indulged in what I can only call childish behaviour. In the second Test at Edgbaston some of them made petty comments to the fourth umpire – nothing less than squealing to teacher – to try to ensure that Simon Jones was fined for giving Hayden a send-off after dismissing him. And then at Trent Bridge, because they were unhappy at some comments made by the grounds-man before the game, they deliberately bowled during warm-ups on a pitch being prepared for a county match – causing much damage.

If I was miffed by Ponting, though, it was nothing compared to my ire at Malcolm Speed, the chief executive of the ICC no less. What is it about these Australians and their radio interviews? This one occurred during the final Test at the Oval and Speed said on the subject of substitutes: 'I think Ricky Ponting has a point there. We need to be careful that we keep it under control, define what's acceptable and that the captains buy into that.' Speed was taking sides, during the decisive Test of the series.

But at the time I thought it best that I did not react in any way to any of this. In fact, I was pleased when David Morgan, the ECB chairman, later praised me for the manner in which I dealt with this situation. Not only that but Bob Merriman, his Australian counterpart, phoned Morgan to add his praise.

Even before the Test series there had been signs that the Australians were under pressure. As you might have noticed, I was never one for a war of words with an opposition coach but, rather unwittingly, became involved in one with Australia's coach John Buchanan at the end of the NatWest one-day series (a triangular also involving Bangladesh), whose final ended in a thrilling tie at Lord's. In that match I had seen little signs which encouraged me enormously; little things I had not seen before from an Australian side. A couple of their batsmen had looked gun-shy against the quicker bowlers for a start. Then there had been the sight of the side being captained by committee as Ponting was surrounded by a group of players every time a crucial decision had to be made. And finally Glenn McGrath had been protected by Mike Hussey at the end of the innings, with singles being turned down. That had never happened before.

So when an Australian journalist asked me whether I thought we had gained any psychological advantages out of the match I was thinking of those instances. I wished I had not, because as soon as I had answered yes I knew that I would have to qualify it. So I did.

Naturally those points were soon put to Buchanan. His reply was touchy. 'It would be interesting for him [Fletcher] to reflect on how Trescothick has got out,' he said, 'how Strauss has got out, how Vaughan has got out through the course of the series so far with the Test matches in mind. I just don't think we've really exposed the weaknesses of the English team at the moment as well as we should have done. That's partly a credit to England – Flintoff's bowled well, Harmison's bowled some good balls and they've had some support at times . . . But I think they've got three fieldsmen only. Collingwood is obviously a very good fields-man; Solanki, who they bring on, Pietersen is quick to the ball . . . but other than that I think they are quite lumbering in the field.' As I said, touchy. Surely this was a man under pressure.

But I knew that already. When we had turned up at Lord's at our usual time (about 9 a.m.) for the second match of the NatWest series, Australia were already there and they were preparing to warm up exactly where they knew we always warmed up – on the top end of the ground. What is more, when some of our bowlers went to bowl some looseners on the pitch designated for such a purpose on the top half of the square, the Australians would not move out of their way as they tried to run up. So Ashley Giles just bowled regardless, weaving his way through them.

That was nothing, though, if we are talking about confrontation. The most fiery example occurred during the one-dayer at Edgbaston. A Hayden versus Jones clash became all the more pleasurable for me when Paul Collingwood, Andrew Strauss and Michael Vaughan all joined in. Unfair numbers? Huh. We had talked before the series about not allowing the Australians to intimidate us. Hayden tried the bully-boy stuff and we reacted. Reacted well, in my opinion.

Basically what had happened was that Hayden had hit a ball back to the bowler Jones, who, in a reflex action, had hurled the ball back at him. It was obviously meant for the stumps but was badly off target and hit Hayden in the chest. Hayden went ballistic, screaming at Jones and marching down the pitch at him. Jones stood his ground and in rushed his teammates to help, just like we had talked about. Jones was going to apologize but Hayden's over-the-top response gave him no chance. Instead Hayden got more than he bargained for. I am not condoning loutish behaviour on the field, but I liked this.

As indeed I liked a lot about our one-day cricket that summer. It had begun well for us in the Twenty20 pipe-opener at Southampton. We set a tone there with some aggressive cricket, targeting several of their batsmen with the short ball, and generally 'getting into their space' as I always liked to put it. As a result I thought that in the subsequent NatWest series we came of age as a one-day team – the best we played in this form of the game under my stewardship. Briefly I could see that it was possible for us to make the same progression as we had in the Test arena. We were as good as, if not better than, Australia in this one-day series. Injuries ruined this team, though. They were all under thirty then and I had high hopes for the World Cup. But by the time that came around we only had about five of them left.

After that NatWest series we had to play Australia again in three NatWest Challenge matches. We lost 2–1, but that was not my main concern. Rather, I was worried that we had been too nice towards the Australians in those matches. When Ponting made a hundred at Lord's some of our players made too much of a point of walking some distance to shake his hand. You must understand that I was never against congratulation (Andrew Flintoff's consolation of Brett Lee at the end of the Edgbaston Test made for both a magnificent picture and an enduring moment), but there is a time (better once the contest is over) and a manner (not unnecessarily over-the-top).

So my main aim before the first Test at Lord's was to ensure that we rediscovered the devil which had been present in, among other occasions, that Edgbaston flashpoint. And it looked like it had worked when our bowlers tore into the Australians on a ferocious first morning. Skipper Vaughan decided to go against the norm and hand Steve Harmison the first over of the match; he responded with a sustained hostility which began by hitting Justin Langer on the elbow second ball and continued until he had taken his sixth five-wicket haul in Test cricket. Sadly Flintoff received a rather different response from Harmison when he asked him to take the first over in 2006/7 in Brisbane.

And sadly that first morning at Lord's was not as productive as we thought. Bowling Australia out for 190 was soon brought into perspective when we ourselves were dismissed for 155, the only bright spot of that being a combative 57 from Kevin Pietersen in his first Test innings. He followed that up with 64 not out in the second innings as we were eventually hammered by 239 runs. But I was so happy he had succeeded immediately because his selection had been the hot topic all summer.

For, despite his instant one-day success during the winter in South Africa, we had not selected Pietersen for the first two Tests of the summer against Bangladesh (they require no more attention here than to say we won easily). It had been a fiendishly difficult decision but we had gone for Graham Thorpe instead.

It was a complicated situation which I will attempt to explain. Basically Mark Butcher, our established number three, had injured himself in South Africa. His replacement Rob Key had not shown enough form to warrant a place. So we were looking for a number three. But the problem was that we did not really have one. We wanted to play young Ian Bell, who had impressed so much in a single Test against the West Indies the previous summer and had made a sparkling start in county cricket that season, but three was too high for him then. As it was for Thorpe, who was obviously nearing the end of his career and was struggling against the moving ball. And also as it was for Pietersen, whose technique we felt was only suitable for number five at that stage.

Vaughan, in the first of many shrewd moves as skipper that summer, volunteered to move up from four to three to allow Bell to slot in at four, so that left a straight shoot-out between Thorpe and Pietersen for the number five slot. Crucially Pietersen had made a poor start for his new county Hampshire and was also batting at five for them – too low in county cricket for an England aspirant. Thorpe was on ninety-eight Test caps at the time, too, and while we were never in the business of handing out sentimental caps it would have been a harsh call to drop Thorpe. But just after we had made that decision Thorpe informed us that he had accepted an offer to coach in New South Wales that winter, thereby signalling an end to his international career at the summer's conclusion at the latest.

So Thorpe played his two Tests to reach 100, scoring a few runs after the others had dipped their bread against the weak Bangladeshis, but then his recurring back problems resurfaced. By the time we came to the Ashes series he had managed just five innings for Surrey since Bangladesh and probably had as many injections in his back. And all the while Pietersen had been run-drunk in the NatWest series.

But still I was unsure. It was truly a 50-50 decision, one of the hardest I had to make in my time with England. Two things swung it Pietersen's way – if Thorpe's coaching revelation had not already done so because that did irritate me a little. First, that I was worried about Thorpe's lack of batting because I knew he needed time in the middle and secondly, that I honestly thought a right hander would be better at five because of the problems Shane Warne creates when bowling into the rough for left handers.

We also wanted our number five to be positive. That was the only way we were going to beat Australia. And Pietersen did that and so much more. Shame about his catching, though. He dropped Clarke badly at Lord's and went on to drop six in the series. It was strange really, given that he is generally a good fielder. Eventually I picked up at Trent Bridge that, in his natural excitability, he was walking in so quickly that he was on one leg, and therefore totally unbalanced, when the ball was hit. Thank goodness for two things: one that he was sufficiently determined to listen and work hard to rectify the problem, and two that he possesses a strong enough character to put such misses behind him. I had noticed that immediately when he played in Zimbabwe the previous winter. He had scored a duck and then dropped a sitter of a catch in Bulawayo but was still clapping and encouraging his team mates for the rest of the match. Weaker characters would have sulked and retreated into their shell.

Which is what we could have easily done as a team after the beating at Lord's. We were being written off in every quarter. There were some silly things being said. Changes were called for, but thankfully we resisted. Or I did, anyway.

For a meeting of the selectors was called on the Tuesday after the Test. That was unusual. In fact, it had never been done before. Naturally, I queried why and David Graveney said rather insipidly: 'We just want to discuss the performance of the team.' I found that strange.

It was now that I started believing that the other selectors were panicking under pressure from the media. I thought they were keen to make changes. I told them I disagreed with the meeting. As the Test had finished early I was already back in Cardiff and had to travel all the way up to London on the Tuesday. So I was rather aggressive when the meeting began. I knew this meeting was nothing to do with just mere performance. That could have been done over the phone. The other two denied as much, but were in the middle of an unconvincing argument when John Carr popped his head round the door and said: 'The board have agreed for you to increase the squad if you want.' It was obvious then that some talk had already taken place about selection and convinced me I was right in my view of why the meeting had been held in the first place. But I was having none of it. I insisted we went with the same team. The meeting lasted little more than ten minutes and I was back on the train to Cardiff.

When we arrived at Edgbaston for the second Test we did briefly call up Collingwood because the pitch was unusually damp three days before, but soon sent him away again when it dried.

It had not dried sufficiently in the eyes of one crucial person, however. For when Ponting won the toss he decided to bowl first, a staggering decision when one also considers that minutes previously he had lost McGrath to injury; the fast bowler had stepped on a stray ball during warm-ups and twisted his ankle. I remember being in the dressing room when it was announced that we were to bat first and thinking to myself 'Great toss to win, Vaughany.'

Having the chance to bat first was one thing, though; it was quite another to make Ponting pay. I had suggested to Michael Vaughan after Lord's that the batsmen should be more positive, especially against Warne. He was in total agreement. But I said to him that it was crucial that, when telling the players at the first practice at Edgbaston, there was total conviction from the pair of us.

The batsmen needed to be reminded that they would not be reproached if their positive intentions went wrong. All out for 407 in 79.2 overs on the first day says that they had heeded the message and shed their inhibitions. And also that they had played the right amount of cricket in between Tests. There had been the all-too-predictable calls for them to be all sent back to county cricket, but, as I always did, I looked forward and tried to gauge their physical, and more importantly mental, tiredness further down the line, not just immediately. This created a continuous battle with the counties throughout my time with England, reaching another of many low points after the Old Trafford third Test of this series, which unfortunately was quickly followed by the semifinals of the C&G Trophy.

This was an especially sensitive issue because there was an agreement in place that the players would be available for these matches. Six were due to be involved: Vaughan and Hoggard for Yorkshire, Bell and Giles for Warwickshire, Flintoff for Lancashire and Pietersen for Hampshire. But they were all knackered after two gruelling Test matches; they carryied niggling injuries too. They could not play, not if the good of English cricket, and in particular the winning of the Ashes, was to be considered the utmost priority. Thankfully C&G were very understanding. Not so some of the dinosaurs in the counties, however. It was little surprise to me that I copped so much stick, but it really was so narrow-minded. Further controversy was stirred because it had previously been agreed that between these Tests the team would take part in a Twenty20 match for Vaughan's benefit year.

'How can they play in that and not the C&G?' was the common, misguided question. Quite easily, was my answer. Vaughan's match was nothing more than a bit of a giggle, and certainly no mental or physical hardship. For I never withdrew players for fear of their getting injured. That would have been ridiculous. They could get injured in the nets, in the gym, even on the golf course. As it was, the match was rained off anyway.

The reason for withdrawing them here was because mental fatigue was always more of a worry than physical tiredness. They could not just turn up and play in the C&G semi-final. If they were to approach it properly they would need to do some considerable thinking about it beforehand. They would have to practise the day before, play the game and then report for the Test match again two days later.

After Lord's the players were not quite so jaded so there was the odd one-day game for a few of them, including the Twenty20 finals day for Trescothick and Flintoff which noticeably freed them up mentally. From this I began to think that it was a good idea for players to play a one-day game before a Test, but only if they had had a lot of cricket beforehand.

But probably more important was the work done in the nets by the likes of Vaughan and Strauss. Vaughan had struggled at Lord's (scoring 3 and 4) so I went up to Yorkshire to work with him, while Strauss spent hours at Edgbaston using Merlyn, the proto-type bowling machine capable of replicating Warne. I had been worried for some time about Strauss' method of playing spin and had talked to him about it before Lord's. He had said that he was happy with his method, which was fair enough, but I did also stress that it might be exposed against the very top spinners. And, crucially, Strauss had not faced any of these in his Test career up until then.

The experience of facing Warne at Lord's changed his mind, and so he resolved to work hard to change an ingrained habit. He had been trying to play with the spin, but by using his body rather than his hands, and so was finding himself outside the line of the ball. Basically, whether the ball turned or did not turn from Warne, Strauss could only score in one area – behind square on the leg side.

What he needed to do was, as I explained earlier in my technical chapter, to stay inside the line of the ball. So if the ball did not turn he had a chance of playing through the off side with a straight bat, especially if Warne dropped short outside off stump, and if it did turn he could use his hands to hit it on the leg side, so widening his scoring areas.

In truth, though, Strauss did not have quite enough time between Tests to train his brain to do this. He is a quick learner, but not that quick. And it showed. Twice he succumbed to Warne, the first occasion padding up to a viciously turning leg break which bowled him. If he had played the ball as we had discussed and practised, he would have been fine. He admitted as much afterwards. But, at least, two centuries later in the series (at Old Trafford and the Oval) demonstrated that his graft did eventually pay off. And he had helped Trescothick in getting us off to a cracking start at Edgbaston, boundaries flying everywhere as we rattled along at five an over on that opening day. It was the start of a truly incredible match, worthy of the title *The Greatest Test* given to the subsequent commemorative DVD.

It concluded with a heart-stopping finale on the fourth (Sunday) morning. To some victory had appeared a formality that morning, with Australia ending the previous day – thanks to Harmison snaring Clarke with a peach of a slower ball – still requiring 107 to win with just two wickets remaining. Not to me, it had not. And this was not just me being conservative. It is the way modern cricket has gone, with latter-order batsmen working so hard at their games. It took me a considerable time to persuade England's cricketers to appreciate the value of this.

And it so nearly paid dividends for Australia. Through Warne, Lee and Mike Kasprowicz they managed to get to within two runs of victory before Kasprowicz gloved a ball from Harmison to Geraint Jones. Talk about relief. If we'd gone 2–0 down in the series, that would have been it.

And importantly it was at Edgebaston that we first saw definite signs that the Australians were going to struggle with reverse swing in this series. Flintoff and Simon Jones demonstrated their ability to do this both ways (not just into the right hander as had been the previous norm) and caused all manner of problems. And they were able to do this surprisingly early in the innings because we kept the ball dry. That was our secret for reverse swing – as Waqar Younis had confirmed to me at Glamorgan in 1997 – that we should try to keep sweaty palms off the ball and pick it up with two fingers on the seam. One side could be shined, but the other had to be bone-dry. But still we probably did not expect the Australians to be quite so troubled by this. Nor that they would be quite so honest in publicly admitting their problems with it.

Mind you, they could hardly disguise them. They were no more glaringly obvious than during the third Test at Old Trafford. Simon Katich shouldering arms to Flintoff and Clarke doing the same to Jones indicated batsmen who were unsure which way the ball was swinging. Jones grabbed a Test best 6–53 in another nailbitingly exciting match, which climaxed in an extraordinary final day where thousands were locked out of the ground. Never before did I think I might miss the warm-ups because of congestion outside a ground. My wife was so shocked by the scenes when she arrived later in a taxi that she feared there had been a bomb scare.

The only scare was for Australia, who somehow managed to escape with a draw, nine wickets down. They were lucky, both with the weather which lopped crucial time off on the Saturday and with the playing and missing of their batsmen, even on the last day. Captain Ponting was still doing that after he had reached three figures in a rearguard 156.

It was a match littered with outstanding individual perform-ances, however. There was a memorable hundred for Vaughan and the milestone of 600 Test wickets for Warne. He finished this series with forty wickets; some achievement for a man who ended up on the losing side. I cannot really pay him a high enough com-pliment. He is truly a great of the game, a marvellous competitor with an always-thinking cricket brain. What really marks him as a cut above most other bowlers is how easily he can change from attack to defence, and back again. Muttiah Muralitharan cannot do that; he just grinds you down.

Shame then that we could not quite grind Australia down at the death, but an untimely bout of cramp for Simon Jones probably did not help. No matter, we travelled to Trent Bridge confident and it showed, even if Jones, having taken another five-wicket haul in the first innings, broke down with a more serious injury. We made Australia follow on for the first time in seventeen years and deserved to win.

Mind you, what I have not said before is that I probably would not have enforced that follow-on. That is not to criticize Vaughan's captaincy – he is a marvellous skipper who completely out-cap-tained Ponting in this series – but rather to confirm my long-held view about the issue. As assistant coach Matthew Maynard said of the follow-on at the time: 'It is overrated.' And, of course, I could see why Vaughan did it. And he was not to know that Jones would break down.

Interestingly at Old Trafford we had had Australia in a position where we might have been able to ask them to follow on, but we had already decided not to because of the time the bowlers had already spent in the field. Here it was less clear-cut. If we had bowled them out for 150 it would have been simple. But they scraped to 218, 259 behind.

Just before they were all out at Trent Bridge, Vaughan came off the field to go to the toilet.

'What do you think I should do?' he asked me.

'What do you want to do?' I replied.

'I want to make them follow on,' he said without hesitation.

'Do it then,' I said, 'but just ask the bowlers first. Make sure that they want to do it.' They did. But they were getting carried away with the emotion of things. It might have been costly.

I did not want us chasing more than 100 in our last innings. Warne was always going to be a handful bowling into the rough. So when the target was 129 I was a little worried. I still thought we would win though. I was thinking; 'If we played out this chase five times, we should win three of them by five wickets, and the other two by seven or eight wickets.' If only. We won by three wickets, which tells you everything about the tension involved in getting those runs. It was satisfying that Giles should be the one to hit the winning runs. When we had been four wickets down, he had come into the coach's room and said 'I'm not sure how I am going to cope.'

'At least you are one of the players who can do something about this,' I said. 'Once you cross that line, you will be fine. It is programmed into you. This is why you practise so hard – for situations like this.'

With Giles at the end was Matthew Hoggard. I had also spoken to him. 'Just look to score off the seamers. Don't even try and score off Warne,' I had said. Thankfully he did, hitting a Lee full toss through extra cover for four as he made the most important 8 not out of his life. It had been an important match in general for him. His part in the series had been minimal up until then, but here on a ground known for its conduciveness to swing since the building of a new stand, he bowled excellently, especially in taking three early first innings wickets.

But still there were more telling contributions, and not just Jones' wickets. I say without hesitation that Flintoff's first innings century was the finest innings I saw him play. It was pure class; not just random big hitting, but full of judicious decision-making and excellent execution. He put on 177 with Geraint Jones in a priceless partnership. It was Jones' best moment in an England shirt. He'd had considerable stick at Old Trafford after he had made a couple of mistakes with the gloves on the Saturday. It was a rain-affected day and the Sunday newspaper writers had little else to write about than Jones, so he really copped it. So now to bat so well for his 85 in Nottingham, the home ground of his rival Chris Read, was special.

It was the other Jones we were worrying about for the last Test at the Oval. Who would replace him? It was the first time we had to make a change all series, and, as it was, he proved irreplaceable. It was a sad indictment of the county game at the time that there was no young fast bowler screaming out to be selected in such a big game. Chris Tremlett had been involved in the squad for most of the summer but we were not convinced that he was right mentally or physically (he had had a knee niggle). We even considered veterans like Andrew Caddick and Darren Gough, but unfortunately both were injured.

So we called up James Anderson, but I still had concerns about his last Test at the Wanderers in South Africa during the previous winter. There he had come in as a one-off for Simon Jones and struggled. That could easily happen again, so in the end we went for Collingwood, hardly a like-for-like replacement and viewed in many quarters as a conservative selection. But we felt that overall he would offer more than any of the other contenders. He had done well in the one-day series against Australia and was certainly not going to be intimidated by them, even if this was a very different Ashes Test from any other I knew.

It was so different that the nerves almost got to me on the last morning. I was unsure about revealing this in *Ashes Regained* for fear of showing signs of personal weakness, but decided to in order to emphasize what that final day really meant. We were 40 runs ahead with one wicket down, needing to bat out the day. I had had breakfast alone and was returning to my room when I began retching. It took me completely by surprise, and rather disorientated me. All I could think of, bizarrely, was how I might not be able to clean my teeth. But it soon passed and I was fine by the time I reached the ground. Just imagine how the poor players were feeling. And I did not want to unnerve them.

Mind you, that would be pretty difficult to do to Pietersen. Nothing seems to faze him, and it was his 158 which saved us on that final day. He had arrived at the crease with McGrath on a hat-trick – Ian Bell had been out first ball to complete a pair – to survive a ferocious appeal first ball, thankfully the ball brushing his shoulder rather than his glove. That was not lucky, but two reprieves on 0 and 15 were. The first was a hard chance off Warne, the ball rebounding off keeper Adam Gilchrist's gloves on to Hayden's leg. Nobody really remembers that, though. It is Warne's drop at first slip off Lee that everyone remembers. In truth it was a dolly, but I did not go along with those who attributed Warne with losing Australia the Ashes. There were plenty of other factors, you know – and I don't include the bad weather which affected this last Test in them, because I think we would still have been good enough without that.

But Pietersen played quite magnificently, hitting seven sixes in a stunning display. It was confirmation that he is an international cricketer of the highest class. But we probably knew that anyway.

Just watching him at work in the nets had told me that. He is such a smart cricketer; always thinking, always working on different facets of his game, always plotting a game plan for a particular bowler or a particular pitch. His net sessions alone are worth watching, and fellow players do stop and take a look. As for when he bats in the middle, you never see too many idling around doing other things then. It is always must-see stuff.

This innings took Pietersen to 473 runs for the series, top of the pack, but I must make mention of Trescothick who was second with 431. He did not get a hundred, but for me he was the unsung hero of the series. Australia came into the series thinking they had the wood over him, having previously exposed him to catches behind the wicket. So there was proof positive here at the Oval that he had conquered such problems: Lee was bowling to him early on with just two slips. And the ball was swinging around on a bouncy pitch.

Another example of how Australian perceptions had altered came when Giles came on to bowl. Langer went for him immediately, wildly in a way, as fourteen runs were hit from his first over. It was recognition of the role Giles was playing; a sign of respect. However, if they thought that by removing Giles it might overtax the other members of our attack, then they were horribly wrong, especially where Flintoff was concerned. He bowled 34 overs in Australia's only innings, including an unchanged spell of 14.2-3-30-4 on the fourth day. Boy, did he deserve his second five-wicket haul in Test cricket. To borrow my comments from *Ashes Regained*: 'I was going to say that he bowled with the heart of a lion. That would be wrong. Three lions more like.' Throughout the series, too.

However, when Flintoff was out cheaply just before lunch on that last day, leaving us 126–5, I was a little perturbed. In my mind we had to reach 250 for the game to be interesting – they would have had to chase anything – and 280 for it to be safe. But soon we were 199–7. Pietersen needed help. Giles was the man; to the tune of a Test best 59. Some time to do that.

We were eventually all out for 335 and Australia faced four balls from Steve Harmison before accepting the offer of bad light. We knew the match was drawn and the series was ours then, but, ridiculously, we had to wait sixteen minutes until the umpires Billy Bowden and Rudi Koertzen strolled out on to the pitch and removed the bails. The Ashes now were ours.

Or rather the team's. That was how I felt, as always. That was why I did not really want to go out on to the pitch and join in the celebrations. I had never done so before, and never did again. The problem was that others in the management team wanted to join in. And then Vaughan shouted: 'I want all the management team on the stage with us.' What to do? I felt horribly out of place bouncing around on the stage, although the lap of honour was slightly easier because I wanted to say thank you to the fans who had been unstinting in their support all summer. I made sure that I slipped off first, though, sneaking back up the steps so that I could spend a few minutes on my own in the dressing room. I really enjoyed that quiet moment of reflection. It was a moment of pure contentment.

Not much else was quiet that evening. The celebrations were noisy and boisterous. And rightly so. But once we had got the bus back to the hotel – a unique experience in a home Test because we normally travelled in our own cars – I went to bed. I even got in before Marina, who had been out with all the other wives and girlfriends. My 10.30 p.m. turning-in time was obviously considerably before the rest of the team. Their celebrations went on and on.

Even into the next day that is, for we had an open-top bus parade ending in Trafalgar Square. This had been talked about during the Oval Test – even made it into the public domain – and had made me thoroughly uncomfortable. I only wanted to talk about it once the Fat Lady was singing, not while she was still clearing her throat. And I was not even sure that many people would turn out to greet us. How wrong I was. The scenes in front of us beggared belief. I stood there in Trafalgar Square and thought long and hard about what I had achieved in cricket. This was undoubtedly the pinnacle.

And then it was off to Downing Street to meet the Prime Minister before going back to Lord's for the symbolic handing back of the Ashes to the MCC. And there was that text telling me I would be getting a British passport. Some day.

The passport thing had become a real issue around the Test. The media were latching on to it left, right and centre. A reporter even began to pester my daughter, Nicola, at the family home in Cape Town about it. That was out of order, and I made sure I spoke to the journalist concerned.

I wanted to go home to Cape Town after all the celebrations. Marina and I had been booked on a flight that Tuesday evening but there was a press conference on the Wednesday morning. Those blasted things! OK, on this occasion it was not too bad. The questions could not be that searching. And our postponed flight was first class after all. England usually fly business class but this was a nice recognition of what had been achieved.

Once at home in Cape Town I began to realize the stress and emotion my family had been suffering for me. They had been playing every ball of that series with the England team. My mother had watched every ball from her retirement home in Durban, wearing an England shirt at the end too. 'They're going crazy here,' she had told me on the phone. All my brothers were watching too. Colin and his family in Switzerland; John, Gordon and Allan and their families in South Africa. My sister Ann had taken a day off work to watch the final day's play at the Oval. And during that Nicola had sent Marina a text message 'Still watching but feel physically sick.'

Nicola and her husband Jared had put up some decorations to greet us on our return. There were Union Jacks everywhere, interspersed with 'Congratulations' banners. I liked the card they had made me. It had a picture of the Ashes urn on the front and a couple of nice pictures of me on the back; one of them with my hands on my head looking exasperated, with the words: 'Nobody said it would be easy. Eighteen years had proven this.' But below was a happier picture and the words: 'But he knew it could be done and history was made.' And so it was.

12

Anti-climax

I tried my best. I think we all tried our best. But the feeling of anti-climax just got the better of us. There is no other way of describing what happened when we went to Pakistan after the Ashes win. With all due respect to the country and its people – as I have said, I actually quite liked touring the place – it would have been better if we had been going to somewhere like South Africa or New Zealand straight after the Ashes. After all the euphoria, excitement and fanfare of that famous victory, Pakistan was just too quiet.

Michael Vaughan and I had chatted before the trip and made a conscious decision to work the team especially hard, just we had done in Bangladesh in 2003. And to be fair to the team they did not once complain about the rigorous fitness schedule laid out by Nigel Stockill. The hotels were superb and the gyms and swimming pools within them very good. So we hit them with gusto and really tried hard to bond and prepare ourselves thoroughly. I think we did that – even when Andrew Flintoff and Steve Harmison arrived late from the ICC Super Series they dived uncomplainingly into the graft – but throughout I sensed a strange feeling. I had never experienced it before with this group and it could only have been an Ashes hangover.

It was a tremendous honour for Flintoff and Harmison to be selected for that Super Series, but it was far from ideal. They desperately needed a break after the Ashes but could not get it. So I had to allow them to arrive late. I never liked doing that. Whenever England tour everyone should fly out together from London. That is why I always flew into London from my home in Cape Town to do so. Some people asked me why I never flew straight to various venues – which undoubtedly would have been easier – but I knew that I always had to be with the team.

I'll also admit now that I was very miffed not to be selected as coach of that ICC Rest of the World XI, of which Flintoff and Harmison were a part. Instead India's Kiwi coach John Wright was appointed. Sorry, but that did not make sense. We had just won the Ashes and were above India in the rankings. For me, it was obvious why I was not selected. It was because Sunil Gavaskar was manager of the team. You've already heard of my disregard for him.

So, too, my displeasure with ICC chief executive Malcolm Speed's comments during the Ashes. Interesting then that Speed should pitch up unannounced during this Pakistan tour. In Lahore it was, late in the trip. Phil Neale passed on a message that Speed wanted to see me. 'Whoopsy,' I thought. 'He's here to dress me down for my comments in *Ashes Regained*.'

A meeting was duly arranged, although Speed suggested we did not meet in a public place, probably because he had not told anyone about it – not David Morgan or anyone at the ECB. Boy, it was an uncomfortable meeting. I told him of my disgruntlement at not being selected as coach of the ICC team. 'Nothing to do with me,' he replied rather predictably. He asked why there was such an unhealthy relationship between the two of us. So I told him. I went through all my previously mentioned grievances, especially that meeting in Christchurch in New Zealand. He never admitted being wrong. He tried to sweeten me by wanting to talk about my proposed referral system for the umpires' decisions. I had had enough. 'I don't want to talk about it,' I said bluntly and that was the end of the meeting.

Someone else had also come to see me in Lahore, right at the beginning of the trip. In contrast this was someone with whom I had an excellent relationship – bowling coach Troy Cooley. Again this was a meeting I did not want to be having. But for very different reasons. The ECB, in their infinite wisdom, were stalling on his contract and his home country Australia had come calling. I knew that he would want to go home at some stage but it did not need to be this early. I knew that he had wanted to go through to the World Cup with me, as he had mentioned that to be the case on numerous occasions. So it was little short of a disgrace that the ECB did not allow this to happen. I was fuming that I was about to lose a man for whom I had so much respect. He had already made his mind up and I could not stand in his way.

It was good of Cooley that I was the first to know. It had taken me just one practice session with him – I think it was at Trent Bridge – to realize that this was one quality individual. I heard him explaining his theories of reverse swing to the England bowlers and thought, 'Crikey, we're on the same wavelength here.' When I had first tried to explain them to previous England coaches and players everyone had laughed. They are pretty complicated, mind you, dealing with the principles of flight which I had learnt in my Air Force days, so I will not go into too much detail here.

But even the best argued theories can be proved wrong. For instance, I suspect the weight of any given ball has considerable bearing on swing. An example emerged when I toured England with South Africa A in 1996. I had a net session at Shenley with Jacques Kallis and we took six brand-new balls to the nets for throw-downs. I held them all in the same way, but the first four I threw swung conventionally away from Kallis and the last two reversed into him. We marked those last two, and lo and behold every time they reversed. 'Tis a curious business that.

Just as curious as the mood in Pakistan. It was not as if we were a much changed squad. Yes, Simon Jones had not recovered from that ankle injury which kept him out of the final Ashes Test, but otherwise the only pre-tour selection dilemma concerned the backup spinners for Ashley Giles. If I am honest there wasn't an awful lot to choose from – we will come to the Monty Panesar scenario later – so we went for the experience of Shaun Udal, who had had a good season for Hampshire. We did not really want two left-arm spinners then so we went for Udal's off-breaks.

We also thought that Udal might be able to help the third spinner, Warwickshire's off-spinner Alex Loudon, whom we wanted to bring on. We had seen that he bowled a 'doosra', which I deem vital in this modern game. Finger spinners are always going to struggle unless they can beat the batsmen on both sides of his bat. Yes, everyone was saying that Loudon's 'doosra' was slow and easy to pick, but the trouble was that they were comparing it with that bowled by someone like Muttiah Muralitharan. Instead, they should have been asking what Muralitharan's 'doosra' was like when he first started bowling it and how long it took him to perfect it. I will tell you. It was slow and easy to pick, and took a long time to be ready. It is like every new leg-spinner in Australia being compared to Shane Warne. People easily forget how average Warne was for his first couple of Test series.

In Loudon we saw a complete package because he could obviously bat and field, and we thought that continual work in the nets with Cooley and Udal would benefit him enormously. That would certainly be better for him than bowling indoors for most of the winter at the National Academy. And he immediately made an impact, exciting me greatly. He obviously lacked control but he was soon genuinely dismissing our batsmen in the nets. These were not slog-induced wickets. He clean bowled Trescothick a couple of times with his 'other one' and also beat Vaughan and Flintoff on the outside as they came down the pitch.

I thought the more Loudon bowled the better he would get. All you want to do with the use of the 'doosra' is to cloud the batsman's thinking. It is the same with a fast bowler and his use of a slower ball; a smug batsman might be saying, 'Ah, I can read that' and in the process will be concentrating on that rather than the good balls which should be his primary focus.

So with a spinner four off-breaks might have passed by and he will suddenly think 'I should have scored off them' because he has been looking for the 'doosra'. It is why I think spinners should vary their point of delivery – wide of the crease, close to the stumps or even behind the bowling crease. It gives the batsmen a lot to think about, thereby creating error in their decision-making.

The only other selection issue causing us any pre-tour vexation was whether to play Ian Bell or Paul Collingwood in the Tests. Bell had struggled in the Ashes but we were still keen to give him a run in the side. However, we were also worried that if we played two spinners – which always seemed likely – we would need an extra bowler and in that regard, as previously mentioned, Collingwood was some way ahead of Bell. We needed to make that decision early, so when Bell was left out of the second warm-up match against Pakistan A at Bagh-e-Jinnah in Lahore, the writing was on the wall for him.

It was quickly scrubbed off, though, as sport demonstrated its never-ending ability to offer unexpected opportunities. Vaughan injured his knee in that match and Bell was now in at three. And how he took his chance. He finished the series as our leading run-scorer with 313 runs at an average of 52.

Others were not so good at seizing opportunities. What I was seeing immediately was an inability to concentrate for long periods. It was evident in the two warm-up matches, the first of which was against a PCB Patron's XI at Rawalpindi. It was only human, I suppose. Doubtless the players were saying to themselves, 'I've got to use this opportunity', and I was obviously urging them to, but in the main they just could not.

We did, in fact, win the first game but were humbled in the second by six wickets. We were not helped again, though, by two poorly prepared pitches, both filthy green-tops which were bound to be in stark contrast to the surfaces likely to be encountered in the Test matches. Yes, it is another bugbear of mine, but I cannot believe countries continue to be allowed to get away with this. There needs to be a mutual understanding that touring teams need flat pitches for their preparatory matches so that tours do not have to be lengthened, in case too many players do not receive the requisite practice. We always seemed all too eager to please in England, even if in 2006 the pitch at Worcester for the A team game against Sri Lanka was a little spicy. I only wish the Test match pitches for that series had been so! That was what I had asked for.

Those green-tops are as damaging for bowlers as they are for batsmen because they lose appreciation of the length they are required to bowl. However, nothing was quite as damaging as that injury sustained by Vaughan. Batting on the second day he felt his knee lock as he turned for a run and collapsed in a heap. Not exactly what you want five days before the first Test. Vaughan had obviously had knee problems before (he struggled more than people imagined in the 2005 Ashes) but little did we realize then how serious this would be. It was the start of a long road.

Who to captain now? It was not an easy decision. Andrew Strauss was not in the running back then, so it was a straight choice between Marcus Trescothick and Andrew Flintoff. Neither was ideal, if I am honest. But after his Ashes heroics Flintoff was now obviously being seen in a very different light, and Trescothick still appeared keen to do the job he had done once before. We went with Trescothick for the first Test at Multan.

And it proved to be an eventful match for him. Unfortunately it was not all good news, as, like Vaughan, he also began a long and arduous road, his being a mental rather than physical battle. He scored a magnificent 193 but he received news that his father-in-law had suffered a severe head injury falling off a ladder. Trescothick was affected badly, as you would expect, and there was much debate as to whether he should go home. He eventually decided to stay, but it had been difficult to know what to advise in this situation. I mean, what if things had turned out far worse? You just did not know.

What I do know is that we threw away that first Test. We played really well for four days and then botched it up chasing a meagre 198 on the last day. We just did not show any patience in being bowled out for 175, stranded 22 runs short. How different this whole winter's cricket might have been if we had scored those runs.

The second Test in Faisalabad was a draw but it was not without incident, certainly not on the second day when first we had a controversial run-out involving Inzamam-ul-Haq, then a gas cylinder exploding as if a bomb had gone off and then, while that situation was being clarified, we had the unusual behaviour of Shahid Afridi who pirouetted on the pitch, which scuffed it up for Pakistan's spinners, of which he, of course, was one.

Afridi should not have been allowed to continue in the game after that. The authorities should look at introducing a red card for such instances. But it was the furore after the run-out that irked me more. Just to recap, Inzamam had passed his hundred when he played a ball from Steve Harmison back to the bowler. Harmison picked the ball up and hurled it back at the stumps with a bit more accuracy than Simon Jones had shown with Matthew Hayden in the previous summer. It hit and there was an appeal for a run-out. The umpires consulted and called for a verdict from the third umpire, who eventually gave Inzamam out. It was the wrong decision because Inzamam was taking evasive action. I had no truck with it, but I did with the many misconceptions resulting from it.

There was only one person to blame in my opinion. That was the third umpire, Nadeem Ghauri, a home country selection who did not know the laws. Blame was being thrown in all manner of directions. First, some of the British press were berating Harmison. That was disgraceful. As I said, everybody shows aggression by throwing the ball back in that manner. Why should we not do it?

Second, the on-field umpires were castigated for referring the decision to the third umpire. But they had to do that. The laws state that the batsman must make his ground before he is allowed to take evasive action and not suffer the consequences of a run out. You can't wander halfway down the pitch and then jump up and say you were taking evasive action. So if you were ever able to study the incident closely you would see that only about 1cm of Inzamam's heel was over the line before he jumped up. How could the square leg umpire, Darrell Hair, be sure of that? It had to be referred for that reason. Once that was ascertained Inzamam should have been given not out.

We should have drawn the final Test as well, but that issue of being unable to maintain lengthy periods of concentration reared its ugly head again on the final day, as we collapsed dramatically in losing eight wickets for 43 runs in just seventy minutes. As the month of December dawned we lost the match by an innings and 100 runs, no way to end the year in which we had regained the Ashes.

The injury situation was not improving either. Ashley Giles had bravely battled through the series with his troublesome hip, not once using it as an excuse for less effective performances as he struggled to get through his action fully. But it just became too bad in Lahore and we were forced to go in with only one spinner in Udal. That left a tricky decision for the fourth seamer's spot between Liam Plunkett and James Anderson. We went for Plunkett, handing him a Test debut, and he did not let us down on what had become a flat pitch by the time Pakistan batted.

We were criticized for squandering an opening stand of 101 between Vaughan (opening because Strauss had returned home for the birth of his first child) and Trescothick by being bowled out for 288 in that first innings. But the truth is that the opening pair played out of their skins for their respective half-centuries. Rarely will you see such good batting in a Test match. It was incredible, and against quality pace bowling from Shoaib Akhtar, Rana Naved-ul-Hasan and Mohammad Sami too. Paul Collingwood's two innings of 96 and 80 in this match deserve no less praise.

Despite the gloom of a Test-series defeat there were some lighter moments for our entertainment during this tour. At its start when I had been fretting about our mental attitude, I had decided that we needed to be careful about reacting impatiently to the many delays and inconveniences you often experience in the subcontinent, simply because that is what the locals are used to. And then an idea came to me. I had heard some of the players saying the letters 'PT', so I asked Matthew Hoggard what they meant. 'Posh twats!' he said, referring to the jocular nickname used for the public school-educated duo of Strauss and Alex Loudon.

'But PT can also stand for the virtues of Patience and Tolerance,' I thought. I could see that this nickname was irritating Strauss and Loudon a little, so I thought this might be a good way of deflecting some heat from them and using this in a more positive manner. I told the players that whenever they could see such an irritating situation arising someone should shout out the letters PT. This might be, say, if a group of players were waiting a long time for food to be served in a restaurant (which is common) and one person was obviously becoming agitated. It seemed to work, even during matches sometimes, despite it being a bit gimmicky.

PT was required when a trip to a clothing factory near Faisalabad went horribly wrong. We really should have known better. Caution is always the watchword on the subcontinent when somebody offers to arrange a visit to such a place. But this one seemed attractive enough with its promise of designer Ralph Lauren clothing for sale. As soon as we arrived we sensed this was not what we wanted it to be. There were factory workers hanging out of the windows to catch a glimpse of us and it was obvious this was no low-key visit. We were ushered down a corridor which was so narrow that you could barely turn around and into a hall where there were mountains of food laid out. 'Hang on, we only want to buy some shirts,' we were saying. It was a day off and no time for a public relations exercise. But there were brothers, sisters, uncles, aunties, cousins, nephews and nieces of the organizer wanting to meet us. It was chaos. I spoke to the organizer and we were eventually taken down some equally narrow stairs where the clothes on offer were nothing like we had been promised. Underpants were all I could see. 'We're leaving,' I said. There were a lot of people in that factory not happy, but we had been conned. Our only problem was that the organizer was the local chief of police (he was to be seen as very much in charge on the boundary's edge when the gas canister exploded during the second Test). So it was noticeable that things were not quite as easy for us on that front for the rest of our stay in that city.

Not that this trip became easier in any respect. We still had the one-dayers to negotiate. For a start I had not been happy about the selection for these. I had wanted Lancashire's Sajid Mahmood to be picked. He bowls at 90 mph and can reverse swing the ball – that is what you need in Pakistan. But the other selectors would not have it. David Graveney told me that we could not pick him because Lancashire had not selected him in the previous county season. I did not care. It was like Glamorgan not picking Simon Jones in 2004 when we had released him. It was up to them. I liked what I had seen and wanted Mahmood. His like are rare gems and any side should be picking them.

I think Graveney and Geoff Miller were a little embarrassed because they had not thought about him. Instead they gave me the same old names; good, honest, county-standard English bowlers like Jon Lewis, Kabir Ali, Ryan Sidebottom and Glen Chapple. Eventually Graveney made some investigations and found that Mahmood had a foot injury and could not come anyway, but I had been outvoted again. This friction with the other selectors was starting to grate. I'd had enough of it, to tell the truth. Mind you, I had to chuckle when Graveney told me later that winter that he had seen Mahmood in the nets at Loughborough and was impressed with his speed. 'He could be useful in India,' he told me. Indeed.

The one-day series was a mirror image of the Test series; we started well – winning the first match in Lahore – but just could not sustain it and lost three on the bounce before grabbing an inconsequential win in the last match of the series. And injuries reared their ugly head again. Vaughan and Giles had gone home with their respective knee and hip ailments, and Pietersen was to join them after just two of the one-day matches with a rib problem. He was struggling and there was no way he could continue. But I did have a word with him before he left, telling him I did not want to hear stories of his swanning around, living it up in clubs while we were still battling away on a difficult trip. 'You don't hear of Vaughan doing things like that,' I said. To be fair, Pietersen agreed and I did not expect to hear a peep from him when he went home.

Lo and behold he had scarcely been home a minute when there was an article in the *News of the World* in which he was supporting the inclusion of Darren Gough in the one-day team. So, all of a sudden, he had become a selector. And then, even more gallingly, he was seen on television in the audience as Gough appeared on *Strictly Come Dancing*.

I was straight on the phone. I was seething. Rarely did I give a player such a blast. Trescothick overheard the conversation and later said he had never heard anything like it. 'Who do you think you are?' I screamed. 'You've only been on the scene two minutes!' I do not swear very often, but I could not help myself here. He said that he had not written the article – that old chestnut blaming the ghostwriter. Take the money, take the rap, I told him. 'How can you look the likes of Liam Plunkett in the eye now?' I asked. 'You've basically said they're useless.'

As for the television appearance, he said that he was big mates with Gough. 'What? Have you not got any mates out here?' I bellowed before slamming the phone down. I think he got the message. To his credit he has talked honestly since about that period of his life where he was young and impressionable, and making mistakes. He has since learnt from those errors in his judgement then, and my relationship with him after that was always very good. In particular I always really liked the way he thought deeply about his cricket on and off the field.

There was another good reason for my disgruntlement during the one-day series – the BBC *Sports Personality of the Year* scenario. Not the fact, of course, that we won team of the year and that Flintoff won the main prize, but the reporting of what exactly happened and its possible consequences to the next day's heavy defeat, leading to an all-too-inevitable slamming from my old friend Geoff Boycott. The awards show happened the night before the second one-dayer in Lahore – the time difference doing us no favours – but what was misreported was that we all stayed up late. In fact, nobody bar Flintoff stayed up beyond midnight. That was not ideal for us but it was hardly all-night stuff as reported by Boycott. We maybe lost two hours' sleep. Flintoff stayed up till four. The BBC had wanted all of us to do the same, but I had refused. In fact, they had wanted Flintoff to fly home and miss the match. Again I refused. It was a huge honour – I fully appreciated that – but the timing was just unfortunate.

I think we got our timing right with Steve Harmison, though. We made a decision to drop him for the fourth one-dayer, at Rawalpindi. As he can, he was cruising again, not practising with the required intensity, especially during warm-ups. He wanted to play, but we said no. We told the press that he had flu – he did have a bit of something – but he knew why he was not playing. It worked, too, because for the last match he prepared with purpose again, running in rather than just turning his arm over. And he was rewarded with good figures of 10-3-27-1, as we won by six runs.

Talking of rewards, they were in order before our next tour, of India in February 2006. By that I mean receiving the awards bestowed upon us by the Queen in her New Year's Honours List. It was a great honour to go to Buckingham Palace and receive my OBE, a wonderful day to cherish and remember for myself, my wife Marina and my daughter Nicola who accompanied me.

Selection for India was tricky. With Ashley Giles injured, we needed another spinner. And I will admit that I did not want Monty Panesar to go. With the benefit of hindsight I know I was wrong and it was a very good selection, but 'Where did he suddenly come from?' was my first question.

He had not been among that winter's academy intake, yet suddenly after Pakistan his name was on everyone's lips. I thought a media bandwagon had started. I recall one very heated phone call with David Graveney while I was back at home in South Africa, because I was insistent on Alex Loudon going along with Shaun Udal.

I have already stated why I like Loudon's bowling. You have got to spin the ball both ways in the subcontinent. The ball obviously turns consistently there but if it is only going the one way it is easy to play. Having said that, though, I do think that for the right-handed batsman playing the ball turning into him – when it is turning big – is more difficult to counter. That goes against the old-fashioned thinking, and I also think the ball swinging into a batsman early on is more difficult to counter than the ball swinging away. But if the batsman knows where his off stump is then leaving the ball turning sharply away from him is relatively easy; when it is coming back at him that judgement is all the more difficult. That is why I wanted Udal.

Anyway we ended up taking Udal, Panesar and Ian Blackwell as spinners to India. Sadly Giles was not to be the only injury problem as a catalogue of misfortune overtook us before the first Test in Nagpur. India is a hard enough place to tour without such bad luck. On our last tour there we had been similarly affected and lost 1–0 with a young side, so we had to hope this time we could fight even harder. For that was our only option when four days before the first Test Trescothick broke down and had to return home with his stress-related illness. And then two days later Vaughan and Simon Jones were on a plane home too with their dodgy knees. We faced criticism for taking Vaughan in the first place. But what do you do? Do you leave him at home and then find out he is OK? How annoying would that be? Or do you bring him out for a couple of weeks and monitor him? We obviously decided on the latter and unfortunately it did not work out.

Vaughan broke down in Baroda and we immediately asked Trescothick to take over in the three-day match against the Indian Board President's XI. Sadly, it proved too much for him. I had heard that he had not been sleeping well, but that is not unusual for anyone on tour so I had thought little of it. But when Trescothick was batting during our second innings on the last day somebody mentioned, 'Tres is acting very strangely.' Sure enough, after he was out for a decent 32 (he looked in good nick despite everything) he walked off with head bowed and clearly in distress. Immediately somebody said to me 'We've got a problem.' I walked into the dressing room to see this young man crying his eyes out. He was finished, gone. I said 'What's wrong, Tresy?'

'I don't know,' he said very emotionally.

'What are you going to do?' I asked. With that he got up and walked outside in full view of all the Indian side and their officials.

'No, no, Tres, you've got to get back inside,' I said anxiously. He was embarrassing himself by going outside. I fetched the doctor Peter Gregory and suggested he take Trescothick back to his room at the hotel.

It was then that Gregory told me that he had been staying up most nights with Trescothick. I did not realize it was that bad. 'He just won't sleep, Duncan,' said Gregory. There was nothing else for it but for Trescothick to go home. He did not even want to go back with someone else to his room to pack. But he did so eventually and we booked him on the first available flight. We even sent a security guard to fly with him just to check he was OK. They had to fly first from Baroda to Mumbai, then on to Dubai where the guard left him, making sure he was on the flight back to London. The whole episode was awful. I like Trescothick very much and I think that made it worse. I never wanted to see someone in that sort of state again. Sadly, I would.

There were other problems, too. As well as back trouble for Paul Collingwood and Kevin Pietersen we also had real problems with stomach ailments. In fact, it was the twelfth day of the tour before every single member of the party was together on the bus going to practise. Previous to that there was always someone being left in their sick-bed at the hotel.

Mind you, by the time we got to Nagpur for the first Test nobody wanted to stay in the hotel. I have never stayed in a worse establishment. Never before on any cricket tour had I asked to change rooms but when Vaughan departed for home I asked if I could have his. The problem was that the place was situated in the middle of a triangle, which had the main highway running on two sides and the main railway line on the third. Talk about noise. All those blasted horns. Indian drivers all use their car horns, all of the time. They use them to say that they are on the road rather than to get out of the way. The airport was not too far away either, just for good measure.

Things could have been worse, though. The original itinerary for this tour had been horrendous. It had been concocted by former president Jagmohan Dalmiya but, with him gone, the ECB could negotiate more sensibly. The initial itinerary had Tests in Ahmedabad, Nagpur and Mumbai and seven one-dayers in outposts like Goa, Indore, Guwahati, Faridabad, Cuttack, Cochin and Visakhapatnam. That was just not on; the travelling would have been awful. We would now play our three Tests at Nagpur, Mohali and Mumbai and the sequence of the one-day internationals was changed to Delhi, Faridabad, Goa, Cochin, Guwahati, Jamshedpur and Indore. Not exactly a breeze, but a vast improvement, in logistical terms anyway. However, with our patched-up side we lost the one-day series 5–1 (with one rained off).

We drew the first Test at Nagpur, which I considered some achievement given those problems presented to us beforehand. We had an instant decision to make on the captaincy and Andrew Flintoff keenly took the reins. He really did want to do the job and it was good to see him accepting it so readily and seriously, a fact emphasized when he made the decision not to return home for the birth of his second child.

The injury crisis meant a late call for Essex's young left-handed batsman Alastair Cook. He had come out to Pakistan as cover and had immediately impressed with his character and work ethic. As I have said before, Nasser Hussain was someone I often phoned to bounce ideas off and enquire about various players. He never plugged anyone without good reason. So when he had raved about

Cook I was genuinely excited. Even more so, when I saw him. He was definitely one for the future.

That he suddenly became one for the present was a shock. But not to the young man himself. Flown from the A tour in the West Indies along with James Anderson he immediately stepped in to score 60 in the first innings and an incredible unbeaten century in the second. Not bad for starters.

He did not do quite as well in Mohali, like the rest of the team really, as defeat came by nine wickets complete with another injury as Steve Harmison left for home with a hurt shin. And even Cook himself fell victim to an upset stomach on the morning of the third Test at Mumbai. It was a shame because he missed a thrilling win, against all the odds, if the truth be known. His absence gave Owais Shah, also summoned earlier from the West Indies, a Test debut which he grabbed with both hands – even if they seemed to have cramp in them quite a bit! – to make a first innings 88 as we took control of the match with 400.

But that was not enough. When India reached 75–3 at lunch on the final day we needed something else and it was provided by one of the most motivational moments I have ever witnessed in sport. The players were sitting around the dressing room, looking very weary after another long session in the heat. Then all of a sudden Matthew Hoggard put the Johnny Cash song 'Ring of Fire' on the iPod, and as it blared out of the speakers every single member of the team joined in, singing at the tops of their voices and clapping too. The Indian team dressing room was right next door and they must have realized that this was now a team seriously up for the challenge. And we were. Upon the resumption India lost seven wickets for 25 runs in just 89 balls. It was one of those moments you could never repeat. You could never stage such an off-the-cuff act of togetherness again.

For such an inexperienced side to win this match really did

give me pleasure, and it did not pass without notice that, on that final day when wickets were needed under pressure, they were provided by Udal (4–14), who outbowled Panesar.

That was why I wanted Udal to start the next home series against Sri Lanka as our sole spinner. I was adamant about that. If you are playing one spinner he has got to bat, in my opinion. I will always stand by that. And I always did, even when it became a hugely contentious issue in Australia the following winter. It is so important in today's cricket that you perform in at least two of the three disciplines.

But the other selectors wanted Panesar and that was that. I was happier with the other awkward selection problem, though – the preference for Cook over Ian Bell. Bell had done well in Pakistan but not so well in India. Some were saying that he was mentally weak, especially after his problems against Australia, but I never thought it was that.

To me it was more a technical problem. Bell's top hand was positioned too far round the front of the bat, so, biomechanically in order to keep his front elbow up, he had to open the face of the bat slightly. When the ball came back at him he therefore had a problem keeping the blade straight. There was no doubt in my mind that talent-wise Bell was the better player than Cook, but at that stage we felt that Bell had become so obsessed with his batting that he was neglecting other areas of his game, like his fielding and fitness. I spoke to him in India about that and, to be fair, he took the advice in the appropriate manner.

If only the respective county groundsmen, probably under instruction from their bosses, had been so receptive when we advised them of the type of pitches we required that summer. Because the three presented to us for the series against Sri Lanka were terrible. The Sri Lankans could not have been happier if they were playing in Galle. We knew that whenever we went to Sri Lanka we would find pitches to suit the home team, but even there one – usually Kandy, where we often did well – was more conducive to our strengths.

Here the Sri Lankans had all three to their liking. What we wanted against this team were three fast and bouncy strips with a good covering of grass. So what if the matches only lasted three days? If you want to be the best team in the world you have to be ruthless. But no, the counties wanted their five days of action and in doing so brought Muttiah Muralitharan into the equation.

People will say that we did not win the first Test at Lord's because we dropped an inordinate number of catches, and we did, but our quicker seamers were nullified there, the pitch annoyingly suiting their dobbers like Chaminda Vaas. As for the catches I have no real explanation. It did often happen for some reason to England sides at Lord's. It was as if when one or two went down a disease was spreading. Even our better catchers like Paul Collingwood and Andrew Strauss were affected. Maybe it was because we had only been back from India a couple of weeks. It is always in the field that the tiredness gets you.

The second Test victory at Edgbaston by six wickets looks easy on reflection. Was it heck. The pitch again. Chasing just 78 to win was difficult, let me tell you, with Muralitharan spinning it like a top. I was asked before our final innings what sort of total we would not mind chasing. 'One hundred and ninety,' I said. I was being very generous. I knew even 120 might be beyond us, given the conditions. Thankfully Cook showed good composure to score 34 not out and see us home.

I took a gamble during this game. I did something I think I may have only done once before. I exerted pressure upon the medical staff to go against their wishes. Liam Plunkett had been struggling with a shoulder injury which required an injection. As a result I was told Plunkett could not bowl in Sri Lanka's second innings. He had bowled excellently in the first innings, taking 3–43, and I could see this match slipping away. I needed him to bowl. 'On your head be it,' said the medical people. Plunkett took 3–17. Phew, it paid off.

Did Kevin Pietersen's outrageous reverse hit for six pay off, though? That shot off Muralitharan was the talk of the Test. There is no way I would ever berate him for that, but I knew he had to be careful. Sooner or later he had to go on and get the really big scores to be a great batsman. But he was still learning his trade then. His dismissal immediately afterwards here triggered a collapse in which we lost our remaining four wickets for 5 runs. Ah, that worry about the tail. That is why the spinner has to bat. Plunkett may become a Test number eight one day but not yet. It will take time.

It was a summer when the seam bowlers came under much scrutiny, as did new bowling coach Kevin Shine. For all my ire over Troy Cooley's departure I was happy with Shine's appointment. But he had a thankless task with so many inexperienced bowlers to deal with. In fact I am not sure Cooley would have been able to do any better in such a short time.

Gloucestershire's Jon Lewis was constantly being championed. 'He's got to play,' the media kept saying. So we played him at Trent Bridge for the third Test. 'Why's he playing?' they now asked. Because we wanted him to play. Sajid Mahmood needed a break, and, as Matthew Hoggard had proved the previous year against Australia, Trent Bridge favours conventional swing bowlers. But in saying that, we probably did misread the pitch. It started too dry and the cracks opened up so that Muralitharan wreaked havoc at the end. The difference between the two sides, though? Probably the 102 runs their lower order cobbled together in the first innings so that they just scraped a lead. Please do not tell me lower order runs do not count. They do.

So does experience in one-day cricket. Our 5–0 beating in the subsequent one-day series was lambasted as our worst performance ever in such a series. I strongly disagree. First, Sanath Jayasuriya, with his unorthodox methods, has destroyed much better attacks than any we could put out here, with no one of any experience or character to turn to when the going got tough. Secondly, there were much darker days with an experienced side under Nasser Hussain, when we were so poor that we could not bat out the allocated number of overs.

Injuries killed us here. That is not just a lame excuse; it is a pure fact from which there is no escaping. The list was both extensive and expensive: Michael Vaughan, Andrew Flintoff, Simon Jones, Ashley Giles, James Anderson and even Ian Blackwell who had become an important part of our one-day set up during the winter. On top of that Kevin Pietersen and Paul Collingwood missed games during the series through injury.

There were other matters to irritate, not least Lancashire's intransigent stance over their all-rounder Glen Chapple. We were meeting in Southampton on the Sunday before flying to Ireland for a warm-up match ahead of the one-day series. That meeting on Sunday night was important because it was where we would set our goals and discuss key issues about one-day cricket. But Lancashire, and especially their chairman Jack Simmons, were adamant that Chapple should play for them in the C&G Trophy on the Sunday.

I said emphatically no. What really annoyed me was that Lancashire then approached the ECB behind my back and were permitted to play Chapple, as long as he flew by helicopter down to Southampton immediately after their game against Derbyshire. What sort of support was I getting from the ECB there? None.

When we had nets in Ireland on the Monday I even forgot that Chapple had played the previous day. So there he was bowling as much as the others during practice when I suddenly realized. 'Stop bowling, Chappy,' I shouted. 'You've had enough.'

Surprise, surprise, Chapple broke down during the match against Ireland, his sole one-day international at the time of writing. Lancashire should take a long, hard look at themselves. Chapple had waited so long for this opportunity and in an instant of selfishness his county could have ruined his England career. Oh yes, and that was another one to add to our injury list for the series.

It made life extremely difficult for skipper Andrew Strauss. I thought he did well in the circumstances. Indeed, I thought he had done so in the two Tests after he had taken over from Flintoff, whose ankle had played up after the first Test at Lord's. Whether that was because he had bowled over fifty overs in the match we will never know for sure, but it would appear so. Monty Panesar should have bowled much more in that match to give the seamers a break, but did not do so because he was ineffective.

But now towards the end of the one-dayers I felt we needed some clarity on the captaincy issue. Between Strauss and Flintoff that is, because I still considered Vaughan the captain of England. Just because he was injured you could not take away the captaincy. This was the man who had regained the Ashes, remember.

I met with the selectors after the fourth one-dayer at Old Trafford and we agreed that Strauss should be appointed for the rest of the summer. This was even though Flintoff was still planning a comeback that summer (as it was, he broke down again playing for Lancashire at Kent). David Graveney said he would speak to Strauss and Flintoff.

So off we went to the last one-dayer at Headingley and I thought it a good idea to have a chat with Strauss about the composition of the Test side for the forthcoming series against Pakistan. 'Why are you talking to me about this?' asked Strauss.

'Have the selectors not told you you're captain?' I stuttered.

They had not. I immediately phoned Graveney. He said he still needed to speak to Flintoff. Fair enough. Soon Graveney called back. 'We've got a problem,' he said. 'Fred has said he doesn't mind as long as he gets confirmation that he will be captain for the Ashes.'

'We can't guarantee that,' I said.

'That will really upset him,' replied Graveney.

What most annoyed me about this was that I was being used as a filter. The player/coach relationship was being harmed by this to-and-fro of opinion. And if Flintoff was unhappy, then so was Strauss. So Strauss called for a meeting. He had his doubts about captaining if Flintoff was then going to get the job for the Ashes.

I had a feeling that Flintoff would not be fit anyway so we persuaded Strauss to take the job. Flintoff was due to be right for the second Test at Old Trafford. That would have meant Ian Bell dropping out after the first Test, even though he had scored a century. But because I was not convinced in my own mind that Flintoff would be right, I did not release Bell to play for Warwickshire after Lord's. Warwickshire were not happy, but it did not do Bell any harm. He added two more hundreds in the next two Tests when Flintoff did pull up.

We drew the first Test at Lord's and were criticized for not declaring earlier. We controlled that game by scoring 528 in our first innings, a reflection of an increased work ethic after the doom and gloom of the one-day series. So why should we risk losing by setting Pakistan something easily attainable on the last day? Always in such situations you find that you are slated by people in the media who have no accountability for their words or decisions. It always amused that those in the media might get, say, one in five decisions or predictions right. But we would never hear about the four wrong ones, just the one right one. And, boy, would we hear about that.

After that 5–0 drubbing the last thing we needed was another loss. Just imagine if that had happened. Imagine how those same critics would have rounded on us even more vitriolically. They wanted us to set Pakistan around 290 on the last day. Did they not remember Headingley in 2001 against Australia where we had been set 315 on a pitch doing plenty and when we won by six wickets it was termed a generous declaration? So we set Pakistan 380. It was a flat pitch, we only had four frontline bowlers and as it was they reached 214-4 with ease, without even trying to push the score along. Two hundred and ninety? You were having a laugh.

Three England batsmen scored centuries in the first innings – Bell (100 not out), Alastair Cook (105) and Paul Collingwood (186) – thus seeing their names posted on the honours board in the Lord's dressing room. It set me thinking. It set me calculating too. Was not it Mr Boycott who questioned my ability to coach players to score hundreds at Test level? I had a look at the board. Since I took over in the English summer of 2000, thirty-two hundreds had been scored by England at Lord's in those seven summers. I counted how many there had been in the previous twenty summers – only sixteen. I know that in not all of those summers had there been two Lord's Tests, but I reckon I did OK.

And so did Old Trafford groundsman Peter Marron in his preparation of the pitch for the second Test. At last we had something which suited us. Marron did get it slightly wrong in saying that it would not turn (Panesar took eight wickets in the match, including 5–72 in the second innings) but I did not think it would either. It had tremendous pace and bounce which suited Steve Harmison down to the ground (sensationally he took 11–94 in the match), but it was a very good pitch on which to bowl both pace and spin. It was not a 'Bunsen Burner', as they say in the trade, with every ball turning square, but one where some balls just went straight on and others ragged wildly. That was because of the platelets on it. When the ball hit the middle of one of those it went straight; when it hit the corner it would spin viciously. There is nothing worse for a batsman, and as early as lunch on the first day Marcus Trescothick had said how hard it was to face Danish Kaneria because of it. It confused everyone.

I caused something of a stink in the media afterwards when I was portrayed as damning Panesar with faint praise because I mentioned he still needed to work on his batting and fielding. I found this annoying because it was already being built up as a personality clash between me and Panesar – just as it always was with Chris Read – but it was nothing of the sort.

It began because we had called up Jamie Dalrymple, who had been our one find of the 5–0 one-day drubbing by Sri Lanka, into the thirteen-man squad for this Test. It was suggested that we were thinking of playing him instead of Panesar. That was rubbish. We had brought him in because we were considering playing two spinners. At Lord's I had spoken to Andrew Flintoff and he was convinced that was what we needed at Old Trafford. If that had been the case we would have left out Sajid Mahmood. But it was not.

All I did after Old Trafford was reiterate the views aired earlier in this book about the role of a finger spinner in international cricket. It was obvious that Panesar needed to work on his batting and fielding, and we also needed to see him bowling on a less helpful pitch. That was all common sense, but there was not much of that flying around after Old Trafford. People were getting carried away with the entire performance and already talking about how we could retain the Ashes. That worried me.

I had spoken to Panesar and explained my philosophy. And I wanted to help him improve. Of course I did; not doing so would be cutting off my nose to spite my face. It was the same with Read. I was always willing to help if requested.

And I was soon helping Read again after Manchester. For Geraint Jones was dropped after this Test. And it was my idea. He was keeping really well and it was interesting how Pakistan's Kamran Akmal – who had supposedly been the bright young thing in keeping when we had been in Pakistan – was struggling in so-called 'difficult' English conditions when Jones has always had to keep in them for half of his games.

But Jones just was not making runs and in losing confidence had forgotten how to construct an innings. Matthew Maynard and I had discussed before this series that this was now a crunch time for Jones and I had said to Maynard that we should give him two Tests. So when Jones did not bat too well at Lord's, Maynard suggested I tell him it might be his last chance. I phoned the selectors and told them my thoughts. It was decided it was best not to tell Jones, mainly because it might affect his keeping. At least then if he was dropped, all he would have to do was sort his batting out, which he could easily do. If he was not keeping well then there would be the same old questions of why we were selecting a keeper whom the critics thought could not keep.

So when Jones only scored 8 in Manchester he had to be replaced. Well, I thought so. The selectors did not. More disagreement. This was the reason why on two occasions in that summer I tendered my resignation as a selector; the second at the end of the Pakistan series when I travelled up to London from Cardiff alone, not even telling my wife what I was going to do, but was talked out of it by Dennis Amiss and John Carr. It was not that I was doubting my ability, just my role. I had had enough.

The selectors thought we should keep a winning side after Old Trafford. I have never agreed with that adage. It is much better for a new or recalled player to go into a confident dressing room rather than one deflated by a defeated player, as is often the case. Also it is worth reflecting that, if a player is not making runs in a winning side, then he must be really struggling.

Just as we had dropped Read during a winning run in the West Indies in 2003/4 so we had to do the same here. It was very hard telling Jones that, but if he was annoyed it was nothing compared to my anger at being overridden in the naming of his replacement. I wanted Sussex's Matt Prior. The other selectors wanted Read. As I have said before, Read will always struggle in Test cricket with the batting technique he has.

Ian Bell has the required batting technique though, and his second hundred on the trot at Old Trafford was nothing short of a masterclass, confirming that he had at last come of age in demonstrating the necessary desire and commitment to play for England. What is more he made it three hundreds on the trot at Headingley in the next Test, a fine achievement, as we made 515 (Kevin Pietersen also made 135) in our first innings. We thought that enough to boss the game but Pakistan, through Younis Khan and Mohammad Yousuf, surprisingly took a lead of 23.

This was a bloody good Test match if you do not mind me saying so. We managed to set them 323 on the final day thanks to a fine skipper's hundred from Andrew Strauss and a gutsy, important 50 from Read. And yes, talking of declarations, we would have batted on into the final day if we had not been bowled out just before the close on the fourth day.

Then it was time for Mahmood to come to the party – ah, I cannot believe I have not used that phrase more – with four excellent wickets as Pakistan were shot out for just 155. Lucky he did, because Steve Harmison and Matthew Hoggard both looked innocuous. But Mahmood showed good signs of learning here, as we had spoken to him about not trying to bowl too quickly, using his fastest ball as a variation rather than the norm (just as we had with Simon Jones previously). And he did that brilliantly.

Panesar also took three good wickets, including a belter to bowl Khan, but I think it was our fielding that won us this match. Throughout it was so much more superior to that of the Pakistanis and no better illustrated than by Paul Collingwood's stunning direct hit to remove Yousuf on that last day. It was 2–0 in the series and the Pakistanis could not catch us. It was a most satisfying win. But, predictably, the questions afterwards again centred around Panesar.

'As a finger spinner there is probably no one to match him in world cricket at the moment,' I said. It was not a tongue-in-cheek comment because, in truth, there was very little competition at the time. New Zealand's Daniel Vettori was injured and then there was Nicky Boje of South Africa . . . and that was it. And what I could not say at the time was that Panesar did not even have an arm ball. I had spoken to Dave Parsons, our spin coach, about that and asked him to work on it. But I had also told Parsons to be careful because I could already see doubts creeping into Panesar's mind. They were especially evident during the fourth Test at the Oval where Pakistan went for him early, his very first ball being hit for six by Imran Farhat. He also dropped a catch – easy for anyone but Panesar – and he was out on the outfield before play bowling overs he did not really need to.

But that is not something I would ever really complain about. In fact, I was pleasantly surprised by the general intensity of practice before that fourth Test. With the series already in the bag it would have been easy for the players to take their feet off the gas, as it were, but there was no such thing. Everyone was still intent on improving their techniques. I spoke to Alastair Cook about his batting and mentioned that I thought his hands were too high on the handle, probably the reason why he was struggling so much with his play of spin. In this instance the bat can become too whippy in one's hands, making it difficult to stop when playing defensively, explaining the hard hands Cook was often showing against the slower men.

Coincidentally Sajid Mahmood also had the same problem. He and Cook tried moving their hands lower down during pre-match nets and both announced themselves pleased with the results. 'I feel like I've got more control of my bat,' Cook said. And I had not even explained the reasons behind this move because sometimes it is best not to do that. Overall I had never seen a group of batters striking the ball so well.

Sod's Law then dictated they produced their worst batting performance of the summer the next day, being dismissed for just 173 by the Pakistanis. By the close Pakistan were 96–1. I said to the players that, in all my time with the England cricket team, if that was not the worst day then it was certainly very close. 'You've got four days to put it right,' I told them. They went out the following day and Pakistan amassed 336–3. Oh well.

There was rain around and it was something I noticed about England cricketers that they often struggled in such circumstances. It can only stem from county cricket, where rain can often signal the end of a contest. Not so in Test cricket. It obviously lasts much longer (with time also being made up, which is not the case in county cricket) and you have to be able to switch off and then switch back on quickly.

But we did rally eventually. So much so that by the time an early tea was taken because of bad light on the fourth day we were 298–4 in response to Pakistan's 504. And you all know what happened then. That was the end of the game. Yes, this was the infamous 'ball-tampering' match. Pakistan had been fined five penalty runs just before for 'unfairly changing the condition of the ball' and would not initially come out to field after tea, causing umpires Darrell Hair and Billy Doctrove to award the match to us. It was clearly a massive story at the time and the full details have been well chronicled elsewhere. All I want to do is clarify my role – or not – in it, as well as any background concerning the England team.

We were interested in what the Pakistanis were doing with the ball, that is for sure. We just could not understand how they were able to get it to reverse swing so early in the innings. With the lush outfields it had been a problem for us all series. We had done it so effectively against Australia in 2005 when the pitches were much drier and rougher, easily scuffing the ball up, but now we could not manage it. Using binoculars, we began examining the Pakistanis closely in the field because we thought we had picked something up.

It seemed that for the first fifteen to twenty overs of our innings every member of the Pakistan team was shining the ball – on both sides of the ball too – probably to get rid of the lacquer quickly and make the leather soft. And then after that period only a couple of players seemed to be entrusted with the duty.

I became implicated for my actions on that fourth morning. I went to see the umpires before play. I was seen doing so by Mike Atherton and Nasser Hussain who, because of the drizzly weather, were shielding under cover near the umpires' room. But it was not, as Atherton was later to write, my primary intention to speak to the umpires about the ball. I wanted to speak to them about the light. Atherton wrote that it could not have been about the weather because it was fine. Why was he then sheltering under the pavilion roofing?

It was always an irritation to me that the umpires rarely gave you any steer on this when you arrived at the ground. Why warm up if the light is so bad that you might not start on time?

So I went out on to the ground, dropped my kit off and then ran up the steps past Atherton and Hussain towards the umpires' room. As I was doing this, it occurred to me that I should have a look at the ball. Pakistan had only bowled eighteen overs at us the previous evening and I was interested to see what sort of state it was in. Normally you would only look at a ball after fifty or sixty overs.

Unfortunately Hair and Doctrove were not there. But TV umpire Peter Hartley and reserve umpire Trevor Jesty were, so I asked them if I could see the ball. They said no, telling me that I had to wait until Hair and Doctrove arrived. Crucially, before the summer's Test cricket had begun, there had been a meeting in which it was stipulated by the match referee that no one could see the ball without the permission of the umpires. That surprised me a little, because that was the first time such a thing had ever been mentioned. It obviously meant that other coaches were having suspicions about balls elsewhere in other series.

Anyway I left and went out on to the ground to begin the warm-ups. Not long after, Hair approached me in the middle. 'I'm not going to show you the ball,' he said bluntly, 'but we've got a handle on it and are monitoring the situation.'

'No problem, we are more concerned about the start of play,' I replied, pointing out about the low cloud and drizzle.

He seemed nervous and fidgety. He said that I should not mention this conversation to anyone. That was not a problem to me because all I was really worried about was the weather and when we could start the warm-up. I was merely being inquisitive about the ball.

But I did not tell anyone, not even Matthew Maynard who had seen Hair talking to me and asked what he had said. 'Nothing,' I told Maynard, 'I was just querying about the light.'

Soon afterwards match referee Mike Procter came out into the middle. I mentioned to him about umpire Doctrove being too lenient towards the Pakistani bowlers, who were running on the pitch. It was noticeable that at Hair's end they were not, but at Doctrove's end they were.

I did not mention to Procter anything about the ball. It was insinuated afterwards that I was tapping up my mate Procter, with some newspapers even saying we were so close that he had been best man at my wedding. He had not been. I hardly knew him then because he had only just joined Rhodesia from Western Province. He is a mate, certainly, but it is simply not true that I was tapping him up. In fact, I did nothing to stir up anything about ball tampering. It annoyed me that I was dragged into it, and in particular I was angry with Atherton's writing of a story with accusations based solely on assumption.

Amidst everything that happened that day I especially recall the meeting which took place afterwards, attended by myself, Andrew Strauss, David Morgan, Inzamam-ul-Haq, Zaheer Abbas (Pakistan manager) and Shaharyar Khan (PCB chairman). Interestingly Bob

Woolmer, the Pakistan coach, was not there. At this meeting Hair completely lost his temper. Inzamam asked him why Pakistan were being accused. 'You know what was going on out there,' said Hair sternly, and got up and left. To be fair Doctrove backed him to the hilt, but it was Hair who subsequently copped all the flak. That was unfair, and doubtless it will mean that from now on umpires will not want to make the big decisions. That is not good for the game.

But the tour continued and we duly met Pakistan again at Bristol in a Twenty20 match to precede the official one-day series. There was always going to be a strained atmosphere. And remember that I was still being implicated then. So what I probably did not need was an audience with the whole Pakistan squad, all on my own!

We had finished our practice the day before the match and I was last out of the dressing room. I turned right out of the Bristol dressing room and headed towards the car park where the whole Pakistan squad were filing their way down for practice. I knew I had not done anything untoward. But they did not. And I just wanted to disappear. But you know what? There was not one word of ill-feeling. Not one hint of animosity. A couple of them even said hello.

We drew that one-day series 2–2 (with one match rained off) after being 2–0 down, which was a pretty good effort. All credit to skipper Andrew Strauss for that, in his coaxing of a raw side. But still there was further evidence for me of English players only really wanting to listen to advice when they were losing. Only when that was happening did the batsmen realize that it might be a good idea to start walking down the wicket to Mohammad Asif to disrupt his length. Throughout my time with England it frustrated me how little of the action players – especially young ones coming into the side – actually watched and learnt from accordingly.

In general, playing too much cricket at county level does not make thinking cricketers. So before the second match at Lord's I decided to try something I had never attempted before. I told every batsman at nets that if he blocked one ball his net was over. At first it met with some strange looks but most said that it was an incredible feeling, having to smash every ball, making them relaxed as well as aware of what they could accomplish if they tried. They were keen to try it again.

There were other frustrations. First there was the question of the pitches, which were again green and spicy, in direct contrast to our instructions. When will the counties learn? Secondly there was continued controversy about ball tampering. At Lord's we were astonished that the ball was reversing after just sixteen overs when conditions were overcast and damp. And then in the third match at Southampton Shoaib Akhtar was at the centre of some television footage which showed him 'working' on the ball. It was soon glossed over though. The authorities were far too scared of the tour being cancelled to do anything strong about this. And thirdly there was a silly question from BBC radio reporter Pat Murphy during an interview. Before the Trent Bridge match – in which, incidentally, we played exceptionally well in winning by eight wickets – he surprised me on air by plucking a figure from nowhere and using it to illustrate what he considered a selection policy under my tenure which was more revolving-door than previous ones.

He said there had been seventy-one new players selected in one-day internationals in my time. I had no idea about this figure, and, even though it stunned me, I replied that it would be interesting to see how many of those had had to come in because of injury. Anyway I went away rather angrily and immediately asked Mark Garaway, our analyst, to do some research on the figures. One of the players must have overheard this and quick as a flash said: 'It can't be true. Stuart Broad's number is one hundred and ninety-seven [he'd made his debut in the opener at Cardiff] and

Darren Gough's is one hundred and twenty-six. He's just done a quick subtraction and got seventy-one.'

And I knew Gough had not made his debut under me. It was in 1994, in fact. Chris Read had been the first to make his debut under me in South Africa and his number was 156, so in fact the figure was only forty-one. They had actually come in 153 matches. The thirty before my time and since Gough had come in eighty matches. You do not need to be much of a mathematician to work out there was a higher percentage of turnover before I took over, and because they played fewer games there was less likelihood of injury. I tackled Murphy about this. 'Some anorak told me,' was his lame excuse. There is nothing like some detailed research.

In fairness, after a rather sticky period between the two of us, Murphy and I got on well at the end of my tenure. But this was another example of my frustration at journalists and broadcasters just blithely throwing facts and figures out into the public domain without proper investigation.

13

Winter from Hell

Retaining the Ashes Down Under in 2006/7? It was never going to be easy. With the ICC Champions Trophy and the World Cup straddling it this was always going to be the most arduous winter ever faced by any England cricket team.

Australia is a hard enough place to go anyway without being shorn of key players. Some very good sides have gone there with their full complement and been heavily beaten. For instance, South Africa had gone there with a full side around the turn of 2005/6 and got hammered. We went without our skipper (Michael Vaughan) and an important fast bowler (Simon Jones), and soon found ourselves without an opening batsman (Marcus Trescothick). And remember that this Australian side will probably be remembered as one of the top two Test sides of all time.

It does not matter who you are, if you are without top players you will struggle. Even the Australians did so when they went to New Zealand without skipper Ricky Ponting, Adam Gilchrist, Andrew Symonds, Brett Lee and Michael Clarke just after we had left their shores. They lost 3–0. But everyone said it was because they were under-strength. I just wish we had elicited the same sympathy in this Ashes series.

Sadly there was no chance of that. The expectations heaped upon us were far too optimistic, even if maybe we should have taken that as a compliment of our improved world standing. But I do think a lot of commentators enjoy being overly optimistic, because they can then slate the team mercilessly when things go wrong. Too often it is all about sensationalism rather than a measured, analytical view of what might happen.

We knew what might happen. We knew we might struggle for leadership on the field. Yes, what I am saying is that the captaincy was always going to be a problem in Australia.

Everyone knows that it was a choice between Andrew Flintoff and Andrew Strauss. But I had some doubts in crucial areas about Flintoff as a captain. Yes, he is a fine cricketer and would be influential in any side, but the areas which concerned me were his tactical nous and man-management skills under pressure. And there was always going to be a worry about his self-discipline. Sadly, I was soon to discover he was unsure of what true leadership is.

As for Strauss, he had impressed me when he had been captain, but I just felt that he still did not have the respect he needed from a couple of members of the squad. He had tough disciplines and a strong character but just had not quite established himself as a commanding enough player.

One selector (Geoff Miller) wanted Strauss, the other (David Graveney) Flintoff. So it was left to me to decide. It was some decision. I agonized and agonized. My brain was saying one man (Strauss), my heart the other (Flintoff). On and on went my vacillation. I was edging towards Flintoff when something clinched it for me.

Colin Gibson (ECB head of corporate communications) was showing us a motivational DVD at Loughborough, where we were having end of summer fitness tests and meetings, when the following words came up on the screen: 'The team has to be together to beat Australia.' That was it. It had to be Flintoff, then.

I was not confident that we were making the right decision, but I also knew that if Flintoff was not captain he would be a huge hindrance to the side. It was his benefit year and he would have concentrated on that. He would also have teamed up with his mate Steve Harmison and they could have been difficult to manage, as the team management had discovered previously, and especially for someone like Strauss who would still have been learning the captaincy business on such a difficult tour.

This appointment would, I hoped, get the best out of Flintoff and maybe he could do the same to Harmison. However, even though I believe it took some time, Flintoff came to realize how difficult it is to motivate Harmison at times.

After seeing that DVD I walked out and immediately told Flintoff he was captain. That was the easy bit. I then had to tell Strauss he was not. Naturally he was very disappointed, and rightly so. But I said to him: 'You might thank me for this one day.' For I always saw him as Vaughan's successor in the long term. 'What do you mean?' he asked.

'One day I'll talk to you about it,' I replied. I doubt if I will now.

Did I talk to Vaughan, who was rehabilitating his injured knee in Perth with the rest of the academy squad, enough during the Ashes? I was rather surprised when he said after I had resigned that I had not; that he had felt underused during this Ashes series. Because together we had agreed that there was no way he could be seen to be imposing his authority too much. We both knew Flintoff's character and we knew that we had to be careful not to affect his leadership. But I still used Vaughan often enough. I phoned him on occasions and he moved into the hotel with us when we were in Perth.

Matters with Trescothick were even more complicated. There was obviously a lot of talk about him in pre-tour selection. During the summer of 2006 I had heard a whisper that he was not going to go to India for the ICC Champions Trophy, but would be OK for the Ashes. That worried me. I had had these problems before with Alec Stewart and Darren Gough when I felt, rightly or wrongly, they wanted to pick and choose tours. My view was always that players could choose their form of cricket but not their countries to tour.

So I was going to arrange a meeting with Trescothick to tell him as much when chairman of selectors David Graveney advised me that, before I did so, I should speak to the clinical psychologist who had been treating Trescothick. Fair enough. So it was decided to organize a clandestine meeting at Trescothick's house for all of us, Graveney included. I cannot name the psychologist, but he was saying that Trescothick could not go to India because it was where the problem had first occurred and it was too recent in his memory bank for a return.

'Give me another year working with him and it would be fine for him to go to India,' the psychologist said. He also said he had successfully treated all manner of professional people – including anaesthetists and consultant surgeons – who had had this same problem. But I said to him: 'That's OK, but they are not performing in the public eye.'

He said it did not matter. He was still convinced that he could 'cure' Trescothick. This was highly specialist advice we were taking. Who were we to go against it? We took it. We decided to pull Trescothick out of the Champions Trophy and select him for the Ashes.

It was the first of many decisions for which I was lambasted. I was going to say 'we' but, as we shall see, it was invariably me who was copping the flak on this tour. The next topic was the preparation. For years the press had been trying to hang me on this point; tour after tour using the word 'undercooked' and then having to shut up when we started the proper stuff (the international matches) well. But here they had their chance to harp on and on about it. And did they enjoy it.

But I stand by our preparation. That was not the reason we lost the Ashes so badly. In fact, I know we prepared better than for any other tour. At the end of the summer we had had that two-day meeting at Loughborough, at which I had decided upon Flintoff as captain. We had never had such a detailed gathering as that before. There were presentations made to ensure the players were aware of how difficult a winter it was going to be. They could then ponder over this while on their short breaks before leaving for the Champions Trophy.

Of course, all our physical preparation did have to take place at the Champions Trophy in India. In normal circumstances this tournament, with so much spare time on our hands, would have been considered an awfully organized event. But we actually used that time for our own good by turning it into an Ashes training camp, with lots of net practices followed by gruelling fitness sessions. We probably would not have done that much work normally, although, of course, this tournament did reduce our rest time before the Ashes.

Results-wise it was a huge disappointment as we lost first to India and then Australia. As consolation we did beat the West Indies in our final game by three wickets and we did play some good cricket in chasing down their total of 272, with Kevin Pietersen making 90 not out. But this match highlighted to me yet again the problems England cricketers have with the one-day game. They struggle to think on their feet. I saw this time and time again throughout my time as coach. And I could hardly believe what I was seeing here. This was a skiddy pitch, the type on which we had spoken about the need to play straight. We had spoken about the West Indian off-spinner Chris Gayle and about how, on this sort of pitch, he was like India's Anil Kumble in that you must not look to sweep him early on because he undercuts the ball and can easily creep under the bat.

All was going well as Andrew Strauss and Ian Bell put on 82

by the twelfth over, when Gayle was introduced to the attack. This was as good a start as we had had for a long time, so there was no rush, no panic. Just the need to remember what we had spoken about.

So Strauss was facing Gayle, who came round the wicket to him. First ball Strauss played forward defensively for the spin, which was understandable, but the ball did not spin, hitting his pad. He was plumb lbw. Amazingly, he was not given. Next ball he tried to sweep, another close shout not given. Third ball he went back to cut a ball which would have hit leg stump and was bowled off his pad. What was he thinking? He could have just seen out that over and had a look at Gayle as there was no rush. One could have understood it if we had been well behind the required run-rate.

So that was one wicket down. Next to go was Flintoff, in at number three, who inexplicably hit one straight down deep mid-wicket's throat off Gayle. There was more. Gayle, as he did to Flintoff, naturally bowled over the wicket to Paul Collingwood. Remember – skiddy pitch, must play straight. Collingwood was caught at slip for a duck trying to work the ball to mid-wicket. We were now 127–3. And then to top it off Bell was run out at the non-striker's end because he did not dive. That would have saved him, so a while after he was out I asked him what had happened. His reply? 'I didn't know where the ball was'! I could not believe it. International batsmen do not say things like that. You can excuse one or two players making errors of judgement in a game, but when all of your top four do so it really does make you wonder as a coach.

Our early elimination in that tournament caused something of a dilemma. Go home for a few days or go straight to Australia? Amidst a predictable storm of criticism, we decided to go home. Why? Because if we had gone to Australia we would have given the players three days off anyway. As I said, we had trained so hard in India for a solid two weeks that they needed the break. So we thought it would be nice for them to see their friends and families, however briefly, before embarking on a very long winter.

So to Australia. If there was one thing wrong with our preparation it was the fact that we had to play the Prime Minister's XI in Canberra. We should have had another net session that day. That came too early for us and I never see the point of playing one-day games when you are preparing for a Test series and do not have your proper one-day team. But I thought the two other warm-up matches, four-day games against New South Wales and South Australia, went well. My philosophy was always that I did not want players tiring themselves out before the Test series started; I preferred them slightly underdone as opposed to overdone.

I remember passing a comment at nets before the first Test about how good the batsmen looked. They were all hitting the ball in the middle of their bats and playing good aggressive shots; signs of well-prepared players. And the bowlers seemed to be coming into nick, except Steve Harmison who missed the final warm-up match in Adelaide.

We were slated for using fourteen players in the first four-day warm-up match against NSW, but if the Australians felt so strongly about it why did they not just use eleven? They used the match in exactly the same manner as we did. Glenn McGrath would bowl a few overs and then walk off; Brett Lee, too. And they had had five months rest beforehand. We had not. We had been playing non-stop since February.

We had an early decision to make on this tour. There was no point dithering about who the keeper was going to be for the Tests. That man had to play in all the warm-ups. It was a unanimous decision that it had to be Geraint Jones. Flintoff preferred him, I preferred him and the four or five other senior players we spoke to all preferred Jones. None of those questioned even thought Chris Read should have been on the tour, let alone in the Test side. So it was not just a Fletcher/Read thing as everyone made out.

You must remember that, even though Read had done reasonably well at the end of the Pakistan Test series in England, he had struggled with his batting in the Champions Trophy (scores of 2, 0 and 4) looking at sea against the spinners again, and he had not done much in the Pakistan one-day series either.

It was also interesting that before the tour Jack Russell sent me a text saying that Read's keeping channel was too narrow due to a technical flaw and asking if he could help. As I said earlier, within the camp we had been talking about that problem for years. Even Russell had taken time to spot it.

And when I said in a press conference that Read could not handle the pressure, I meant it, but only because of the technical deficiencies with his batting. As he does not really have a defensive technique he always has to look to smash the ball. I would have preferred Matt Prior, as I had the previous summer.

And I was not the only one who wanted Jones on the tour management team, another easy point of criticism from the baying media. I always picked the management team in consultation with the captain and here Flintoff wanted him, too, to join Strauss and Collingwood on that group. This was first because we valued Jones' thoughts on the game – they are better than most – and secondly because we thought it was a good way of reviving his confidence after being left out of the side for a while.

Of course, Trescothick would have been in that group but sadly his stress-related problems resurfaced early on. We had seen signs of them at Canberra in the first game and it had been suggested that we bring his wife and child out early. For the families were not to arrive until we reached Brisbane for the first Test. That very decision had actually caused a serious disagreement between me and the players during the Pakistan series. It was at Old Trafford during the second Test that the players were saying that they wanted their families out in Australia from the very start of the tour. I said 'no way'.

'We're not landing in Australia with prams and all that sort of stuff,' I said. I wanted the families to come out after two Tests to meet us in Perth and I wish that I had stuck by that. But I relented and agreed that they could come out after the warm-ups, but insisted that they had to arrive in Brisbane three days before we came from Adelaide so that they could get over their jet lag and not be disturbing the sleep patterns of the players too much.

By then Trescothick had returned home. During the match against NSW in Sydney it became clear that he could not carry on. I had decided that he must go home even before he came off after being bowled by Brett Lee for 8 and broke down again, just as he had in India. During a break beforehand I had called a meeting with Flintoff, Matthew Maynard and the team doctor (Nick Pierce) and told them there was no way we could have these problems with Trescothick so close to the first Test. Not only that it was obvious the problems could be there for some time. I thought the problem needed to be addressed firmly straight away. The pros and cons of bringing Trescothick's family out early were discussed. I let the others say their piece, with most saying we should wait on the issue, but there was little doubt to me that he had to go home. The others eventually agreed.

As things panned out I had a migraine soon afterwards and had to lie down in the physio's room. Lying there I was deliberating how I would pass the news on to Trescothick when Pierce came in and said, 'The problem with Trescothick is worse than we thought. Can you clear the room please, Duncan?' Trescothick had come in from his innings and then broken down in tears. Sadly it ensured that the right decision had been taken, but it is one decision I am not happy to have got right.

I did not feel remorseful about picking him in the first place.

Although, of course, there was the inevitable criticism. Bob Willis was one critic I recall in particular. When the tour party had been announced, he'd said we had got it spot on. Now he was asking: 'Why did they ever take Trescothick?'

That was nothing compared to the storm about to erupt when we announced the team for the first Test, though. Ashley Giles or Monty Panesar as the spinner? That was the burning question. There was little doubt whom the public wanted. Panesar's exploits against Pakistan had very obviously endeared him to them. But they were not examining the true facts. First there was the problem of our batting order and who should bat at number eight. You will know by now that it has long been my contention that you have to bat deep in Test cricket. Australia have good batsmen down the order – Shane Warne, Brett Lee and Stuart Clark can all bat – but they were still keen to play Shane Watson in an all-rounder role in this series. He was eventually injured but it was interesting that the Australians wanted him to bat after such a quality batsman as Adam Gilchrist at seven.

We already had problems with Flintoff not being consistent enough at six and Jones was having to feel his way back in at seven, so it was imperative that we had someone who could bat at eight. It would not have looked right with Panesar in the side because then we could not have someone who could bat at eight.

Giles simply had to bat at eight. And he was bowling better than Panesar at the time. That much had been obvious in the warm-up matches. For instance, why in Canberra against the Prime Minister's XI did skipper Flintoff turn to Giles, who had been out injured for so long, rather than Panesar, who had been playing regularly, when the flak was flying? It was the same scenario in Sydney against NSW until Giles tired towards the end.

We took a gamble with our selection for the match against South Australia in Adelaide, selecting Panesar because we wanted to look at him when the pressure was only on him. And we asked

Giles to bowl 36 overs per day in the nets to ensure he was match fit. But Panesar was ineffective in the middle so that at one stage Flintoff preferred Kevin Pietersen's off-spin.

Crucially Flintoff wanted Giles to play in that Test. Something also happened which I had not seen before, when some senior players not on the management team approached me and pleaded that Giles be picked. Not one of the management group even hesitated in nominating Giles.

I had asked both selectors, David Graveney and Geoff Miller, back in Loughborough who they would pick for the first Test. Giles they said, and Jones, too, for the wicketkeeper's spot. I thanked Graveney sarcastically for that, knowing that I would be the one who would take all the flak when the crunch came, with him hiding behind the fact that the other selectors do not have a say on away tours. It was always going to be seen as my personal selection.

I knew we needed aggressive characters to beat Australia and a side containing Read and Panesar, along with other already established members who were quiet, did not stack up. It made me laugh when commentators like Ian Botham said that England had to stand up and fight, and were then advocating Panesar and Read. A slight contradiction, I feel.

I could have taken the easy route and played Read and Panesar, but I did what I thought was best for the England team. It was nothing to do with favouritism or blind loyalty to the 2005 Ashes heroes. I spoke to a large number of people, and I mean a large number – including the likes of commentators Jonathan Agnew and Mike Selvey – but only a couple advised me to pick Panesar. One of those was Nasser Hussain. 'You've got to go with Panesar,' he said. 'It might not be the right decision but you must do it for your own good. The public like Panesar and you have to be careful of your job.' That settled it for me. I was going with Giles. I was not going to let a selection process worry me about my job. I wanted the best side for England, not the one which might keep me in a job.

But I still knew what I was letting myself in for. After the selection meeting it is normally the job of the captain to tell disappointed players (as Hussain and Vaughan had done), but on this occasion I asked Flintoff if he wanted me to tell Panesar that he was not in. 'Yes,' Flintoff said. So I spoke to Panesar and explained the reasons. As I walked away, I went past Matthew Maynard and bowling coach Kevin Shine and said, 'I've just put my job on the line.'

'What do you mean?' they asked.

'You just wait and see,' I replied. And we did see. Obviously, I still think about that selection a lot even now, but I have not altered my view. I still maintain that we picked the best side for Brisbane.

The toss was crucial in that first Test. It was a beautiful looking pitch and we needed to bat first on it because halfway through the second day big cracks would start appearing. They can create havoc with a batsman's mind, especially when pursuing a total as large as the 602 Australia amassed.

But the most disappointing moment of that first Test was Steve Harmison's first ball of the match, which embarrassingly ended up in Flintoff's hands at second slip. I had not wanted Harmison to take the first over. He had done so in 2005 at Lord's with good effect, but he was bowling well then. Now he was not. And it has to be said that Matthew Hoggard normally took the first over anyway. But understandably Flintoff was adamant that he wanted his mate to open up, even though, as I have mentioned, Harmison had missed the last warm-up match in Adelaide with a stiff side. As it was, Harmison's nerves typified those of the team in general. I had never seen the team bus like it was on that first morning.

And I had never experienced such personal targeting as that which came my way after this Test. It was very obvious that I was bearing the brunt and that Flintoff was getting off lightly. ECB chairman David Morgan told me that he fielded a call immediately after the match from an Australian journalist, who asked: 'So what are you going to do with Fletcher? Are you going to sack him?' After one match! Mind you, Geoffrey Boycott had done even better than that. As mentioned much earlier in this book he had started it all by calling for my head before we had even left for Australia.

So it was inevitable that he had plenty further to say during the winter. There was one particular piece in which he talked about an unnamed England captain asking him to dinner. But he said that the captain was 'frightened' of being seen with him in case I found out, adding that the captain had said the dinner must be 'under the radar'.

I knew about the dinner. I knew it was with Andrew Flintoff and I can remember the exact circumstances.

Boycott was always asking England players to dinner and sometimes they returned the invitation. I would hear it time and time again in the dressing room – 'Boycott has asked me to dinner again and I don't want to go.' But what he would do is pester them – and pester is the right word – until eventually they joined him. And as the individual was off to dinner you could always hear the rest shouting 'Good luck' sarcastically.

I would not have minded if players wanted to go and see Boycott for one-on-one sessions. Players did that with other coaches, and it is common practice in many teams. But I do have to say that Boycott's coaching thoughts are relatively old-fashioned. I remember a former Australian batsman once saying that to me after doing a Channel 4 masterclass during a Test match lunch break with him. And my gut feeling is that players do not want to be coached by him.

Anyway, other critics queued up to say we should have played Panesar in that first Test. It tickled me that Nick Cook, once a coach at Panesar's county Northamptonshire, should be among them. He was once a left-arm spinner himself yet he sent Panesar to us without an arm ball. He and his county also sent Panesar to us when he was scarcely able to bat or field. We worked our socks off with him to improve those two disciplines and both were coming on really well. Could they not have done that at Northamptonshire? It just goes to show what is wrong with a lot of counties.

We'd talked at length before Brisbane about how we had succeeded at home in 2005, about how we had been aggressive as a team, never letting anyone get isolated and always sticking together. But it was very, very sad to see that this did not take place. Only two players, Kevin Pietersen and Paul Collingwood, incidentally our two most successful batsmen with 92 and 96 respectively in the second innings, showed any spirit and aggression. They got stuck into the Australians. Nobody else was interested, even the captain, who went out of his way to be friendly to the bowlers Brett Lee and Shane Warne.

The Australians seemed to have a plan and that was to suck Flintoff in. They had identified him as a player who should not be sledged because then he will come back hard at you, as he had in 2005. Some you have a go at, some you do not. Matthew Hayden is one you do go at; Warne not, thus Collingwood's later sledging of him was probably not a good idea.

Ironically, Warne made an early mistake by throwing a ball at Pietersen. That riled him and urged him to better things. But, cleverly, Warne did gradually get back on side with Pietersen so that he then dropped his aggression. That left Collingwood on his own to take on the whole Australian team for the rest of the series. That really irked me. Not as much as the manner of the Australian sledging, though. In fact, you could not call it sledging because it was so foul-mouthed as to be a disgrace to the game. It was the sort of stuff that belongs in the gutter and not on a cricket field.

At least if we said things on the field they had some sharp wit, which is how I think it should be. I particularly liked Pietersen's comments to Andrew Symonds, who was introduced for the third Test in Perth. Symonds was quick to try to get at Pietersen, but immediately Pietersen put him down with the line that he thought it was good that the world's best 'fielding all-rounder' had at last been given a game. And every time Pietersen hit the ball near Symonds he would shout 'Fetch it! Fetch it!'

But when we moved on to Adelaide for the second Test I knew that somehow we had to stand up to the Australians more than that. First, though, I thought it best we try to sort out the bowlers, because there was no hiding from the fact that they had performed very, very badly in Brisbane. So we called a meeting just with them as a group and it went so well that even Flintoff remarked afterwards how constructive it had been.

That was fine, but I still needed to find a way of making Flintoff as aggressive as he had been in 2005, especially in his leadership. I was not sure how best to approach it. So I spoke to our psychologist Steve Bull. I told him we needed to address this business about 'getting into the space' of the Australians, just as we had in 2005. It was only going to work if Flintoff got into their space first.

Bull suggested that a meeting should be called by Flintoff, and that he should lead it. So I mentioned this to Flintoff. 'No, no, Duncan, we're having too many meetings,' he said. I stressed to him its importance and reluctantly he agreed. This was all rather ironic considering Flintoff was subsequently to receive much praise in the media for calling this meeting.

But we had it, and it also went really well. Flintoff had been primed by Bull and underlined to the players how they had to be aggressive and stick up for each other. It was a rare moment of strong leadership in a meeting from Flintoff, who was generally quiet in such affairs. Nasser Hussain and Michael Vaughan would always be vocal and strong, but Flintoff tended to take a back seat role and let the senior members talk.

But sadly that meeting was all talk and no one walked the walk, apart from Collingwood. When it came to the Test Collingwood was again left isolated. Flintoff even laughed at him once when he chirped Warne while he was making vital first innings runs.

And everyone laughed at me because they thought I had got the selection wrong again in omitting Panesar. But I can state categorically here that I wanted Panesar to play at Adelaide. I wanted to play both spinners, Panesar replacing James Anderson from the first Test line-up. I also wanted Sajid Mahmood to play instead of Steve Harmison because I thought his skiddiness would be more effective at Adelaide.

I had thought even before the tour started that I would like two spinners at Adelaide; at Perth (although that was proved wrong) and Sydney too. When I spoke to Hussain before this second Test I reiterated these thoughts, so that afterwards he felt moved to come up and ask me why I had changed my mind.

Well, I will tell you why. We went into our management meeting and every single person there, bar me, wanted just one spinner and wanted him to be Giles. This included people like Phil Neale, Mark Garaway, Kevin Shine and Matthew Maynard, all with considerable experience in the game, the first three all having coached county sides. The only person who hinted that he might agree with me was Collingwood, who said, 'Maybe we could play two spinners.' But that was it. I should have been stronger, but what do you do when the vote is so convincingly against you? It was why I made my much-publicized 'I'm not the sole selector' comment after this Test.

That provoked much comment, with Ian Botham predictably piling in with his contention that I was not supporting the captain. He knew I wanted Panesar. My relationship with Botham deteriorated over time, so much so that when I finished he did not even have the decency to come and shake my hand. It was the match against the West Indies in Barbados and as usual I came on to the playing arena first. Hussain was there in the middle doing his stuff for Sky TV and came over and shook my hand, congratulating me on what I had done. In a very unusual show of public emotion he even gave me a bear hug. Mike Atherton also walked some distance across the field to shake my hand warmly. But Botham, he just stood there and did not say or do anything. And to think he then passed the comment afterwards that I had 'taken being miserable to a new level'. What about him that day?

Botham thinks the players listen to him, but they do not. Often you would go into the dressing room and hear the players in exasperation saying things like, 'Have you heard what Botham is saying about the wicket?' In contrast, I felt they were quite happy to listen to other commentators. However, it did worry me that Botham influenced Flintoff too much on this tour.

Botham's commentary has long caused problems. Back in 2004 in Jamaica, Sky had called a meeting with Michael Vaughan and me, intended to improve the relationship between the broadcasters and the team. Present at a restaurant, owned by a relation of Michael Holding, were Holding himself, executive producer Barney Francis and David Lloyd.

It was interesting that Botham was not there because most of the conversation then centred around him as he appeared the one obstacle to improving the relationship. Some critics said he was inconsistent in his thoughts and did not do enough investigative work before a day's commentary.

I knew that Rod Marsh would be vindictive at some stage during this Ashes series. Our association had been such that it was predictable. And so he was vindictive, bringing to mind that breakfast I had been to on the previous Ashes tour when I had been asked about Marsh undermining me. That inquisitor clearly knew something.

An article by Marsh appeared in the *Observer* during the first Test. It began: 'It hurts me to say this . . . but the England set-up looks a shambles at the moment. And they have played accordingly. Take the selection process. It's a farce . . .' etc., etc.

I am glad Marsh mentioned about selection. He was a very average selector, with some of his suggestions and statements about players in selection meetings defying belief. Take the following as an example. At one meeting he was championing one of his academy players and, when asked why, remarkably said: 'I've got to have credibility with my academy players.' Nothing to do with selecting the best side, of course. I felt that, for him, Rod Marsh's academy was much more important than the success of the England cricket team.

And what did he actually do as head of the National Academy? Granted, he signed Troy Cooley. That was a smart move, a great signing for England cricket and an equally grievous loss when he left. Doubtless Marsh also improved his golf handicap during the summer. What about the academy's (or A team's) record on tours? It has been poor.

Because he was unaccountable to anyone this was soon glossed over. Not highlighting this was a glaring omission from the Schofield Report. With the depth of England's highly paid professional structure they should be able to field A teams which beat most other equivalent teams from other countries. What about the statistic that upwards of 80 per cent of the batsmen who attended the academy then performed worse the following season than they had in previous years? In fact, the only one who showed any real improvement was Middlesex's Owais Shah, who put that improvement down to speaking to India's Mohammad Azharuddin.

Many had to go away and re-establish their games before challenging for an England place, Andrew Strauss being a classic example. It took him two years after leaving the academy to force his way into the England team. In fact, how many players graduated straight from the academy into the England team? I do not think there were any. Most needed a couple of years out of it before they made the grade. James Anderson joined the Australian tour of 2002/3 in Adelaide from there but even then they told us he was not ready. Andrew Flintoff was also called from there to India but had hardly been there any length of time. In fact, he mentioned how excited he was to get out of there when he got the call. There were even instances where I received requests from players that they did not want a second term at the academy. If the academy was so good how come it has changed its name and focus on a couple of occasions?

Botham and Marsh were not the only people scathing in their criticism in Australia. Former players like Graham Gooch, Mike Gatting, Phil Tufnell and Graham Thorpe all dived in with their so-called words of wisdom. It annoyed us that people like that, who were out in Australia, were piggy-backing our 2005 success and making money out of it. That success was the only reason there was such incredible interest in this series after all.

Thorpe was the one who upset us most. He had a real go at Giles, a former teammate and good friend. Thorpe clearly has a short memory. He had obviously forgotten how good Giles had been to him when he was struggling with his marital problems on one particular tour of India. There Giles had spent endless hours in Thorpe's room, comforting him and playing computer games to keep his mind occupied. Now, knowing that Giles had been through injury hell, he was slating him. It was truly appalling.

Poor Giles had a bad Test at Adelaide. The media had finally got to him. He had bowled well in Brisbane, people forget that. He did not bowl badly in the first innings here but struggled in the second innings when the chase was on. And, of course, there was 'that' catch, dropping Ricky Ponting on thirty-five at deep square leg in the first innings off Matthew Hoggard, who nonetheless returned the astonishing figures of 7–109 from 42 overs on a slow, slow pitch.

Giles was a very good fielder. Usually in the outfield if he got his hands to the ball he caught it. And he got to more than you might think. He may have looked cumbersome but he was quicker than he looked. Flintoff came off at the break and said that, after himself (he has bucket hands), he would have backed Giles as the next most likely to take such an important catch.

It was not that catch which lost us the match, though. It was our batting on the final morning. Still to this day I do not understand what happened. I do know, however, that the result of the Test – a loss by six wickets – changed the lives and careers of quite a few people, especially me. I might not be writing this book now if the result had been different. Who knows how the rest of the series might have panned out?

We should have drawn it. Our first innings batting demanded that. We had batted really well, Collingwood and Pietersen putting on a mammoth 310, with Collingwood becoming England's first double centurion since Wally Hammond seventy years before. I did not find out that last statistic until a while afterwards. That is mightily impressive.

I had been really worried about the fourth evening session. Australia had been dismissed for 513 and we faced one of those tricky sessions before the close at which England were never especially good. We were always vulnerable to allowing the momentum to shift dangerously away from us during periods like this. So I was pleasantly surprised that we were 59–1 at the close off 19 overs. Andrew Strauss and Ian Bell had batted positively and it boded well for the final day.

That was the instruction on the final day: to bat exactly as we had the previous evening. The upshot could not have been more different. Australia were very shrewd in opening the bowling that morning with Shane Warne and Stuart Clark rather than Glenn

McGrath and Brett Lee (we played the latter two pretty well over-all in the series) but still that was no excuse for us going so timidly into our shells and succumbing for 129, with Warne grabbing 4–49. It was eerily reminiscent of Multan a year before, even if there the obvious purpose had been to win and here it was to draw.

I asked the batsmen afterwards what had happened. Nobody could give me an answer. They said the Australians had bowled superbly. They had. But the crucial dismissal was that of Kevin Pietersen, bowled around his legs sweeping at Shane Warne. It was a shame, because he had padded away most similar deliveries in the first innings.

Pietersen now became the topic of debate in Perth during the third Test. He batted extremely well there but was left with the tail on both occasions, in making 70 and 60 not out. It brought into focus his position at number five in the order. He was adamant that was where he wanted to bat. But we suggested that four was a better position. That is where all the top batsmen bat in my opinion. I was asked at a press conference by a reporter I had never seen before why Pietersen was batting at five and I replied that was where he wanted to bat. 'But you're the coach, tell him where to bat,' was the reply.

This comment showed an ignorance of what happens at the top level of sport. If you make a top player do something he does not want to do, you are in trouble. It is crucial that the player is happy. He must be comfortable and confident in what he wants to do. At the time Pietersen did not even want to discuss the matter. As it was, being stuck with the tail for a third consecutive time in the first innings of the fourth Test at Melbourne finally persuaded him. And he immediately made the move up to four for the second innings and has remained there ever since.

A chat with Andrew Flintoff before the third Test at Perth did not yield such instant reward. I was not happy, and this was not just because he and Steve Harmison had been in the Australian dressing room drinking till midnight after we had lost in Adelaide. I told Flintoff we had reached the crossroads. He had made a commitment to the team before Adelaide that he was going to lead from the front in terms of aggression, but he had simply not fulfilled it. You cannot tell the team that they must play in a certain manner and then not set the example. That is the basis of any leadership. He lost some respect from the players because of that.

The press kept asking me what mistakes I had made. The only mistake I had made was in not being stronger. Yet again I thought about resigning as a selector because I could see there were going to be problems with the one-day squad. But eventually I decided not to because it would not have been a good idea in the middle of a tour, especially when considering what had already gone on regarding selection.

We obviously had to leave Giles out in Perth. But that bad news for him was soon put into perspective when it was discovered that his wife, Stine, was seriously ill at home. We had lost yet another player, a fine man, too, who always contributed enormously to the cause whether on or off the field.

And Panesar took his chance well, claiming 5–92 in Australia's first innings. But let us be honest, this was a pitch which was very responsive to spin, certainly much more so than Adelaide, where Warne had toiled away for 85 overs for just five wickets (and one of those, Andrew Strauss, was wrongly adjudged out). Panesar did again demonstrate his magnificent control, though.

But we also demonstrated the fragility of our tail. They were just not helping out with any decent scores. It was fair enough for critics to be pointing out that the top six should score the runs but they were underestimating the pressure on those six, knowing that from seven down few runs were going to be added. And, of course, poor Geraint Jones was at seven. Just like Giles, the media had got to him. Those two could have done so much more if they had been backed. Jones had actually been keeping very well. But he reached the end of his line here with a pair.

His second innings dismissal showed how much the pressure had got to him, run out from silly point after the ball had come off his pad sweeping. But it also underlined a minor technical point I had been making to all of the batsmen for a long time. Such pieces of advice can seem unnecessary and niggly until too late, but I had been saying that everyone must be careful to get well behind the crease when playing spin, because your back foot always moves forward whether playing defensively or sweeping. That might have saved Jones here. So too Flintoff in the last Test, where he played forward off Warne, overbalanced and was stumped.

We battled hard in our second innings to save this game, but Alastair Cook's wicket on the fourth evening, after a gutsy hundred, was crucial. He and Ian Bell had put on 170 and the Australians were looking tired, but, once Glenn McGrath returned to find his edge and immediately bowl nightwatchman Matthew Hoggard, it was over for us. Not just this Test, but the Ashes too. It was 3–0 and the urn was Australia's again.

For the first time in my career as England coach I sensed people around me were going into 'secretive' mode. It was not a great atmosphere to work in. There was so much bad press flying around that nobody wanted to talk about it and give me more bad news.

Bad news came in a rather peculiar form in Melbourne during the fourth Test. This was the story of our bowling plans falling into the wrong hands. As things were already going so badly on this trip it naturally caused much merriment and ridicule, but for us it was pretty annoying and also a little suspicious.

The first thing to say is that we had been extra-vigilant about these plans since an incident during the first Test at Brisbane. There our lucky mascot (a toy lion, named 'Dave' by Ashley Giles for some reason) had disappeared overnight and we realized that we had left the bowling plans pinned up on the walls in the strategic positions we always used (next to the urinal was always a good one!). Anybody could have photographed them, so we decided from there on to take them down every evening.

And it also meant that we were never going to be as careless as some people accused us of being in Melbourne. It was even suggested that they were stolen from our dressing room during play, in effect blaming our security staff. That was rubbish and upset me because Reg Dickason, who headed our team, is a top man and also very good at his job.

What happened was that analyst Mark Garaway's printer, which we normally used, broke down. So we sent Steve Bull up to the administrative offices of the Melbourne Cricket Club with a memory stick to get the plans printed. He was well aware of how careful he needed to be. He spoke to a woman there and stressed the confidentiality required. The trouble was that the printer was in a separate room and when Bull went through nothing appeared. He went back through to the offices and asked again.

Eventually the printing was done. We wanted these A4 sheets, always carefully compiled by Garaway, in colour, so when two came out in black and white Bull folded them up together and put them in his back pocket. When the story broke it was said that one was found on its own. How did that become disentangled from the other then? The one found was clearly not one of these two.

This was just another distraction we could have done without. Criticism was flying in from everywhere by now. The subject of the wives and families being with us now became an issue. I have already mentioned my thoughts on that, but it did become tiresome when things began to be inferred from the absence of some players and their families at the Christmas bash before the Melbourne Test. This was not a problem at all. The Christmas 'do' was not compulsory. As ever it was magnificently organized by

Medha Laud from the ECB as a way of providing something for those who did not have friends and families they could see in Australia over Christmas. Otherwise where else would they go? It is not easy booking somewhere on Christmas Day. It was not a problem and it was a thoroughly enjoyable day.

Not so the Test which followed; another thumping defeat, this time by an innings and 99 runs, as Shane Warne took seven wickets in the match. The Australians were so on top that we were struggling to compete.

But however tough it was, there were always some lighter moments to lift our mood. More often than not they came from what we called 'Maynardisms', as Matthew Maynard sometimes humorously got his thought processes a little muddled. The best came at a practice session where I gave him the fielders to organize. 'Right, you two halves go with him, the other half come with me!' he shouted.

Then in Adelaide we were waiting to take the bus to the ground when he was accosted by an England supporter, who proceeded to bend his ear for some time about how he loved Australia and wanted to emigrate there. Eventually the chap left and Maynard turned to the rest of us and said: 'God, these locals are annoying'!

I took copious notes throughout the tour but glancing back I can see very few about the cricket in the last two Tests. But I was miffed enough with Ricky Ponting in the final Test at Sydney to do so. For it was here he indulged in some poor sportsmanship when Kevin Pietersen was batting. You need to remember that this is the same Ponting, my old mate from that incident at Trent Bridge in 2005, who complained then so much about us supposedly not playing in the spirit of the game. So as Glenn McGrath was running up to bowl Ponting moved from second slip to fifth. Everyone knows you cannot do that. Pietersen turned around afterwards and asked him what the heck he was doing. Ponting just laughed. What the umpires were doing I will never know.

The one bonus for us in that last Test was that Flintoff at last scored some runs, making 89 in the first innings. But 5–0 in the series it was, as we lost by ten wickets and the whole of Australia gloried in that, while also celebrating the retirements of Warne, McGrath and Justin Langer. We had got what we deserved in terms of the inexperience of our cricket, but we had been more competitive in patches than people wished to give us credit for. It was just that we could not sustain that competitiveness for long enough.

Then at the end in Sydney came the bombshell of the Schofield Report. As well as its timing and the fact that it was looking at a period (2003–7) when we had been so successful bar one series, the make-up of its review team worried me. I had had no dealings with Ken Schofield. In fact I thought it a good idea to have someone from a different sport in charge. And, of course, I had no problem with Nasser Hussain. I always appreciated his confidentiality but he is also a person who is not afraid to speak his mind. Nick Knight was fine, a recently retired modern player whom I thought had a decent grasp of the game. Micky Stewart was OK. I have already stated my respect for him, the only question mark being whether he had stayed with the modern game. If you stay out of it for more than two years it will go past you, unless you are in a dressing room. As for Hugh Morris I obviously knew him well from my time with him at Glamorgan but I was seething about the fact that neither he nor Schofield came to see me in Melbourne during the Commonwealth Bank one-day series. They were both staying in the same hotel, for goodness' sake.

But two members of the review team particularly concerned me. Brian Rose first. Who is he, with all due respect? And secondly Angus Fraser. You needed people on the review team who had a track record of success. Middlesex under his leadership had been unsuccessful. Could he contribute? Maybe. But he is also a journalist and showed a total lack of confidentiality. He went out to dinner with Andrew Flintoff and Flintoff said to him something like, 'If you think you are going to get out anything out of me for the Schofield Report you can bugger off.' But Fraser then reported that in his newspaper column.

I was not sure media people should be on the committee at all, but Fraser justified it by saying that he wanted to help English cricket. That is all well and good, but is it really helping English cricket by calling for the head of the England coach three days before an important World Cup match against South Africa? No, it is not and it was not at the time. As a result I have to doubt Fraser's sincerity.

And why did Fraser not come and speak to me about the report? He had plenty of opportunities to do so. Every member of that review team should have spoken to both captain and coach. It was a travesty that did not happen.

Anyway, to the one-day series. The big selection surprise was the call up of veteran wicketkeeper Paul Nixon. And full credit to Michael Vaughan for that. Again, I wanted Matt Prior, but having spoken to the people who were at the academy with him, it created some doubt in my mind. I made some enquiries about Nixon's form in the previous season and heard good reports of his one-day batting, as well as some sound keeping.

But still I was having my problems with the selectors. David Graveney was arriving at the start of the one-dayers and, when a press conference was called, I spoke to him beforehand to clarify who was the number one keeper now with Read staying on. I was sure I would get asked the question. I was getting so much stick about the keeping situation that I did not really want to be contradicting Graveney.

Graveney told me Nixon was number one and that he would announce it because he was doing another press conference with

Michael Vaughan after me. So I presumed I could pass the question to him if asked.

But, as it was, at my press conference I was never asked the question. So, as I was coming out, I saw Graveney and mentioned to him not to forget about the Nixon scenario. Huh. When they had finished I spoke to ECB media liaison officer James Avery, whom I had asked earlier to monitor this situation. 'What happened?' I asked.

'It was the very last question,' he replied.

'And what did Grav say?' I asked.

'He said that we would have to wait and see.' Unbelievable. Was I being set up again?

In truth Nixon was what we wanted; someone who is lively, positive and full of spirit. One of the more depressing incidents in the Ashes had come in the last Test at Sydney where Paul Collingwood, from slip to Monty Panesar, had been having a go at Shane Warne. It got quite heated. But from behind the stumps and standing in between the two Chris Read did not utter a word. He would not even make eye contact with Warne. He just put his head down and let them get on with it. Imagine Nixon in that scenario. He would have piled into Warne with some verbals in support of his teammate. So too would Mark Boucher, Adam Gilchrist, Kumar Sangakkara and indeed any other keeper with some fight in them.

I wish that I had shown a bit more fight when it came to our one-day strategy. I was faced with exactly the same dilemma as I had been with the team selection for the second Test. Everyone thought I ran the team with a steel rod, but that was far from the case. I wanted us to be more aggressive in our approach during the power plays, yet everyone else on the management team wanted to adopt the 'wickets in hand' tactic, the old-fashioned approach which attracted so much criticism.

You have got to come up with a strategy with which everyone is happy and one in which the players believe. As I have said before, it is no good forcing something upon the players, and it was clear to me the way they wanted to go here. It was just that I was not totally convinced. I should have been more emphatic in stressing the strategy I thought we should adopt.

My theory on this has always been that the top three batsmen must take advantage of the new ball. In telling them that, there is still room for a lot of thought for the individuals. They need to assess different situations and play accordingly. It does not just mean that they must go out and biff the ball in every game. A good example was the Champions Trophy in India, where every team lost early wickets because of the pitches. Ideally you then have two batsmen in the middle order who can stabilize the innings and bat through. When we did well as a one-day side in 2005 we had Andrew Strauss at number four and Paul Collingwood lower down to fulfil those roles.

Of course, more than anything, what you need is an experienced top three to implement this plan. And that is something we rarely had. Marcus Trescothick was our only opener who you could describe as being that, but otherwise we tried unsuccessfully to find the right sort of opener. As I said earlier in the book, for that you have got to be able to cut and pull well, and also drive powerfully down the ground, over the top if necessary. Trescothick ticked all those boxes. Someone like Strauss can cut well, but only pull OK, and not drive straight strongly enough. I felt Andrew Flintoff would struggle with the job because his technique is not suited to facing the new ball, and also could not work the ball around if that was required.

To say that this one-day series in Australia did not begin well would be the biggest of understatements. Kevin Pietersen, our best batsman by some distance, cracked a rib in the first match defeat to Australia in Melbourne, and then in our second match in Tasmania, although we crept past New Zealand for our first win of the tour, returning skipper Michael Vaughan tore a hamstring.

Yet another huge decision loomed. Who was to captain now? I thought we had had enough of this palaver before we left. Vaughan had joined the squad after the Ashes and noticeably energized it – as had others like physio Dean Conway – but now he was out for a considerable time (he did eventually play in the final qualifying match before succumbing again).

It was Flintoff versus Strauss again, although Collingwood was a slight outsider. Our worry about Strauss was that he might not be a certainty in the one-day side if everyone was fit. And, as badly as the Ashes had gone under Flintoff's captaincy, it would have been a huge slap in the face if he were not to be asked to do the job.

As was often the case we were rushed into a decision by the media. It was made quite clear to us that if we did not act quickly then it would lead to all sorts of wild speculation. But our biggest concern was that we did not know then how long Vaughan was going to be absent. So when we arrived in Brisbane at 6 p.m. for our next game I went to Flintoff and asked him: 'Are you keen to captain?' He was not sure. 'Can I think about it overnight?' he asked back.

'No. Sorry. We need an answer by nine tonight,' I said. He came back and said he wanted to do it. I will be honest and say that I did not expect him to be lifting the Commonwealth Bank Series Trophy on 11 February at Sydney. Especially after we had lost our fourth match of the series, to Australia in Adelaide, being thumped by nine wickets after being bowled out for just 110. So bad were we that day that I felt moved to apologize to the public afterwards. We were bad, but I will again point to injuries as some sort of justification. For, by the third match of the tournament, we only had four players (Strauss, Flintoff, Collingwood and Jon Lewis) from the 2005 one-day side which had been so successful.

When we then lost to New Zealand in Perth it meant that we had to win our two remaining matches – against Australia in Sydney and New Zealand in Brisbane – if we were to have any chance of qualifying for the finals.

We won in Sydney because something remarkable happened. One of our top order batsmen scored a hundred, that is what happened. Not for seven months had anyone done that and the situation had become so dire that we had stopped mentioning it in team meetings. It was clearly getting to the players.

But it was Irishman Ed Joyce who stopped the rot, scoring 107, as our total of 292 was too much for an Australian side which never recovered from Adam Gilchrist's first ball dismissal to a beautiful in-swinger from Liam Plunkett.

This was the sweetest of victories after nine successive defeats to Australia on this trip, and not least because the home side were arrogantly resting the likes of Ricky Ponting, Brett Lee and Glenn McGrath. And also because their coach John Buchanan had made some ludicrous comments bemoaning the fact that England and New Zealand had not been testing his side sufficiently. Apologies for that, John. I just cannot understand how anyone would want to humiliate an opponent in public. It just makes them more determined. We certainly were here.

And I was happier all of a sudden. I received many messages of support and congratulation after this win, making me realize how important your loyal friends are. One of them I would like to mention is Malcolm Ashton. He had been the England scorer when I began and his role expanded to that of analyst before, unfortunately, we had to let him go in 2004. In his cricketing ability, unlike Tim Boon whom we brought in then as analyst, he could not cope with the multi-tasking I wanted from my support staff. But Ashton is a thoroughly decent individual who loves the game of cricket and always stayed in touch thereafter, sending his texts as he did here.

Just as I thought, once one batsman had scored a hundred, then so another followed immediately, Collingwood making 106 against the Kiwis to secure our place in the finals. That was of particular relief to him because he had lost his form badly and had looked so mentally shot that we toyed with leaving him out of the previous game. As it was, he was taken ill anyway and missed out. But the break seemed to have done him good, and he played superbly here. As he did in the first final, too, this time scoring 120 not out to win the game almost single-handedly. Ponting, McGrath and Lee were all back and I hope Mr Buchanan was pleased with the workout we had given his team.

Collingwood did not do too badly in the second final either, top-scoring with 70, but I was pleased with myself in this match, if you do not mind me saying so. Pleased that I had at last put my foot down, that is. Throughout this series I had been debating long and hard with Flintoff and Kevin Shine about Liam Plunkett and whether he should bowl over or around the wicket to left handers. Initially with the new ball I thought he should bowl over the wicket, as he had done when getting Gilchrist first ball in Sydney, but when the ball is swinging the margin of error is small, as the ball easily slips down the leg side. So after that initial period, if he was not getting it right, I thought Plunkett should immediately go around the wicket. We had seen in the 2005 Ashes how vulnerable Gilchrist was to this as he opened himself up. But Flintoff and Shine wanted Plunkett to bowl over the wicket.

So he had been doing this with no success as Australia chased 247 to win, when luckily there was a rain break. As they came off I grabbed Flintoff and Plunkett, and said, 'Look, guys, I think this is really important. When you go back on Liam must bowl around the wicket to Gilchrist.' If only I had been so strong elsewhere on this trip. But that is what happened when they went back on and Gilchrist was immediately bowled. There was no way back for Australia after that.

The team had shown tremendous character in fighting back from the brink. How many sides could have done that? It was the first time an England team had won an Australian tri-series for twenty years and ten years since one had won a one-day tournament (Sharjah 1997) away from home.

After we had won Andrew Flintoff said: 'The one person I really want to thank is Duncan Fletcher. Throughout the trip he has kept taking the knocks for us, but he has kept backing us.'

I had certainly kept backing Flintoff. He may never have been captain that day. Not because I might not have picked him when Vaughan was injured, but because I might have dropped him after a drinking misdemeanour. This was alluded to when the infamous 'Fredalo' incident emerged during the World Cup, but was probably more serious than anybody realized.

It had begun when it came to my attention that, after one of the one-day matches, Flintoff had spent the whole night drinking with Ian Botham and had only got to bed at 7 a.m. the following morning. I did not do anything about it at the time because you have to be careful with rumours, but I made a note and carried on without mentioning it. I never minded players having a drink as long as they didn't go overboard and were mindful that you should leave at least forty-eight hours before a game when drinking.

You just hope the players will not let you down. Sadly Flintoff did. We went to Sydney for the vital match against Australia and there a fielding practice was arranged for 10 a.m. Flintoff turned up still under the influence of alcohol. We were doing one drill called the 'cut and pull' with two groups either side of me, requiring an accurate throw from one side so that I could cut. Flintoff was in such a state that he could not throw properly. He had to pass the ball to the bloke next to him to do so. And then when it came to him trying to catch the ball I honestly thought that I was going to hurt him, so uncoordinated was he. I was fuming and stopped the practice early. Remember this was the England captain in this state. I had to calm down and think what to do; how to react, how to act.

It was a terrible bus journey back to the hotel. I sat at the front, as I always did, trying to analyse what was best to do. My instinct was telling me I simply had to drop him as captain. But then again I was thinking about how much pressure I was under anyway and how I had already been targeted by the media. Imagine what they would do now if I demoted Flintoff, the national hero.

When we got back to the hotel I told Flintoff I wanted to see him in my room. I asked Matthew Maynard to come along as well, because I wanted somebody else there to witness what was said. I then phoned Michael Vaughan. 'I'm going to drop Freddie,' I said. Initially he agreed, but then cautiously said: 'Just have a chat with him first and see what he says.'

Flintoff came to my room. He sat down and I said: 'I just want to ask you one question, Andrew. Why should I not drop you as England captain? Tell me now.'

He just sat there. I could not get an answer out of him. I just could not get him to talk at all. I went at him: 'Come on, give me an answer.' Nothing. 'OK, I'll give you time to think about it,' I said. 'If you've got anything to say to me, come and see me later.'

I sat stewing in my room all day, but eventually I came to the decision that I was not going to drop him. It is a fine line between doing the right and wrong thing. Would we have won the one-day series if I had dropped him? Who knows.

But what it did mean was that when the 'Fredalo' nonsense broke in the World Cup, there was no way Flintoff could escape censure.

Let us deal with that now. It was the day after we had lost to New Zealand in St Lucia in our opening match. I walked downstairs in our hotel ready to give a press conference (another 'Duncan Day' after we had lost) and saw Andrew Walpole and

Reg Dickason speaking in the lobby. I do not know why, but I just knew immediately that something was wrong. I wandered up and said, 'Right, what's happened?' in a rather jokey manner. It was the way they then looked at each other that betrayed the seriousness of the matter. Dickason filled me in as to what had happened, that Flintoff had been out drinking and had been involved in a dangerous incident with a pedalo in the early hours. 'Bloody Flintoff again,' I thought to myself.

I asked Walpole and Dickason if it had got out to the press already and they said no. Dickason said that he had spoken to the security people and that they would keep it quiet. 'Yeah, I've heard that before,' I remember saying to Walpole.

Poor old Walpole. I have so much admiration for that man. I really appreciated what he did for me during my time with England. He had this incredible ability to understand my problems (and there were plenty where the media were concerned) and I know I must have annoyed the hell out of him so often, but he was always calm and helpful.

And he had to be here. I was not happy. I told him to get hold of Phil Neale because I wanted a team meeting at twelve noon. But first I had to do my press conference. I was hoping and praying that nothing had leaked out about this affair. Thankfully it had not, and all I had to field were questions about why we had lost. For once that could have been a lot worse.

Before the team meeting I had an idea. I decided to get hold of a flip chart and on it I wrote down the names of the whole squad in a list. The players arrived and I seated them in a semicircle, as we always did in team meetings so that they could look each other in the eye. I then asked them one by one to come up and write beside their name what time they had got to bed the night before and then speak to the team about the reasons why. You have to remember that we had another match the very next day against Canada.

They all did this and then I spoke. As I did so I looked around the room and there were a number of players with smirks on their faces, most of them on the faces of those who had been out late. 'Right, all of you who were out after midnight, you're fined,' I said. I cannot divulge the amounts involved but they were hefty. Six players were fined: Flintoff, James Anderson, Ian Bell, Jon Lewis, Paul Nixon and Liam Plunkett. Suddenly there were not any smirks. I could see the players thinking, 'That was an expensive night out.'

I was so disappointed. You put your trust in these players and then they go and do something like this. They do not realize it is the coach who gets it in the neck afterwards.

Afterwards two members of the management team, Kevin Shine and Jeremy Snape (with us for a short time as a sports psychologist), admitted they had also been out late. They had not been in the semicircle for the meeting, but had sat at the back of the room. I felt especially sorry for Shine because he is such a good character, and I know it was the first time during the whole winter that he had been out after midnight. He had been out with his brother who had flown over from the UK and they had met up with the players later on. Because this was such a difficult scenario for me I just let the ECB deal with Shine and Snape.

But not Flintoff. I had a meeting with Vaughan afterwards and we agreed that Flintoff should be dropped from the Canada game and stripped of the vice-captaincy. It was only right and proper.

But I was still adamant that I was not going to impose a curfew. I had never done that with any side I had coached, ever since the days at the University of Cape Town. I was not going to start now. It is all about individual responsibility and that was what I was stressing to the players when we had a meeting after the Canada match. 'You're earning a lot of money and you should know what you can and cannot do,' I told them. 'If any of you are

out late again you will be on the first plane home.' It saddened me
to discover that some players later went to members of the senior
management and asked, 'When he said late, how late did he
mean?' They just did not understand.

Neither did Ian Botham, who said on television that he could
see nothing wrong with what had happened and that Flintoff's
only 'crime' had been in getting caught. That was a silly thing to
say. Even Flintoff knew that he had been stupid.

Therefore an incident soon afterwards pleased me a lot. Some
time before the 'Fredalo' incident we had all been invited by
Hampshire chairman Rod Bransgrove to spend the day after the
Canada match on his boat. But Andrew Walpole had advised me
against this trip, because the media might pounce again and see it
as another drinking spree after 'Fredalo'.

But I had no problem with the trip. We had been cooped up in
hotels all the time and I thought it would do the guys good to get
out. They did not have to drink, after all.

In the dressing room after the Canada match Kevin Pietersen,
who obviously knows Bransgrove well at Hampshire, was asking
the other players who was going to go on the boat. At least four or
five of the senior players asked: 'Is Botham going?'

Pietersen got a response from Bransgrove that Botham was
indeed going, and, when Pietersen relayed this loudly in the dressing room, a unanimous call of 'no thanks' rang out.

None of the players went. For once they were standing up
to someone in the media. I could never understand how players could sit in the dressing room and slate someone like that
and then the very next minute walk out on to the field and greet
him as a friend. I had first seen this in my first home Test at
Lord's in 2000 just after David Lloyd had published his autobiography. Some players were upset by what had been written
and were cursing Lloyd, yet minutes later out in the middle they
were saying 'Hi, Bumble, how are you?' To me that is double

standards. I could never do it, and it was one of the major reasons why my relationship with the media was so strained.

But at the start of the World Cup I had been attempting to put everything else aside. I did not want anyone to have even an inkling that I might be contemplating resignation and certainly did not want my last assignment to end in a flop.

And I was pleasantly surprised how positive and chipper the vibe was among the squad as we prepared in St Vincent. That was a decent place to be, with the Arnos Vale Stadium an excellent venue, even if the practice facilities left a little to be desired. It was not just the standard of the surfaces but the fact that they were positioned right next to the airport. The Australians were also practising here and one of their practices was curtailed when a plane crashed, but miraculously all three people on board survived when it finished upside down in a creek on the side of the runway.

Our problems centred more around lost balls. Batsmen kept hitting them into the airfield and we could not go and retrieve them. I counted fourteen that were lost in one practice. 'Gone for ever,' I was thinking. Then something very amusing happened. From nowhere a fire engine appeared, hurtling off the runway towards the long grass where most of the balls had been hit. And out of it came Reg Dickason!

Talk about ingenuity from our security man. The fire engine was the only vehicle permitted to go down the runway, so Dickason had pleaded with the authorities to allow him a quick ride in one. He found all those fourteen balls and plenty the Australian team had hit there the day before. I told you he was a top man.

We began the competition slowly. I always found England teams did. It stems from county cricket. You always hear comments like 'the Championship is not won until July' there. It encourages a mindset where not every match is vital. In the southern hemisphere every match is vital. There are only eight or ten to play.

It was also vital to win the toss in that first match against New Zealand in St Lucia. We did not and it cost us. It was hard work batting first on a pitch where the groundsman had been unsure how much water to use so that it would last the distance. Early on in the competition a lot of the pitches were like this because they were relaid and so created doubt in the groundsmen's minds. We did, however, play some poor shots as well in only scoring 209–7; nothing as ill-advised as the antics that night though.

But what happened there was put firmly into perspective two days later when, during the match against Canada, we heard the shocking news of Bob Woolmer's death. To say that hit me hard would be a huge understatement. I knew Woolmer well. We both lived in Cape Town and did the same job. We had a lot in common. And again this set me thinking: 'Is all this really worth it?'

It certainly would not have been worth it if we had lost to Kenya. That became a must-win game, otherwise we would be out of the tournament like Pakistan and India. But we came through by seven wickets and moved to Guyana to play Ireland.

I can honestly say this was one of the most boring periods of my whole cricketing career. And I think most of the players would concur too. We just had too much time to kill. It brought home how poorly the tournament was run but it also brought home how tired the players were. The non-stop schedule was catching up on them. I could see their mental tiredness the day before the Ireland game. We had a heavy practice two days before the match, as we always did, but unusually this left the players noticeably jaded. People can say that it was the World Cup and that they should have been able to raise themselves, but we had been going for eleven months. It was too much, and it was catching up.

We scraped home by 48 runs. It was not particularly emphatic stuff. But the pitches in general helped the minnows in this tournament. Slow, uneven pitches always do that, bringing sides closer together rather than faster, bouncier pitches which can expose the limitations of the lesser sides. I remember talking to Adrian Birrell, Ireland's South African coach, later on in the tournament and he said exactly that to me without my raising the topic first.

I probably knew around the time of that Ireland match that we were going to struggle to win the World Cup. But what people forget about this campaign is that we were only one shot away from reaching the semi-finals. This is not to heap blame on Essex's Ravi Bopara, who had played superbly in a seventh-wicket partnership of 87 with Paul Nixon against Sri Lanka, but if he had hit the last ball of that match off Dilhara Fernando for four rather than being bowled, then victory would have been ours. That would have been enough for us to make the semi-finals. Who knows what might have happened then? Remember the Commonwealth Bank Series.

We should have won that game anyway. If you play Sri Lanka and Sanath Jayasuriya only scores 25 and Muttiah Muralitharan concedes 48 in his 10 overs (even if he did grab the vital wicket of Kevin Pietersen) then you should win. Those two are such influential players that to nullify them and not succeed is almost a crime.

As it is a crime not to have your fielding in good shape in one-day cricket. I am not sure if it was ever picked up on, but our fielding improved a lot during the World Cup. In fact, I think it improved twofold from where it was beforehand. We had made a conscious decision in Australia to work harder at it and I left most of the batting to Matthew Maynard so that I could work on this aspect of the game. I especially worked with individuals on their throwing at the stumps. There were two key components I wanted them to work on. The first was on aligning their shoulders to the stumps before throwing and the second on hesitating for a fraction

of a second thereafter so there was more focus on the target. We
had talked about this a lot but as a good example we noticed that
Andrew Symonds, in effecting a run out in one of the early one-
day games, had hesitated just before throwing at the stumps.
Thank goodness analyst Mark Garaway had taped Symonds doing
this so that the players could see.

But I had to go right back to basics with the team. We had to
run through it as slowly as possible to begin with, and there were
some who thought it too much like schoolboy stuff at first. But
slowly I won them over, working a lot with Paul Collingwood
and Monty Panesar on aligning their shoulders towards the
stumps, and then really beginning to crack on once skipper
Michael Vaughan began believing in it. And, once I had given
them this initial feel, Garaway was then put in charge to monitor
their progress and drive the fielding practices. He did an excellent
job.

After Sri Lanka we lost to Australia, the eventual champions.
No surprise there, you will probably say. But I would just like to
give you a statistic. Since 2004, including the ICC Champions
Trophy match at Edgbaston that year, England have played
Australia sixteen times in official one-day internationals. One was
a no-result, one was a tie and, of the remaining, Australia won
eight and England six. There was also one win each in Twenty20.
That is not bad, is it? One team are world champions and the
other are perceived as one-day chumps. And please do not try
to say that Australia were missing players during the Commonwealth Bank series. We were missing players continually after the
2005 Ashes.

When the Schofield Report was published after the World Cup
it described our one-day performances as 'disappointing in the
extreme'. Yes, they were not good but I wonder if the review
members knew of that statistic against Australia. I also wonder
if they knew that, before the World Cup, we were only one or

two wins away from leapfrogging New Zealand and Sri Lanka in the world one-day rankings. And these were two teams everyone raved about at the World Cup. Were New Zealand and Sri Lanka described as being 'disappointing in the extreme'? Remember, Pakistan and India did not even make the Super Eights.

I think I should just stay on the Schofield Report here and record some brief reactions to it. They will only be brief because I have already stated my misgivings about its very existence.

The report also said that 'exceptional management action should have been taken to retain the services of Troy Cooley'. 'Exceptional' is the wrong word. As mentioned previously, all it required from the ECB was common sense in that all Cooley wanted was to be signed up until the end of the World Cup. Unfathomably the ECB were only willing to sign him for one year.

The report talked of 'inadequate and ineffective communication between the England Head Coach and the First Class County Coaches' and recommended a minimum of two meetings per year. Well, even considering the amount of cricket and small amount of time I had, I still managed to see them once a year after winter tours when I drove around to every county to see their chairman, chief executive and coach to discuss anything they wanted.

I did find the report's choice of words in some cases ridiculous. When it said 'the performance of the England team in Test cricket during this four year period [2003–7] has been one of steady progress' it really riled me. That beggars belief. To think we lost just two series, both away from home, and had come from worst in the world, bar Zimbabwe, to second (and held that position), and that it is considered only 'steady' progress compared to the teams of the last twenty years is very hard to stomach.

It also said: 'By November 2006 the press and public perception in Australia was that England had failed to achieve playing progress since the Ashes success in 2005 and had arrived in Australia ill-prepared.' I have said my piece on that, but one followed the other; the press brainwashed the public into thinking that. I will say it again: we were not ill-prepared. Should the press and public perception in Australia dictate to this report anyway?

But this business about not making any playing progress really annoyed me. It is instructive to look at other sports in this respect. It took Alex Ferguson and Arsène Wenger five or six years to build their great sides at Manchester United and Arsenal. It also took Clive Woodward the same amount of time to build his World Cup-winning England rugby team. And so it took me that time to build the 2005 Ashes team. But thereafter injuries ruined that team, so there was always going to be a period of rebuilding when it was unrealistic to expect too much progress. Once Manchester United and Arsenal lost key players it also took them quite a bit of time to rebuild, and remember that they can buy in players of international experience at club level too. England's rugby team is still battling to rebuild. We only had one year to rebuild after the 2005 Ashes.

I agreed that my relationship with the chairman of selectors was 'indifferent' and 'cannot be repeated', but as I have outlined in these pages I lost respect for and confidence in David Graveney as a selector. I do have to say here, however, that I think Graveney is a good bloke. If we had not been involved in the high pressures of selection then I am sure we could have got on fine.

But whenever there was a tight decision to be made, his response would always be 'you're in the dressing room, you've got a better idea and are in a better position to make the decision'. So naturally after a while I thought I would be better off making the decision with the captain.

*

Reading that damn report has brought back to me all the reasons why I had to pack in. As I mentioned right at the start of this book, I decided to tell the ECB of my intention to resign the day before the Bangladesh game. I did not want anyone thinking that, if we did happen to lose to them, that was the reason for my decision. And we might have lost to Bangladesh. We played poorly and nervously after misjudging the toss and inserting them when we should have batted first.

Unfortunately it was only after the next match against South Africa that we discovered that the groundsmen in Barbados had decided to change their preparation of the pitch. So we got the toss wrong again, this time batting first when we should have fielded. There had been more watering, so for the first ten overs or so the pitch was extremely lively. Having said that, it was no excuse for our slow start in scoring just 7 runs from the first 6 overs. You just cannot do that.

At least we still had the West Indies match with which I could end on a winning note, but two days after the South Africa defeat it was made public what I had known for some time: it was time to finish with England.

I still wanted to coach, and I never ran out of ideas at the end. Some England players were actually mentioning that I had too many ideas. All I was trying to do was introduce more flair into their games. At the end I was even discussing a new shot. It was a new way of sweeping. It had often puzzled me why players could learn the reverse sweep quicker than the conventional sweep. The answer I came up was that it was down to the position of their hands on the bat handle. So I advocated that, when sweeping conventionally, you should swap your hands around. In other words for a right-handed batsman you should have your right hand at the top of the bat. Some of the players tried it in the nets and said they liked it. 'More control,' they said. I even mentioned it to Jacques Kallis and Mark Boucher when I returned to South

Africa and they liked the idea. I await its use in a match some-where.

And I still believe I had the respect of the players, as shown by their reaction to my resignation in Barbados. Two letters I had from Andrew Strauss and Kevin Pietersen emphasized this, with their whole-hearted praise and thanks. On the day we beat the West Indies in that final match I also received this e-mail from Shaun Udal.

Dear Duncan

I hope this message finds you in good spirits as the last few days must have been pretty tough for you.

I just wanted to send you a message to say it was a real pleasure to work with you last winter in Pakistan and India and I learnt more from you about various things, angles, training the brain etc., than I have off any coach I've had in 21 seasons playing the game. I only wish I could have stayed involved for longer but it wasn't to be. You can take great pride and pleasure out of your time as England coach. You did some wonderful things and helped to turn us into an excellent Test match team and of course you will go down in English folklore as the coach that got us the Ashes back.

Whatever you choose to do in future I wish you well and, if it's in cricket, then whoever employs you has an outstanding coach and a hard working, intelligent human being who cares deeply for his players. As I've found out recently with the news that my son has autism, you never know what's around the corner, but I'm sure your excellent coaching will benefit someone, somewhere.

I wish you well.

With kind regards and best wishes

SHAGGY

Thanks, Shaggy. There was plenty of goodwill like this being shown at this time. But there was also some frustration from me. I did not want to do my final press conference after the West Indies match. Everyone in the camp agreed with me that it was wrong to go and speak to people who had slated me mercilessly, but it was also the right thing to do. If I had not gone it might have made things even worse. But where else do you get such a confusing contradiction?

Anyway, no matter. Let us not end this book in rancour. If there has been irritation it has been because I have been trying to explain how difficult a task coaching England is, and I have tried my best to be honest, forthright and insightful.

But I know that all the problems I had as England coach were always far outweighed by the enjoyment I took from the job. I only thought that I would ever do it for two years, so to last for seven and a half years must mean that I was finding fulfilment and having fun. I must have been doing a decent job too.

It has been a memorable journey, full of memorable people and memorable places. My final conclusion is that I doubt if there are too many people in cricket who would not have fancied taking the same journey which began playing cricket on the lawn at Carswell Farm back in Rhodesia and ended having the best coaching job in world cricket. I know I am lucky to have taken that journey, and certainly feel immensely proud to have experienced it. I think we will end as we started. Really, it has been one hell of a time.

Appendix: Career Highlights

- Beat the West Indies in a Test Series (3–1) for the first time since 1969 in the summer of 2000
- Won a Test series in Pakistan for the first time in thirty-nine years in 2000 – achieving victory in the final Test in Karachi, a ground where Pakistan had never previously lost in thirty-four matches
- Won a Test series in Sri Lanka in 2001 – England's fourth successive Test series win and the first time this had been achieved since Mike Brearley's captaincy in 1978–9. It was also the first time England had come from behind to win a Test series since the tour of India in 1984/5
- England's 3–0 Test series win in the Caribbean in 2004 was their first in the West Indies for thirty-six years
- Eight successive Test wins in 2004 for the first time in England's history
- England's 2–1 victory in the Test series in South Africa in 2004–05 was their first in South Africa since 1964/5, their first in a five-Test series overseas since 1986/7 and only Australia, twice, had won a Test series in South Africa since the country's return from sporting isolation in 1991
- Named male Coach of the Year at the Sports UK Coach of the Year awards in 2004
- Led the team to an Ashes Test series win in 2005 for the first

time in eighteen years – and their sixth straight Test series win following previous victories over West Indies, New Zealand, West Indies, South Africa and Bangladesh

- The team's victory in the Mumbai Test of 2006 which squared the series 1–1 was their first in a Test match in India since 1985
- The England one-day squad's Commonwealth Bank series win in Australia in 2007 was the first time the hosts had lost the triangular one-day series final for fourteen years. It was also England's first one-day series win overseas since 1997 and their first in Australia since 1986/7

Compiled by Andrew Walpole

Index

(the initials DF stand for Duncan Fletcher)